The Kennedy Case

The
Kennedy Case

by RITA DALLAS, RN

and JEANIRA RATCLIFFE

G. P. Putnam's Sons, New York

To my son, Vincent, from Rita Dallas

To Lunda and Lucille Ratcliffe

from Jeanira Ratcliffe

The Kennedy Case

I

I WILL NEVER forget the morning of Friday, November 22, 1963. Hyannis Port was wrapped in a damp, gray overcoat of fog. During the night, a cold, suffocating mist had moved onto the Cape, enveloping it in a dismal shroud of shadows.

As I walked toward the lumbering white house at the foot of Scudder Avenue, I saw its windows dotted with morning lights that wavered in the fog, signaling that inside the usual routine of the day was beginning.

Mrs. Kennedy's car was idling on the circle drive, with Frank, the family chauffeur, waiting patiently behind the wheel, and I knew she would soon be leaving for mass as she had every morning since I had come on the Kennedy case.

In the kitchen the staff was working quietly during the first morning hours. It was too early for temperaments. No one sulked or brooded as the day got under way; but I knew the house well, and I knew how its occupants could flare up in anger or frustration. It was a complicated household, vacillating between two mistresses, Mrs. Joseph Kennedy and her niece Ann Gargan. It was a house full of division, lonely in the stark loss of its once virile and decisive master, Ambassador Joseph P. Kennedy.

In his suite on the second floor, Mr. Kennedy began his day quietly. He eyed the November sky through the window beside his bed, and I could see he was wondering when the fog would burn off.

He was especially concerned about the weather on this particular morning, because Ann was leaving for Detroit on the afternoon plane to visit her relatives. At first, it seemed doubtful if the weather would clear for her flight; but as the morning passed, the fog thinned, and her departure was on schedule. Her luggage had been stacked in the hall, and only last-minute odds and ends were left to be done.

Ann was excited about her trip, and her aunt was particularly pleased that she had been successful in persuading her to take it. Ever since his stroke Ann had kept an almost neurotic vigil over the Ambassador. Often she was with him day and night, and finally Mrs. Kennedy had almost demanded that she take a brief vacation. She was to spend Thanksgiving with her sister and rejoin Mr. and Mrs. Kennedy at their winter home in Palm Beach shortly before Christmas.

The season was nearly over on Nantucket Sound, and the Ambassador's spirits had sagged after the Labor Day weekend, for the compound had become like a ghost town. The grandchildren were either back in school or ensconced in their winter homes, and I could see that he sorely missed the cheering effect of their laughing, tumbling exuberance. Only the weekends were alive with visits from his immediate family. John, Bobby, Teddy, Eunice, Jean, and Pat would return regularly, bringing with them the vitality that had become synonymous with the Kennedy name, and he would absorb their energy when they visited. The early autumn days with their soft warm air had often left him sluggish and susceptible to blue moods. A recent November cold snap had revitalized him somewhat, but it was still a lonely, desolate time of year on the Cape.

Mrs. Kennedy ached from the cold, moist air and anxiously yearned for Thanksgiving, for that meant they would soon close the Hyannis Port house and head for the warmth of a Florida winter in Palm Beach.

Preparations had been made for the annual Thanksgiving Day festival. The whole Kennedy clan would arrive from around the country, bringing sons, daughters, grandchildren, and an entourage of welcome guests. The holiday was always enriched by birthday parties for the President's children. John was going to be three on the twenty-fifth, and Caroline was turning six two days later. It would be a boisterous, freewheeling holiday, full of Irish humor and family devotion. It was also to be a celebration of the third anniversary of the Presidential election.

I often saw the Ambassador looking out his window at the White House trailer parked in the drive behind his son's house. He would also sit long hours, staring at the Presidential flag which flew proudly from the tall staff in the front yard when John Kennedy was at the compound. The trailer and the flag were symbols which filled Mr. Kennedy with pride because they were tangible proof that he had fulfilled his lifelong ambition to have a Kennedy in the White House.

We had not seen the President for nearly two weeks, and I remember him affectionately teasing his mother during his last visit. "You're getting to be just like a mother hen," he said jokingly. He tried to make light of her worries, but every day we could see she was getting more and more concerned.

"Do you think he looks especially tired?" she would say. Or, "My poor son. So much responsibility, and there is no way for his father to help him now."

Although I understood her worries, I had never seen a happier man than John Kennedy. It seemed to me that the role of President of the United States was made for him, and although he often seemed exhausted, I saw a tremendous joy and fulfillment flowing through him at all times. Therefore, when Mrs. Kennedy and I would talk and she would express her fears, I did what I could to lift her spirits.

She was restless, though, and retained a unique maternal instinct that grew more and more pronounced as his tenure of office wore on.

Despite my efforts to reassure Mrs. Kennedy, there was something about the memory of his last visit two weeks before that hung like a shadow on my mind. Even though his own house was still open and filled with the usual entourage of guests and dignitaries, he had spent most of his time with his father. They absorbed the football games on television and often sat quietly together, father and son. Comrades. Friends. The President seemed determined to share these hours with his father and neglected his guests to do so.

He had arrived Friday evening and was expected to leave by midafternoon on Sunday, but over the weekend his father had taken a cold, so on Sunday morning the President was at his bedside. They had breakfast and lunch together, and the President decided not to leave until late in the evening. This was an unusual, unscheduled decision; it meant a late return to the White House, but he brushed all else aside to remain at his father's beck and call.

It was just before dusk on Sunday when we heard the helicopters landing on the front lawn. The President lingered over his father's bed to kiss him good-bye. He promised he would be back as soon as he returned from his appearances in Texas. I remember clearly how he paused in the door, for a moment, dwarfing it with his size. Then he waved his hand slightly and was gone.

As soon as the door to the elevator closed, Mr. Kennedy began tossing his head and motioning toward the balcony. I asked him if he wanted me to move his bed to the window so he could see his son depart, and he nodded vigorously. Because of his stroke, Mr. Kennedy's speech was severely limited, but we had developed an ability to communicate by signs and gestures over the two years I had been with him.

It was the custom of the staff and members of the family to gather on the front lawn to watch all Presidential arrivals and departures. Therefore, there was no one left in the house to help move his bed. Using the house phone, I called the downstairs porch and requested an aide to come up. In a few minutes we had the Ambassador rolled to the balcony doors. We positioned him so that he had a clean, unhampered view of the lawn.

We waited. And waited. And waited. The aging man kept craning his neck, mumbling to himself, obviously impatient at the delay. His eyes were riveted to the helicopter, his face twisted in deep frowns of concern. I could almost hear his thoughts. Where is he? What's wrong?

Lost in his thoughts, he did not hear the elevator door open. I looked over my shoulder and saw the President. He silenced me by pressing his finger to his lips. After walking softly to his father's bed, he touched him lightly on the shoulder. "Look who's here, Dad," he said. He bent down, put his arms around his father, and kissed him again. He then walked rapidly back to the elevator, motioning for me to follow.

At the door he whispered, "Mrs. Dallas, take good care of Dad till I come back."

The door closed before I could answer him.

I stood at the Ambassador's bedside, and together we watched the President walk across the lawn. He turned once, the cold November wind churning a fury about him, and looked up to our window. Even though he could not see his father, he waved with a high, wide salute, and Mr. Kennedy raised his hand in a silent farewell. The helicopter lifted off, taking him to Washington where he was to meet Jackie. Together they were going to Palm Beach for a few days' rest before the trip to Texas.

After the President's departure, the household staff had been busy right up to the morning of the twenty-second preparing for the Thanksgiving holidays. Mr. Kennedy had not been very active, owing to his cold, but it did not progress to a state that caused him any serious complications. Had he been feeling better that morning, he would have enjoyed seeing Ann off on her trip, for he took any excuse to get out of the house for a long drive.

He and his wife existed on a rigid schedule. He would begin his day watching the national news on television, keeping a sharp eye and ear tuned for comment on his sons, then devour the New York *Times*. Mrs. Kennedy, on arising, would go to mass. When she returned, she would breakfast with her husband, quite often with Ann joining them. Mr. Kennedy's midmornings would be taken up with a swim and some therapeutic exercises in the heated pool. If the weather permitted, he would lunch on the *Marlin*, his beloved boat. Otherwise, he would join his wife and Ann in the dining room. Immediately after lunch he took a lengthy nap, as did his wife. This had long been a family ritual, and it was rare for either of them to break the pattern. After his nap, he usually went to the family theater in the basement of the house to watch a movie. Mrs. Kennedy would play golf or swim during this time. The rest of his afternoon would be taken up with television, unless he decided he wanted to go for a drive. Before dinner he would rest again, then join his wife for their evening meal.

They were both faithful to their daily routines, but on this particular day the schedules had been adjusted so Ann could have lunch with them before meeting her plane.

Shortly before she was to leave, Mr. Kennedy was settled in his bed and was soon asleep. Mrs. Kennedy was closeted in her bedroom, with the shades drawn, hoping to be able to rest. The days, she often said, seemed to get longer with each passing year.

While the houseman loaded Ann's luggage in the car, she handed me an envelope and asked that I keep it in my possession until she returned. She explained that it had been put in her charge by the family and that it contained instructions on what had to be done in case something happened to the Ambassador. In it was the name of the priest to call, the funeral director the family wanted, and other pertinent information. I placed the envelope in my desk and wished her a good trip.

Suddenly our conversation was interrupted by wild, piercing screams.

Dora, Mr. Kennedy's personal waitress, came running up the stairs, completely distraught. She was sobbing wildly. "The President's been shot! My God, the President's been shot." Instinctively, I ran down the steps and grabbed her shoulders. "Be quiet," I urged, shaking her. "Be quiet. What are you saying?" She sank down on the stairs and buried her face in her hands. Frank, the chauffeur, came toward us, white-faced, and told us the few details that he had heard on television. Ann was frozen at the head of the stairs, transfixed in terror. She began trembling, then cracked into a wild fit of hysterics and ran to her room.

As I helped Dora to her feet, I could hear Ann's television blaring from behind her closed door. I was urging Frank to take Dora downstairs when Mrs. Kennedy burst through her bedroom door and stomped out into the hall. She was wearing her robe, and she had the disheveled look of someone who has just been jolted out of a sound sleep.

"What's the matter with you two?" she said sternly, looking at Dora and me. "Please, can't you be quiet? I've never heard so much commotion. Now keep still. Do you want to disturb Mr. Kennedy?"

She looked directly at me and said, "You, of all people, should know better than this, Mrs. Dallas." As she started back to her room, she said, "And someone tell Ann to turn that television off."

I had worked my way back up the stairs, unable to say anything. Dora began crying again, leaning her head on Frank's shoulder. When she saw this, a tense look traveled over Mrs. Kennedy's face. I felt her eyes watching me as I hurried to Ann's room to carry out her orders. Ann was sitting hunched in front of her television, tears washing her face. The TV roared at full volume. It was not tuned to a news program, but she seemed unaware.

"Turn it off, Ann," I said. "And come along. Mrs. Kennedy is out in the hall."

Stupefied, she followed me out of the room and shrank against the wall. Mrs. Kennedy looked at first one, then the other. "What *is* the matter?" she asked, her voice dry. "What's wrong?"

I whispered to Ann, "You'll have to tell her. She should hear it from her family."

Ann's eyes pleaded, for a moment, and then she started to cry. Instinctively, I moved toward Mrs. Kennedy, for I did not know how severe her reaction would be to the news.

"Aunt Rose," Ann sobbed. "Jack's been shot."

Mrs. Kennedy's eyes clouded. Then, without making a

sound, she turned and started back into her room. Her hand trembled ever so slightly as she pressed her fingers against her temple. Slowly, she faced us again. Her voice was hollow, but steady. "Don't worry," she said, "we'll be all right. You'll see." With those few words, she walked back into her room and quietly closed the door. Ann stared into space, then shook her head as if to clear it, and quickly ran to her room. I hurried in to look at Mr. Kennedy. I was relieved to find him still asleep. I walked unsteadily to the small area that served as the nurses' station and sat down. I felt a shock wave sweep through my body.

Time, in such moments, loses all meaning . . . and I'm sure only a few minutes had passed when I was jolted by Ann's running past me into her uncle's room. At the same time Mrs. Kennedy opened her door and called, "Mrs. Dallas. Mrs. Dallas. Don't let Ann say anything to Mr. Kennedy. Don't let her tell him. I've just called my children, and they are coming up this evening. I want them to be with him. I want them to tell him."

Hoping to intercept Ann, I hurried into the room just as she was saying, "Uncle Joe, there's been a terrible accident."

Mr. Kennedy, groggy from being awakened in such a way, was slow to comprehend and did not notice when I put my hand on Ann's arm and said, "Please come outside for a moment, Ann." She looked puzzled as I brought her out into the hall.

"Your aunt doesn't want you to tell him," I whispered. Before I could explain any of the details, she darted back to Mr. Kennedy, who was nearly asleep again, and speaking in a rapid, high voice, she babbled, "Uncle Joe, it's Wilburt. He's been hurt." Mr. Kennedy's eyes became alert, for Ann was talking about the head gardener, who was a great favorite of Mr. Kennedy's. Ann quickly said, "But he's all right, he's all right. It wasn't serious." Mr. Kennedy looked bewildered but finally settled down and went back to sleep.

In the meantime, Ham Brown, the Secret Service agent assigned to Mr. Kennedy, had been contacted by his superiors in

Washington and was issued orders to secure the grounds. The family had to be guarded against the possibility of a nationwide conspiracy.

I checked again on Mr. Kennedy, who was still asleep. Then I turned up his intercom and quietly left the room. I looked up and down the empty hall. Ann's door was closed. The domestic staff was somewhere downstairs. Ham Brown was busy checking spare rooms throughout the house as a security measure. I knocked softly at Mrs. Kennedy's door and said, "It's Mrs. Dallas. Don't come out. I just wanted you to know I'm here if you need me."

I could hear the television on in her room, very low. In a muffled voice she replied over it, "I think I'll be all right, Mrs. Dallas, but thank you. Don't worry about me. Just stay with my husband, and don't let anything happen to him. I'll be in to see him a little later, but I can't right now."

As I turned away, I heard her say, "Perhaps you should call Dr. Boles and see if he can be here when our children come."

I returned across the hall to my station, and keeping a sharp ear for Mr. Kennedy lest he should awaken, I called Dr. Boles in Boston. He had already heard the news and was planning to leave for the compound within the next hour or so. He inquired after Mr. Kennedy and first directed me to keep him under a mild sedation, but when I explained that some of his family would be arriving early in the evening, he adjusted his order.

We had to be extremely careful in the dosage administered to the Ambassador, for he never liked to be tranquilized. The rapid effects of some medications upset him, for he was a man who, despite the serious nature of his illness, rebelled at heavy sedation. He always wanted to be alert and aware of what was going on.

My conversation with the doctor was cut short when I heard Mr. Kennedy calling me over the intercom. When I went in, he seemed in good spirits and indicated that he wanted to see a movie. I phoned for Frank to come after him. "I can't face the boss," he said at first, but in the end, he came and put up a

courageous front. Frank had worked for the Ambassador for a
long time, and they were close friends. Usually they chatted
pleasantly, but Frank was full of tension trying to cover his
feelings. However, if Mr. Kennedy noticed, he gave no indication.

But there were other things out of the ordinary. The five
phone lines coming into the house had begun to ring, insist-
ently, and Mr. Kennedy cocked an eyebrow questioningly. I
motioned Frank to get him on the elevator as fast as he could.
As soon as they were on their way, I sat down at my desk and
began answering the phone. Unfortunately, there was no one
else to take the calls, because Mr. Kennedy's secretary had left
for the day to attend her sister's funeral. It was up to the rest
of the staff to handle the crisis.

Captain Baird, pilot of Mr. Kennedy's plane, the *Caroline*,
phoned from Hyannis Airport to say that he had Eunice
Shriver's luggage. He asked if I could send someone for it. He
told me that she and Teddy were coming in on an Army transport plane and would be arriving shortly. His orders, from the
Attorney General, were to stand by the *Caroline*.

Father Cavanaugh, former president of Notre Dame and
longtime friend of Mr. Kennedy, called to say he was coming in
that evening to stay with Mr. and Mrs. Kennedy as long as he
was needed.

A moment or two later a call came from Cardinal Cushing,
who wanted to know if he should come to the compound. He
said that he had been asked to offer the mass, and it was then
that I knew the President was dead.

In less than a half hour, Mr. Kennedy became restless at the
movie, and I received a call from his aide warning me that he
was afraid he could not keep him there much longer. Agent
Brown was in the room with me when the call came, and he
immediately decided to jimmy all the television sets, for we
knew that when Mr. Kennedy returned from the movies, he
would immediately want to watch his usual afternoon pro-
grams. When a second call came that Mr. Kennedy was insisting on returning to his room, I went after him. In the elevator

he motioned that he wanted to get off on the first floor. He then wheeled himself into the small study. When the television did not come on, he was quite angry, and he signaled for me to get someone to fix it.

Agent Brown and Frank busied themselves pretending to make adjustments. We were all terribly anxious, for Mr. Kennedy was becoming impatient. He began beating his left hand on the arm of the chair. After a few minutes he indicated he wanted to go upstairs to his own bedroom and watch from there. We held our breath, for we knew that he would probably explode when he found the set in his bedroom was also out of order. All of us were extremely tense, but, to our surprise, when the television tube remained dark, he merely shrugged and motioned for a magazine.

Fortunately, Mr. Kennedy's secretary had heard the news report and returned to the house immediately after her sister's burial. But later, Mrs. Kennedy, sensitive to another's grief, told her to go back to her own family. "They need you, too," she said.

Mr. Kennedy was an extremely perceptive man, and he could not help noticing that something was amiss in his house. For one thing, Ann had not left as planned, and this must have puzzled him. Also, Mrs. Kennedy, without showing any visible effects, had frequently come to his room to say just a word or two. This was very unusual, for Mrs. Kennedy rarely departed from her normal schedule. However, although he seemed puzzled, Mr. Kennedy did not become disturbed, to our great relief.

Time again lost its meaning, but when the afternoon nurse came on duty and assured me she could handle Mr. Kennedy without help, I decided to get out for a while. I wanted to take a walk. I needed time away from the house and its trembling tragedy.

I walked across the lawn, and the icy wind bit into my face. The air was brittle and harsh. As I walked, I saw Mrs. Kennedy huddled on the back steps of the President's house.

She wore her old familiar black coat, pulled tightly around

her shoulders. The wind ripped loose strands from her hair, and her face was hidden in the shadows.

"Mrs. Kennedy," I said softly, approaching her. She raised her eyes. They were hollow and dim.

"I had to get away," she said.

"I know, but it's terribly cold. Shouldn't you come in?"

"I walked the beach for a while, but the sound of the ocean against the breakwaters was so rough. Angry, in a way."

She shivered. It was not good for her to sit in the damp air. "Let's go in," I suggested. "I'll fix you a strong cup of tea."

She pushed herself to her feet wearily. As we walked back to the house, I told her the doctor would be in and assured her that Mr. Kennedy's condition was stable. She thanked me by resting her hand on mine. It was as cold and as brittle as the air.

"It's so hard," she groaned, "so hard," but her eyes were dry, and I knew that only in the privacy of her room, where she could pray alone, would she give in to her deep grief. Neither her family nor the rest of the world would ever see her falter. Once, after looking in on Mr. Kennedy, she had whispered to me, "I'll be back shortly, as soon as I compose myself." That was the only time I saw an indication that she might break.

Dr. Boles had arrived by the time Mrs. Kennedy and I returned to the house. He and the Secret Service agent sat in the nurses' room. The afternoon nurse was not having any trouble with Mr. Kennedy, so I sat with them and waited. None of us spoke. We were each lost in our own thoughts.

Then I saw Eunice racing up the stairs. She never entered a house or a room; she exploded into it. She stomped up the steps angrily, cold fury written on her face. She shook off her mink coat and threw it over the banister. She ran her hands over her face, then motioned to her brother Teddy who was hesitating on the stairs behind her. The Senator came up slowly, his face white, his eyes glossy with tears. They stood for a moment in the nurses' station and spoke to us. Teddy pressed his lips together and then gave a long, trembling sigh as Eunice asked about her father. Dr. Boles told them that he had not seen Mr.

Kennedy because we wanted nothing unusual to disturb him. We knew he would have questioned the doctor's visit. He then suggested that I go in with them to watch Mr. Kennedy while they told him. Eunice gave her brother a firm look, and he straightened his shoulders and walked behind her into their father's room.

I felt that the Ambassador should be left alone with his children at this time, but I realized that I had to be there in case of an emergency. None of us knew how he would react, so I slipped quietly into the room and leaned against the dresser.

He was puzzled and surprised to see them. Teddy and Eunice stood by their father's bed, and after a moment's pause, Eunice took his hand in hers. She looked up at me, and I managed to nod. Teddy clenched his hands behind his back. Eunice bent down to kiss her father tenderly.

"Daddy," she whispered. "Daddy, there's been an accident. But Jack's okay, Daddy. Jack was in an accident, Daddy. Oh, Daddy. Jack's dead. He's dead. But he's in heaven. He's in heaven. Oh, God, Daddy. Jack's okay, isn't he, Daddy?"

Mr. Kennedy looked at her and then at his son. Teddy cried out, "Dad, Jack was shot."

Mr. Kennedy's eyes darted back and forth, a streak of panic discoloring them. There was a small footstool near the bed, and Eunice pulled it over and sat down. She laid her head on her father's hand. Teddy leaned across her and kissed his forehead, then walked around the bed, still dazed, to rest his hand on his father's shoulder.

Mr. Kennedy looked up at me, and I saw a sea of sorrow sweep over his face as he laid his hand on Eunice's buried head. As helpless as he was, something came into his eyes that told me he would be able to give them comfort. Teddy dropped to his knees and buried his face in his hands. I saw his shoulders sag, and Eunice, her body twisted with grief, said, "He's dead, Daddy. He's dead."

I had to leave the room.

I waited for them, along with Dr. Boles and Ham Brown. When they finally came out, they had composed themselves.

Eunice pressed her eyes together for a moment. Through tight, clenched lips, she said, "We'll be in with Mother if you should need us."

They shook hands with the doctor and the agent. Then Senator Kennedy took my hand, his voice cracking, and said, "Thank you, Mrs. Dallas." He wrapped his arm around his sister's waist, and they went in to their mother.

A strange thing had happened. None of us had said to either Mrs. Kennedy or to her children, "I'm sorry." It was as if the tragedy were bigger than that.

A son was gone. A handsome, sometimes reckless man, blessed with the sentiment of his Irish forebears, was gone. A man who romped with his sisters, who took quiet looks at his wife, who impulsively kissed his father and held his children close, was gone. John Kennedy was dead, and the shock was deep; but it was coupled with the realization that it was the President who was dead. Murdered. Blown apart.

Camelot, once so clear to the eye, had vanished.

All through that desolate November night, the world hung on the happenings in Dallas. Lyndon B. Johnson was now the President of the United States. Jacqueline Kennedy, blood-stained and angry, stood aside and listened as he assumed the oath of office. Lee Harvey Oswald, pale and sharp-featured, had been captured. In Washington, Robert Kennedy, laboring under the terrible loss of his brother, continued to execute his office as Attorney General.

The body of John Fitzgerald Kennedy was returned to the Capitol, and the probing eye of television gave to the world a picture of a young widow, caked in dried blood, standing in the doorway of the plane with her hand resting on her husband's casket.

Questions that only history can answer began to creep into all our minds. Why? Who?

And at Hyannis Port the wind died. From the cold Atlantic waters, an impregnable fog slid across the Cape, and a small light burned throughout the night in Mrs. Kennedy's bedroom.

Before dawn she slipped across the hall and went in to her husband. There were no words to be spoken between them. He could do nothing to lift her burden. But their eyes met, and these two people, dimming with age and bewildered in their grief, found comfort together.

2

MANY TIMES during that long night I thought back over the two years I had been on the Kennedy case. They were two years filled with memories of the whole Kennedy family. It had been a challenging period of my life, and I had run the gamut of emotions from pure joy at seeing the family in its robust happiness to deep frustration at some of the contradictions that enveloped them. I thought back to the beginning in Palm Beach, where the Kennedys first entered my life.

I was originally a native of Massachusetts, but I had been living in West Palm Beach for some years working as a staff nurse and also taking occasional private cases. By 1959 the Kennedy name had become a byword in Palm Beach society. In fact, Palm Beach was never the same after John Kennedy won the 1960 Presidential election.

Its sun-drenched elegance was rudely interrupted by a carnival of shirt-sleeved tourists and souvenir hawkers that caused even the stately palms to shudder to their roots. The moneyed residents of the beach were appalled by the brassy invasion of prying reporters and peering television cameras. Even more disconcerting to their sun-baked security was the platoon of Secret Service agents with their stoic faces, darting eyes and Brooks Brothers suits.

The traumas suffered were not too unexpected, however, for over the years the Kennedy clan had frequently caused the Establishment to blanch behind its well-guarded doors. Long after John Kennedy had taken his oath of office and was firmly ensconced in the White House, the cultured dowagers of Palm

Beach society continued to suffer regular attacks of the vapors whenever the Kennedy name was mentioned.

The Kennedy estate, and those who lived there, had never been known as *crème de la crème*. Despite its enviable location on the best stretch of sand, it was a battle-scarred architectural oddity. Compared to the surrounding, breathtaking luxury, it was a dull, cumbersome conglomeration of Spanish stucco called Moorish architecture by some, "boorish" by others.

Palm Beach, Florida, boasts some of the most famous estates in the world, palatial and elaborate beyond comprehension, but the Kennedy house, with its peeling paint, crumbling privacy wall, and weather-beaten gate, showed a defiant lack of luxury and pretension. It appeared deliberately ignorant of what money could and should buy. But it was more than the Kennedy estate that seemed so out of place; it was the whole Kennedy life-style.

From the time the Ambassador had purchased the estate, there had always been too many guests peppering the beach. Too many loud, impromptu parties and too much new money floating around to satisfy the established gentry. Actors! Blacks! Untitled foreigners! Cigar-chewing politicians! Snappy show-girls! High-powered cars! All this, coupled with gaggles of climbing, shrieking children, grandchildren, in-laws, and assorted relatives, had always seemed to be "too much." But there was little the bluebloods could do, other than sigh in despair and groan, "They're terribly Irish, you know."

Over the years, even though the social registry had not thrown open its arms to the "Irish Mafia," there had been a kind of wary truce. The genteel residents simply had to endure the clan because the Kennedys simply could not be ignored. They would not go away. They brought with them such a tidal wave of boisterous energy that one was left with the feeling of having stood in the path of a hell-bent tornado.

Meanwhile, the working people from the "other side" of the beach loved the family. We who lived there were caught up in the excitement of sirens tearing through the night and black, spit-polished limousines looming into town at all hours.

There were times, of course, when we were inconvenienced. Often certain streets were blocked off for security reasons; but no one really minded, for this meant that the President was home, and somehow just knowing he was there charged the air with excitement.

Then, on December 19, 1961, as the winter season was coming into full swing, the town was suddenly alerted by piercing sirens and roaring escorts racing down the streets, all converging on St. Mary's Hospital.

The emergency room was abruptly jolted into a turmoil of hysterical activity, for Joseph P. Kennedy, the President's father, had suffered a stroke while playing golf and was being rushed to emergency.

I was on private duty at Good Samaritan Hospital nearby, and throughout the day I heard repeated rumors that Ambassador Kennedy had suffered a massive stroke. We were told that his right side was paralyzed and that he had lost the ability to speak. I received a phone call from Mother Josephine, the administrator at St. Mary's, who confirmed that he had suffered a cerebral vascular accident. She then asked me if I could take the Kennedy case. She knew of my work at St. Elizabeth's Hospital in New York, and I had worked at St. Mary's for eight years. Also, she was aware of my intense interest in caring for people who were disabled, in any way, through paralysis.

After hearing her brief but comprehensive report on the Ambassador, I knew, if he survived, he would be in for a frustrating and painful period of convalescence and rehabilitation. I was flattered by the confidence she was placing in me, and I was excited by the possibility of such a challenge; but in good faith, I could not abruptly sign off my current case. My patient's disease was terminal, and I could not confront his family with the news that I was leaving him to care for someone else. He was a huge man, more than three hundred pounds, and this excessive weight, plus the constant care relating to his terminal condition, would present major problems in getting another nurse to take my place. It was impossible for me to leave him. Mother Josephine understood this obligation and was satisfied when I agreed to take the Ambassador's case as soon as I was free to do so. Several weeks later, when my patient succumbed, I accepted the Kennedy case.

My adult life had been spent in service as a private-duty nurse, and it had never been required of me, or of any other nurse to my knowledge, to be interviewed prior to going on a case.

Nurses are usually assigned according to qualifications and doctors' specifications. Therefore, I was surprised to be requested to report to the Kennedy house the day before I was to begin my duties, in order to meet my patient, and go through the formality of an interview.

The Ambassador was recuperating at home, but from the first day of his attack, there had been frustrating difficulties in keeping nurses on the case. I had, of course, heard all the gossip from the other nurses, and I was aware that there had been a rapid, unheard-of turnover of personnel and aides. However I always believed in finding things out for myself, so I went to the interview with an open mind.

An appointment was made for me at two o'clock the day before I was to start on the case. I drove to the Kennedy estate, parked my car on the road that fronted it, and walked up to the front door. I pressed the doorbell repeatedly, but there was no answer.

There was a high stucco wall along the street side of the property, broken by three garage doors that faced the road. A double iron-grilled gate closed off the driveway. One of the garage doors had been left open, and when no one answered the front door, I walked to the garage, peeked in, and spotted an inside door. It was locked.

I walked again to the front door, and thinking the bell might possibly be out of order, I began knocking. There was still no response.

It's been said the Irish become quickly exasperated, and, admittedly, I was. I had given up a part of my last free day in order to come for an interview, and I was determined to see it through. I peeked through the gate into the driveway and rattled it, but it was also locked. I walked down past the garages and finally came upon a small break in the wall. There was a magnificent palm tree, and evidently, when the wall was built, someone had decided to break the wall on either side of it rather than cut it down. There was barely enough room for me to squeeze through, but I managed.

Once inside the estate, I was on a small concrete patio adjacent to the side of the house. I had to duck under several clotheslines in order to follow the walk that led back to the house itself. I looked around, but there was no one in sight. I finally found a door that was unlocked and knocked on it repeatedly, but there was no response. I pushed open the door and entered an exceptionally long, wide living room. I called a couple of times but nobody answered. Corinne, the nurse I was to replace, had told me she worked on the first floor, so I decided to try to find her. I started exploring and kept calling out, but there was no answer.

Next to the living room was a fair-sized dining room, and directly across from it was a small library with a well-worn couch, a man's swivel chair, rows of books, a small bar, and fireplace. Above the mantel was a framed copy of President Kennedy's inaugural address.

I roamed through the main floor, finding many doors that appeared to lead nowhere. The stairway to the second floor was housed in a dark, windowless room. I searched through the halls and peeked into rooms until I eventually ended up in a deserted kitchen. It was a well-equipped room, with several cooking and working areas. Adjoining it was a large, comfortable butler's pantry. I peeked into a few other nooks and corners and finally found my way back to the living room. I took some time to look around the room and found it comfortable and cheerful.

One side of the room was a wall of windows that faced the ocean. Looking out, I was struck by the unique view. Leading down to the ocean was a well-tended span of grass, sprinkled with an occasional palm.

In Florida, even in the most modest surroundings, there are always flowers, and usually in wealthy homes there is a lot of landscaping; but here the simplicity of the grass, the sand, and the ocean made a very peaceful impression.

I had begun to feel strange wandering around the main floor of this large empty house calling and getting no answer, so I stood at the window, looking down at the ocean, trying to collect my thoughts. As I was trying to decide what to do next, Corinne came rushing into the room and said, "Hi, Rita, I'm sorry I didn't hear you." We were old friends, and I began telling her about my "forced entry" when another woman, wearing a white uniform, bounced in, stuck out her hand, and said warmly, "Hi! I'm Louella Hennessey." The three of us started talking, and they chuckled over my story of how I managed to get in. They explained that everyone must have decided to take a rest at the same time, and then Corinne shook her head in good humor and said, "That's the way it is around here."

Before taking me to meet my patient, she warned me that I would have to be extremely firm with him.

"He's a strong-willed man," she said. "He is also stubborn, defiant, and difficult. He gets frustrated and angry at the slightest provocation, so you'll have to watch out for him." Then she said, "And you'll have to adjust to the niece."

I had heard much about "the niece" from the doctors and other nurses who had been on the case, especially during the period when Mr. Kennedy was in the hospital. I was curious about why she carried so much authority where the Ambassador's health was concerned. However, I knew it was not uncommon to run into a member of a family who was overprotective in cases like this.

Louella offered little comment but nodded knowingly while Corinne briefed me on the problems. We decided not to go over the case history until after I had met Mr. Kennedy, so the three of us headed for his private quarters.

On the way, Louella told me that he was being housed temporarily in the President's bedroom until an elevator could be installed to the second floor, where his room was. This was to be done during the summer season while the family was at the Cape.

I thought it a bit peculiar when she did not go in with Corinne and me to meet Mr. Kennedy; but the whole situation was obviously unusual, and I decided to meet each problem as it came along. So while Louella remained outside in a small room that was about the size of a modest closet, which they told me was the nurses' station, Corinne took me into a long, rather narrow bedroom that was spectacularly light and cheerful. One wall was lined with window after window, all facing onto the patio and pool.

Ambassador Kennedy was sitting up in bed when Corinne introduced me to him, and I was immediately struck by two things: his powerful build and the most brilliant, steel blue eyes I had ever seen. Eyes that snapped with color. Clean. Sharp. And hard.

With his left hand, the hand that had not been affected by the stroke, he motioned for me to step back from him. For a long moment, his eyes went from the top of my head to my toes and back again. Finally he extended his left hand to me and said, "Yaaaaaaa." He nodded his head, which I took to be his approval, and so I smiled at him and said, "If I'm all right with you, Mr. Kennedy, you're all right with me." He nodded vigorously. Not wanting to tire him, we left, after I told him I would report early the next morning. It seemed that my "interview" had been successful.

Corinne and I met Louella and went back to the living room, where the three of us settled down to discuss the case in detail. While we were talking, I realized, that Mr. Kennedy's bedroom wall was the same as the wall of the living room where we were sitting.

"It would be very simple to set up an intercom speaker system here," I said. Corinne shrugged and said, "There's so much to be done, and so much that could be done, but you'll find it difficult to get anything accomplished. We generally seem to go around in circles. Ask Louella, she's been with the family for years."

Louella then explained to me that she was the children's nurse. She had originally come to work for the Kennedys when Pat Lawford was a child. She was having her appendix removed, and Louella had been brought in as the private-duty nurse to care for her. She was later asked to go to England with the family when Mr. Kennedy was made ambassador, for Pat had not fully recovered from the operation. After she accepted the post, she was informed that she was also expected to keep a watchful eye on Rosemary, the Kennedy daughter who was retarded.

As soon as Pat had recuperated, Rosemary became her primary concern until she had grown into young womanhood. Eventually, when Rosemary had to be placed in a private sanatorium, Louella remained on constant call to all the Kennedy women when they had their children. With the growth of the family, this had turned into a fairly perennial job. As I became a working part of the household, I saw that she was loved by all the Kennedys. She was "our Lulu" to each one, from the President on down to the youngest. They also had great respect for her because she had natural diplomatic qualities. Regardless of what she thought, she never expressed her opinions in a way that could offend or hurt anyone. She neither agreed nor disagreed and never took sides, but despite this, she was a warm woman with a strong personality.

I had heard nothing but bitter complaints about the Kennedys until my meeting with Louella, and it was refreshing to meet someone who openly expressed devotion for a change.

Louella had just finished telling me of her involvements with the family when a woman in her mid-twenties entered the room and walked over to us. She nodded pleasantly to the other two nurses, put out her hand to me in a matter-of-fact way and said, "I'm Ann Gargan."

She was wearing a pair of dungarees, a white T-shirt, worn sneakers with crew socks, and she had a heavy shock of clipped black hair, combed straight back. Her clothes and manner gave her a tomboyish quality. She had clear, fair skin with crisp black eyes, and her handsome face bore a resemblance to the actress Mercedes McCambridge. Her chin was strong, even stubborn in its thrust. I later learned that this characteristic was "pure Fitzgerald."

Although she didn't identify herself, I sensed right away that this was "the niece." This impression was strengthened when she sat down in the chair opposite us, and I noticed that she kept darting her eyes from one face to the other as we discussed the medical reports. She listened intently as Corinne briefed me on the routine and care of Mr. Kennedy. While we talked, I studied the sheaf of doctors' reports. The two nurses told me about the Ambassador's habits, his personal attitudes, his morale and his daily care.

When I was told that he was being hand-fed, I asked, in surprise, "In heaven's name, why?"

Ann interrupted, for the first time. "And why shouldn't Uncle Joe be fed? He's a sick man."

So, I thought, *this is my first confrontation with the niece.*

"Of course, he's ill," I agreed, "but he should be learning to use his able hand. He should be feeding himself. There's nothing here in the doctor's report to indicate otherwise."

I glanced at Corinne for confirmation of this, but she just gave a slight shrug. After that, Ann became extremely possessive of her uncle's welfare and treatment, overruling everything Corinne tried to say. Louella kept silent.

Ann fluffed off the doctor's orders and was quite critical of not only the therapy prescribed, but of the therapist. "Uncle Joe," she said firmly and precisely, "does not have to do anything he does not want to do. He's had enough pain and shock. He doesn't need any more. Just wait, you'll see when he tries to walk. It hurts him."

I kept my eyes glued to the doctor's report and nodded as she continued telling me about her uncle.

"He's a frightened old man, and he has reason to be. He's terrified. He hates to take medication. In fact, he's petrified that it might not be the right kind. So I'm here to see that he has everything he wants, just the way he wants it."

She spoke with stern intensity, and I recognized this overprotective attitude as a typical reaction that often occurs in the family of stroke victims. Therapy is, indeed, painful and slow. It often seems to destroy the family as much as the paralysis tends to defeat the victim. However, I am a nurse, dedicated to my profession, and I was determined to give my patient the best of my knowledge and ability. I was hired to carry out the doctor's orders, and on that first day, my patience and expectations were as yet unchallenged.

I finished reading the report and went over the chart and schedule one last time with Corinne. Then I left—this time by the front door.

On the way back to my small home in West Palm Beach, my mind raced with the events of the day. Seeing Mr. Kennedy, for that brief moment, had made it impossible for me to imagine him as Ann had described him—a frightened or terrified man. But the more I considered it, the more possible it seemed.

Joseph Kennedy was, by reputation, a ruthless man who had forged an empire. He was famous for his shrewd financial wizardry, and this know-how had always served him as a protective armor. Now the armor had cracked, and he must have felt vulnerable, for the first time in his life. Mr. Kennedy had been an extraordinarily healthy man all his life, and now he was unexpectedly immersed in pain and uncertainty. I knew nothing about the varied manipulations of financial empires, but I could well imagine the traumas he, his family, and his business associates faced. After his stroke the intricate network of influence and power that Mr. Kennedy had created and held under single-handed control was in the hands of a disabled and seriously handicapped man. His speech disability was most disconcerting because one incorrect, incoherent, or misinterpreted order from him could easily create an economic crisis. I knew that millions were involved. His condition, therefore, was a definite crisis—but was he terrified?

I knew the doctors' and specialists' views were optimistic. It was improbable that he could ever function again to his full capacity, but he could, at least, be rehabilitated to the point where he would not burden himself or his family. There were many reasons why the doctors were optimistic, despite the severity of his stroke. First, Mr. Kennedy was, by nature, a healthy man. He had fine muscle tone, and his posture was excellent. He was a beautifully maintained individual. This alone would tend to make the prognosis optimistic. Another major advantage was that because of his wealth, he could have the finest rehabilitation specialists in the world. But more than all this was his legendary strong will. A self-made man of immense personal wealth he had become an ambassador and virtually placed his son in the Presidency.

In spite of all this I knew he would need all the encouragement and assistance he could get to overcome the unexpected handicaps that he was suddenly afflicted with. It is almost impossible for a healthy person to imagine the sensation of being strong and vital one moment, then suddenly experiencing the pain of a stroke and waking up in a hospital completely helpless in the grip of paralysis. The shock is complete. Your body is not your own. You cannot move and, worse than that, when your speech is affected, you cannot communicate with anyone. The emotional panic is severe and the struggle back is often unendurably slow.

In a massive stroke, such as he suffered, the right leg, arm, and face were affected, producing a paralysis in these areas. The hemisphere of the brain that was involved, in this case the left side, controlled his speech, which was lost. His words were, for the most part, garbled or not in any logical sequence. It was not that he could not pronounce any words. He could. The problem was that, in his brain, he did not know what the words were that he was saying. He knew the words he wanted to use, but the directive mechanism, the portion of the brain that directs this ability, was not operating. This was, in all probability, a temporary condition. In speaking, what he would intend to come out as "no" might easily be blurted out as "yes," and he would have absolutely no control over it. He knew in his mind he wanted to say "no," but the ability to say it was hampered. This is not unusual as an initial condition in a stroke and will often rectify itself.

His right facial muscles were inoperable. He could not control his mouth, and therefore, it dropped on the affected side. This being so, there was no way for him to control his salivation.

During the initial stages of his stroke, while he was still in the hospital, the flexor muscles in his right wrist became spastic or completely rigid. It is crucial to rectify this, if possible, and the doctors placed it in a splint in order to prevent the wrist muscles from pulling the wrist down into total flexion. This means that, without the therapy of the splint, the fingers would be drawn down to the point of almost touching the wrist. It is impossible for one to use the hand or fingers when the wrist is drawn to such a degree. The splint kept the wrist straight and was an initial step in his rehabilitation.

The doctor's report puzzled me for it was definite in stating that the family had given Mr. Kennedy's niece complete authority over him. I learned that it was she who remained on the premises during his stay at the hospital, and the hospital chart stated that it was at her direction that his splint was removed from his wrist. She claimed it was an unjustified indignity her uncle should not have to suffer, and when he became fretful wearing it, the corrective splint was removed. Apparently the removal of the splint caused his hand to become deformed.

There are varying degrees of damage as the result of the kind of stroke Mr. Kennedy suffered. Sometimes the incapacity can become permanent, as in the case of his wrist, and sometimes the condition is not irreversible.

There are a certain number of cells in the brain called motor cells. When we think of moving a finger, for example, these cells make the finger move by initiating the motion in the muscle. This is the motor neuron, and this sends the message from the brain. If the message that comes down to the muscle comes from a cell that is very much upset, the message may be normal or abnormal. If the cell is completely dead, then the muscle this cell innervates will be permanently paralyzed. If the cell is merely damaged, however, then there will be improvement as it comes back to normal. The muscles which are stronger, like the flexor muscle of the wrist or the flexor muscle of the knee, usually retain more function, simply because they are stronger muscles and have more cells directing them.

These cells usually persist, even when other lesser cells disappear. Muscles that are spastic or rigid are those whose brain cells are not so badly influenced. They are overpowering muscles. These are the muscles that pulled the wrist down into flexion.

Mr. Kennedy had reached a point where the doctors and therapists were hoping to ambulate him. To assist in this, a long walking rail was set up in the living room for his exercising. He was a typical patient, unhappy about wearing a leg brace. This reluctance can sometimes develop into a major problem, for a brace can be quite painful until the muscles adjust to it. Since the flexor muscles of the knee, the ones that bend the knee, are stronger, they are therefore overpowering in a paralysis of this sort. When the leg brace is buckled on, the knee is forced straight, against the overpowering muscles, but there is no other way to walk unless the leg is straight. Also, there is a danger of falling without the brace and the hip can be dislocated.

In a hemiplegic or paraplegic, it is imperative that they not be pampered. In any rehabilitation program, overindulgence is absolutely the worst thing that can be done to a patient. It is a crime. A patient needs encouragement, interest, and help, but not too much help. Any unnecessary pampering prevents the patient from helping himself, and the results are often a self-destructive dependency. I felt that Mr. Kennedy could be helped, and I was anxious to take on the challenge.

Later that night it occurred to me that I had not met Mrs. Kennedy. This seemed peculiar, especially when an interview had been specifically requested. I knew Mr. Kennedy had not been capable of making the request himself, so if it had not come from Mrs. Kennedy, I wondered who could have made it. And why? These were only the first of a long series of questions that I was to ask myself while on the Kennedy case. There were innumerable questions and countless problems.

During the next eight and a half years, ninety-three nurses came and went, and I still often shake my head and wonder how I alone managed to survive to the end. Holding qualified personnel became almost impossible, for duties were never defined. The nurses' quarters were constantly invaded by floods of children and adults, who went through cartons of Band-Aids and gallons of ointment. Each demanded personal attention, and as a result, there was no way to maintain any logical order or system. Caring for Mr. Kennedy became terribly complicated not only because of his physical condition but also because the house was always swarming with the conflicting energies of his large, boisterous, loving family.

Despite the problems, one thing stood out over the years: There was never a moment when the love each child felt for Mr. Kennedy was not evident, and if his disability offended them, they never let him know it. It was not easy for them to see him incapacitated because Mr. Kennedy had personally taught them to respect only physical and mental perfection in others. Anything or anyone less than perfect was, in his way of thinking, out of the swim of life. Time and again I would see them stand outside his door and actually seem to screw up their courage from deep inside before entering the sickroom. They went in to him with shoulders squared, but when they left his presence, they would often sag against the wall in despair and frustration.

During those years, I watched life come and go. I saw the newborn take their places in the legend, and I watched a strong family crumble from assassination, murder and scandal. My personal identity often seemed to be completely absorbed by the rush of events that the famous Kennedy magnetism drew to itself. Indeed, from my first day as Mr. Kennedy's nurse I became immersed in history. It was an extraordinary and unforgettable experience.

I decided to spend my last night before taking the case researching through my encyclopedia for whatever Kennedy history I could find. I had followed the Kennedys for years and kept up with them in the papers, but I wanted to refresh my mind and learn as much as possible about this extraordinary family.

Mr. Kennedy's personal ambition had been to capture the Presidency for himself, and much of his initial energy had been directed toward this goal. Politically, his hopes were drowned when, as ambassador to England, he avidly and publicly opposed the United States giving aid of any kind to the Allies in World War II. As Hitler marched freely across Europe, Ambassador Kennedy's appeasement philosophy, coupled with the passive timidity of Britain's Prime Minister, Neville Chamberlain, destroyed all personal chances for his seeking a political career.

He hotly opposed Franklin Roosevelt seeking a third term, and resigned shortly after the election landslide—probably having been given no choice.

In 1968 *Fortune* magazine estimated his wealth at more than $300,000,000. This he had amassed by his own wits on Wall Street. He was the undisputed financial chanticleer, but politically he was a lame duck.

It is now legendary how, after his own aspirations were foiled, his drive for the Presidency centered on his first son, Joseph Patrick Kennedy, Jr. All plans were altered to suit this new direction. It is strange how that decision which marks the beginning of Joseph Kennedy's drive to fulfill his ambitions through his sons also marks the beginning of the series of tragedies that still haunt the family and its name. Joseph, Jr., was killed in 1944 while serving on active duty as a Navy pilot. John was injured permanently when the PT boat he captained was destroyed in the Solomon Islands. A daughter, Kathleen, was killed in an airplane crash in 1948. Shortly after, it became necessary to have Rosemary placed in a private sanatorium. Despite her retardation, Mr. and Mrs. Kennedy had made a valiant effort to keep her part of the family, but the time came when they reluctantly made the only choice open to them. She was permanently hospitalized, as she is to this day.

When Joseph, Jr., died, the mantle went to the next son. The details of John Kennedy's rise to political power are leg-

endary. The Kennedy clan banded together to ring every doorbell in the Eleventh District of Massachusetts during his
campaign, and he was elected with a five-to-one majority. He
took his seat in the House of Representatives in 1947 at the age
of twenty-nine and was twice reelected to this office with the
same vigorous campaigning supporting him.

In 1952 he made his bid for the Senate and defeated the
incumbent Republican Senator, Henry Cabot Lodge, in his
own political stronghold. John Kennedy was reelected to the
Senate in 1958 with more than 75 percent of the votes cast in
his favor. This margin of victory was the largest ever recorded
for any office in the history of Massachusetts.

The Kennedys had produced a vote getter.

The political stigma attached to his father's name had apparently been erased. John Kennedy had been wildly received
over national television at the 1956 Democratic Convention
when he nominated Adlai Stevenson for President. During the
next four years, an unprecedented campaign was launched to
put John Kennedy into the Presidency. He received his party's
nomination and won the office of President over his opponent,
Richard Nixon, in 1960. He became not only the youngest
President in history, but the first Catholic to hold the national
office.

The Kennedy phenomenon was in full swing, and every
member of the family shared the heady mace of success with
the exception of Mr. Kennedy. As Eunice, Teddy, Bobby, Jean,
Pat, Rose, Ethel, Jackie, Caroline, and John-John became
household names, every effort was made to disassociate the
father from the son in the public's eye.

I often wondered during the years I cared for Mr. Kennedy
what his thoughts must have been when the praise and glory
went to others. Power, of course, was unquestionably his, but
his ruthless and controversial reputation labeled him as an
undesirable associate to the President. Great caution was taken
to dispel any thought that the President or his administration
was under his father's influence, so much so that he was literally smuggled in, under wraps, whenever he visited the White

House. The public soon forgot there was, or ever had been, a father image.

Some political historians feel that the New Frontier was often more celebrated for its image and style than for its accomplishments. Even though John Kennedy and his family were idolized the world over, it is felt by some that it was only during the first year in office that he was able to electrify the political field.

His father's stroke occurred in the eleventh month of John Kennedy's term, and I often wondered how history might have been different if this powerful, driving source of energy and vitality had not been suddenly incapacitated. His illness prevented him from active participation in the lives of his family and suddenly to be deprived of the force that had steered the course for all of them had to make his family vulnerable.

As I finished my research, I thought back to my first impression of Mr. Kennedy. His face was still full of strength, even though it sagged from the effect of his stroke. His body disputed his seventy-odd years, for he was still a powerfully built man and his unaffected muscles were still perfectly toned. But what I remembered most about him and still do were the piercing blue eyes. They were unforgettable, almost mesmerizing. Stubborn. Suspicious. Curious. Penetrating. I also remembered one of my first thoughts when I heard about Mr. Kennedy's stroke: *The President is on his own.*

I realized as I read about the tremendous influence and accomplishments of Joseph Kennedy how much he had done for his family. It was obvious that the driving factor behind the Kennedy rise to power had been instilled in his sons by Mr. Kennedy. I knew that they had to feel his absence if only as a father. Above all, I thought of the challenge of his rehabilitation if only for the sake of his family. There was much that could be accomplished through therapy to restore Mr. Kennedy's vitality, and I was eager to begin.

3

THE NEXT MORNING I reported on the Kennedy case prepared to undertake his rehabilitation. When his breakfast was brought to him by Dora, his beloved personal waitress, I said, "Well, Mr. Kennedy, what do you say to the idea of feeding yourself?"

He looked at me sharply, his eyes flashed hard; but after a moment I sensed a change in them, and finally he nodded his head yes. Since he did not have the use of his right hand, he picked up the glass of juice with his left and guided it to his lips. His eyes glinted as if to say, "Don't look so surprised. I can do it."

I encouraged him throughout his meal, and when he finished, we both shared a feeling of success after his effort. And it had been just that. Effort. After I removed the tray, he lifted his left hand slowly and offered it to me. Nodding his head, he attempted to tell me he was pleased.

The morning had gone well.

I had heard that it was impossible to do anything with Mr. Kennedy when he was disturbed. I had also learned, through long years of practice, never to discount a nurse's report, and Corinne had said, "He'll fight you like a tiger, when it's time for his morning sunning."

Therefore, when I noted on his chart that it was time for him to be taken for his morning air, I was on guard. I managed to get him in his chair, but as I started to wheel him through the patio doors of his bedroom, he grabbed for a bedside table. We then had our first battle. Books, medicine, water, magazines flew in every direction. He threw whatever he could reach, and it was such a violent outburst that I left the room until he calmed down or exhausted himself.

I knew, since this was a daily occurrence, that something had to be drastically wrong. So I headed for the kitchen in search of Dora.

Corinne had told me that she had been in his service for many years, and Mr. Kennedy considered her an essential part of his personal staff. She, in turn, had great respect for him. I thought, if anyone would know about his habits, she would. I found her in the kitchen and we talked openly about his anger. I asked her, "When Mr. Kennedy was well, was he a sun lover?" She replied quickly, "Oh, my, no. He would spend a short time in the bullpen taking a little sun; but he was never one to sit around the pool, and he never would be out in the sun without his hat."

After talking with Dora, I returned to his room. He was still furious and started yelling, but I yelled louder.

"Mr. Kennedy, we're going to have to learn how to talk to each other," I shouted over and over. He kept bellowing and flinging his left arm as if to strike me.

"Now, wait a minute," I thundered. "You hired me to take care of you, and that's what I'm going to do."

The shouting match continued, but finally his agitation began to subside.

"We'll have to figure out some way for you to tell me what's wrong with you or what you want to do. Isn't that right?"

Leveling off, he shook his head vigorously and pointed toward the patio.

"Do you want to go outside?"

"Nooooo," he bellowed. "Nooooo."

"All right, all right. Now let's be logical and I'll tell you how you can signal me when you're in the wheelchair."

He watched me carefully as I promised him that if he would cooperate, I would always try to understand what he wanted.

"Mr. Kennedy, if you're going to be wheeled somewhere and you don't want to go there, all you have to do is put out your left foot and we'll stop. Then simply point to where you want to go. Is that clear?"

He shook his head yes.

I got behind his chair and said, "Now you show me where you want to go. Show me."

It puzzled me when he pointed to the patio, but nevertheless I wheeled him to the door. Then he stuck out his left foot. I stopped.

"Now where?" I asked.

He pointed to an umbrella table and said, "Thaaaaa."

I wheeled him to it. He let out a long, deep breath and relaxed back in the chair. "Mr. Kennedy," I asked, "do you like the sun?"

"Noooooo," he roared and began pounding his fist on the table.

"Then you've been taking sunbaths against your will?"

"Yaaaaa!" he bellowed. "Yaaaaa! Yaaaaa!"

His eyes were panicked with frustration, and hoping to calm him, I offered my hand. He grabbed it. I felt his grip grow strong as he pumped up and down. I emphasized again that I would always try to understand and reminded him that so long as he remembered his signals, he would never be taken anywhere he didn't want to go.

We sat under the shade of the umbrella and I talked to him for a long time. At one point I told him that Dora had said he used to sun in the bullpen, and he pointed to a roofless concrete boxlike building, a short distance from the pool.

"Is that where the men sunbathe?" I asked. He nodded. By the time his sunning period was over I felt we had made a good start.

During the rest of my shift, I learned a great deal about him. He religiously devoured the New York *Times* and was developing strong television habits. He particularly enjoyed the afternoon game shows and especially the *Lucy* reruns.

I learned that he dreaded his daily sessions with the therapist, but it was marvelous to watch him endure the buckling on of his leg brace and see his determination to walk the parallel bars. The muscles in his shoulders bulged as he pulled himself along, and after these daily sessions he would be so exhausted he would lie limp on his bed.

Without my assistance, he was able to handle his noon meal and afternoon snack. He was flushed with pride. As I was leaving for the day, I told him, "I'm going to check with your doctor, and maybe I'll have a surprise for you in the morning."

His eyes brightened with curiosity as he held out his hand to say good-bye. I shook it generously and said, "Feed yourself at dinner, Mr. Kennedy. If you do, I think I can guarantee a surprise." He nodded agreeably, almost like a small boy.

As soon as I reached home, I phoned his doctor and asked if there was any reason why he should not go to the table for his meals. The doctor said, "If you can swing that one, Mrs. Dallas, we're on our way."

He further said that the great frustrations he and the specialist were having were due to lack of encouragement and discipline. "He's being treated like a spoiled child. If he doesn't want to do something, his niece puts a stop to it. And you know, Mrs. Dallas, as well as I, that sometimes a patient must be coerced into a rehabilitative routine."

"Then I have your permission to take him to the table?"

"You not only have my permission, you have my heartfelt support."

I mentioned the discovery I had made regarding his sunbaths. The doctor informed me that he was also objecting to using the pool for therapy, even though a whirlpool had been installed for him.

"That figures," I said, "he's in the sun, and he hates it."

The doctor suggested a solution. "I suppose the pool could be covered and heated. Of course, there won't be any problem with the family, for they want him to have whatever he needs, so I'll talk to the Attorney General about it."

Soon construction got under way, and a corrugated plastic building was set up to enclose the pool. It was like a house. Later the same type of building was constructed over the Hyannis Port pool. I often loved to compare the Kennedys' taste to, for example, the adjoining estate in Palm Beach. A glimpse onto the grounds was like looking back to Rome at its zenith, accented by tons of glistening marble of high columns and wide steps, leading down to an enormous pool. Silk-covered lounges, fountains, and graceful walks gave the elaborate villa a breathtaking beauty. The display of flowers and manicured shrubbery was true artistry.

To look then at the plastic shed on the Kennedy estate was startling; but the family was satisfied with it, and I realized, for the first time, that money per se was not really important to them. Only what money could do mattered. It was the strength of money that was important to them, and the Ambassador had taught his children how to use it to its fullest advantage.

After my conversation with his doctor, I could hardly wait to tell Mr. Kennedy the news the next day. He was awake when I came on my shift and was itching with curiosity.

He remembered!

When I told him about his "surprise," he took a deep breath, and a proud and anxious man began to emerge. He immediately wanted to select the dressing gown and pajamas he would wear to the breakfast table the next morning. I wheeled him to his closet, and he pointed to a heavy blue silk robe that matched the blue of his eyes. He picked velvet monogrammed slippers to wear with black silk hose, and to complete the outfit, he selected a pair of rich ivory-colored raw-silk pajamas and a muted striped ascot.

"You won't need to wear that, Mr. Kennedy," I said, referring to the ascot. He fingered it a moment or two, then laid it aside, and I was relieved that he did not object. I didn't want him to wear it because I had to watch his swallowing carefully. The paralysis had affected his throat, and although his swallowing had improved and he was able to eat most anything, there was still the danger that something could choke him accidentally.

All through the day he made a great point of helping himself. He ate breakfast and lunch off his tray and did exceptionally well, using his left hand. He kept eyeing me for approval, and both of us enjoyed his astounding capabilities.

That afternoon I told Louella and Ann that he was going to the table the next morning for breakfast. Ann immediately objected. "And what makes you think Uncle Joe's going to do that?"

"I don't think," I replied, not wavering. "I know. I checked with his doctor, and he agrees that it should be done." When Louella raised her shoulders, as if to say, "I wish you luck," I was beginning to feel I might need it.

Ann objected strongly to the idea that her uncle was being "forced" to go to the table for his meals. In her opinion, he should stay in his own room, where his meals were brought to him and then be hand-fed. In this way, she reasoned, he would not use up his already-sparse strength.

She raised many arguments, which I repeatedly answered with "doctor's orders." At the end she finally said, "Well, take my advice, and don't start making plans until you see Aunt Rose about this."

This was my first real confrontation with Ann, and over the years that I was on the case I was in very close contact with her because of her relationship with Mr. Kennedy. In some ways Ann had been allocated the role that often falls to a less affluent relative. I once asked one of the members of the staff what Ann had done before Mr. Kennedy had become ill, and the reply was: "Walked ten paces behind, and carried his briefcase." Whatever her duties were before his illness, she was to become a predominant figure on the scene during the years that followed. Her authority became indisputable.

Ann had a perplexing trait which grew more pronounced as time went on. She was constantly buying puppies. She would scour the want ads in search of a new one, regardless of breed, then devote herself to making the little animal totally dependent on her. The puppy would sleep with her and be hand-fed by her, until the little creature had become completely absorbed by her love and attention. When it had reached the stage of crying and pining after her, she gave it away, usually to some member of the Kennedy complex.

As soon as she had disposed of it, she would buy another. Invariably, the old dogs were around, and when they would see Ann, they would dash to her with tails wagging, but she would pat them absently and then shoo them away.

Ann had many controversial and complex sides to her nature. In one respect, she was a delightful slapstick comedienne. Interestingly, her antics had varied effects on the members of the family. Usually the boys were casually amused by her comedy, whereas the girls, though exceedingly fond of her, studied her performances with cocked brows, as if to say, "Oh, well, that's Ann for you."

Mrs. Kennedy, it appeared to me, was so absorbed in her dilemmas and ever-mounting responsibilities that it never appeared to penetrate that there were times when her niece had the tendency to behave like a roguish jester. Mrs. Kennedy had the rare ability to "block out." Her formula for survival seemed to be based on: see what you want to see and hear only what you want to hear.

Considering the tragedies that shattered her life, this formula might well have been her only course to self-survival. And regardless of the grief and despair that flooded her waking hours and haunted her dreams, she possessed an extraordinary determination to survive. Ann's presence was a great relief to her with all her burdens, and Ann's drawing-room behavior never bothered her perhaps because it meant so much to her to have Ann there.

It was, however, disquieting when Ann would break into a wild comic routine at the most inopportune and illogical moments. Had it not been for Mr. Kennedy's grave condition, coupled with the serious routine of his therapy, she would have been a charming, witty, original, and quite amusing companion. During the first dreary days after the Ambassador's attack, I imagine this lightheartedness was a diversion for the family, but too much gaiety, even from an expert, can become wearisome. Sometimes her humor seemed to be overdone and suggested a need to be paid attention to—a need to be loved that was rooted in insecurity.

I was keenly aware of Ann's composite attitudes, for she was an ever-present force on the horizon, holding unequivocal dominance over my patient.

Ann could be lovable and amusing one moment and completely exasperating the next. I spent many hours trying to understand her, and I gained some insight from an article in the *Ladies' Home Journal* called "The Kennedy Nobody Knows." Working with writer Gail Cameron, Ann spoke out about herself.

Virtues and frailties have greater creditability when they are confirmed by the subject in question. Opinions ventured on another individual's personality can often assume prejudicial proportions, but self-admission is, for the most part, indisputable.

In the article Ann relates that her mother, Mrs. Kennedy's sister, died when she was two years old and her father when she was ten. She and her brother, Joe, were raised by an aunt and uncle in Lowell, Massachusetts.

Quoting from the article about her experiences in school: "Ann went to boarding school, beginning with the Sacred Heart Academy in Newton, Massachusetts, and winding up, finally, at Marymount in Tarrytown, New York. An enthusiastic student, she nevertheless managed to make enough of a mark for two schools to dismiss her. 'They said my behavior was not what they wanted,' Ann explains. It included, it seemed, among other things, filling up the font of Holy Water with ink, whereby unsuspecting nuns would pass by and bless themselves with Waterman's blue-black. In study halls she communicated with friends by pinning notes onto nuns' robes as they floated by. There was also the night that Ann and a friend rang the chapel bell at 11:10, getting the whole school up for Mass."

In the same article, in response to Ann's stories on herself, Mrs. Kennedy says: "She was always a little angel, at least around our house. I refused to believe the things they'd tell me about the things she did at school."

The article continued to relate how, at nineteen, she decided to become a nun, and joined the sisters of the Holy Cross in South Bend, Indiana. She wanted to become a nursing nun and work in either a hospital or foreign mission. Ann told Miss Cameron, "I had no interest in science, but I was drawn to the human part of nursing; I liked the idea of helping a sick person to feel more comfortable." Unfortunately, two months before she was to take her first vows, she had to leave the convent because she became ill and was diagnosed to have multiple sclerosis. Fortunately, the multiple sclerosis subsided, and when I knew her, she seemed to be in fine health.

The article further elaborates: "I am a great animal lover. And I am also a great animal giver, so watch out."

Upon close scrutiny, these published self-admissions project the life of a girl who, until the Ambassador's stroke, was a quasi-member of a famous family and, as such, had been relegated to the perimeter of its intimacy.

As I became more involved, it was evident that Ann possessed a desperate and, in fairness to her, an understandable need to be loved and noticed. Her humor, which could often be charming, and her role as companion to her uncle were the two main areas of fulfillment for her. Ann attended Mr. Kennedy with a dedicated devotion, which could have been used to his greatest advantage if only she had agreed to train herself or, at least, to understand the technical and professional aspects of nursing and rehabilitation. Since she did not avail herself of the opportunity of learning, her role should have been that of his personal companion. There is no room for "nonscientific" nursing. With her great love and devotion, he would have made remarkable strides and served as a worldwide incentive for other stroke victims and their families. As it was, she was a loving amateur, ill equipped to overrule and override prescribed treatment. She represented his loyal protector, in her mind, and there is no doubt that he projected a powerful and genuine father image to her.

Most of the members on the staff thought it was strange that such devotion was not partially directed to her blood aunt, but

then, Mrs. Kennedy was not the type of woman who solicited
or returned familiarity. Ann always treated her with respect,
but it was "Uncle Joe" who was her ideal and her security.

The private role she played under the Kennedy roof was
often effective and personally rewarding to her, but had destiny
not fitted her into the script, the saga of Mr. Kennedy might
have read differently.

After that first confrontation with Ann about Mr. Kennedy
eating breakfast at the table, I realized that she was not someone to take lightly. Since she seemed to have so much authority
over Mr. Kennedy, I felt I had to watch her carefully. That
seemed to be the key theme in the whole Kennedy case. Watch
out. Watch out for the niece, watch out for the family, watch
out for Mr. Kennedy, watch out for his tantrums, watch out
for his left hook.

I had been on the case for only two days, but already the
contradictions and challenges were amazing.

When my shift was over, I went to the library and called Mrs.
Lester, the Ambassador's personal therapist, to tell her that I
had made the arrangements for our patient to have breakfast
in the dining room the following morning.

"Will you come early and help me?" I asked.

Mrs. Lester, a highly skilled therapist, agreed immediately,
and we made plans for her to come early and help me prepare
him. As soon as Mrs. Kennedy returned from mass, we wanted
to have him ready to join her at the table.

After my talk with Mrs. Lester, I went to the kitchen and
explained to Dora how to set the table for him. I told her he
would need everything laid out for a left-handed service. I cau-
tioned her not to be too obvious about it, but to see that things
were arranged so he could help himself. Dora, who loved him
deeply, was genuinely touched, and I left the kitchen with her
promises to do everything she could to make the meal go
smoothly.

I had been on duty with the Ambassador for two days but
had yet to meet an immediate member of his family. I had
glimpsed Mrs. Kennedy walking across the grounds to her car,

or going down to the beach, but we had never met face to face.

I was a little puzzled as to how I should approach her or, for that matter, find her, but I realized that Ann was right in advising me to discuss the arrangements with her, for I did not imagine Mrs. Kennedy to be a woman given lightly to surprises.

I asked Louella what would be the best way for me to go about seeing her. She told me that Mrs. Kennedy adhered to a very strict routine. Every afternoon she left the house and was driven to the country club, where she played several holes of golf.

I decided to wait in the parking lot, in the hope of intercepting her on her way to golf. When I spotted her chauffeured car pulling out of the driveway, I started toward it. At almost the same moment she saw me and waved her hand through the window, calling, "Nurse, please come over here for a moment."

My first impression of her was somewhat startling. She was wearing a large floppy hat, enormous sunglasses, and pieces of what seemed to be adhesive tape stuck on her face. I later learned that these were what she called her "frownies." They were flesh-colored tape that she insisted should be worn in order to prevent wrinkles. She was especially concerned with the frown line between the eyebrows, and I seldom saw her around the house without a frownie or two on her face.

I attempted to introduce myself to her, but she began speaking right away.

"Nurse," she said briskly, "naturally, I don't like to have anyone dislike me, so there is something I want you to do. Mr. Kennedy has an afternoon nurse who is very unsatisfactory. While my husband was in the hospital, I didn't feel I had the right to judge her, but here in my own home, I simply cannot tolerate the idea of such sloppy dressing."

I knew the nurse in question, and she was right. She was careless with her appearance and seemed to do everything in a loud, clattery, nonprofessional sort of way.

Mrs. Kennedy perched on the edge of the seat and stuck her

head out the window. "And, Nurse, have you noticed that she actually wears sneakers while on duty?"

I nodded, a bit overpowered.

"I want you to call up the Registry," she continued, "and tell them that she's through. If we need an extra nurse, have them send over someone who looks halfway decent."

"Mrs. Kennedy," I said, "I think the Registry would expect the dismissal to come from you or a member of your family. I simply don't have the authority."

"Well," she gasped, drawing back, "I could never do it. You do it. Tell them I said you're in charge. Tell them anything; only get rid of that woman."

I learned a quick lesson right then. Where a Kennedy is concerned, you do things their way! With them, no other way works.

She dismissed the matter by telling her chauffeur to drive on, but I placed my hand on the door and said, "May I have just a moment?" I asked.

The chauffeur patiently set the car in neutral, but Mrs. Kennedy looked impatiently at her watch.

"I'm going to be late for my golf. Perhaps we could spend some time together in the morning."

"But that's what I wanted to talk to you about, Mrs. Kennedy. The Ambassador will be joining you for breakfast."

"What?" she said, whipping off her glasses and squinting at me. "What did you say?"

"The Ambassador will be eating breakfast in the dining room in the morning," I repeated. "I wanted to tell you in advance."

Her eyes widened. "You don't really intend to have him come to the table and eat, do you? Is that what you're telling me?"

"Isn't it wonderful, Mrs. Kennedy? The doctor feels he's strong enough, and your husband is quite excited about it."

"But he'll be so embarrassed," she groaned. "He's a very proud man, and in his condition . . . why, Nurse, he drools . . . without realizing it. If he ever knew, he would die of humiliation."

I explained that he was in the first stages of his recovery and his facial muscles were growing stronger. I assured her the salivating would eventually stop. I attempted to explain more about his condition, but she cut in, saying, "I dine with him in his room every night," she said, "and he seems quite content with the arrangement. He can't even feed himself and, well, I don't see how it can be done any better at the table. I won't hear of him going through unnecessary personal humiliation. He would be offended to be hand-fed in the dining room."

"He's feeding himself now," I said. "Didn't you know?"

"My niece feeds him," she declared firmly, "or didn't *you* know?"

"She doesn't when I'm on duty! He's been doing it for himself and quite well. Your husband is a remarkable man, Mrs. Kennedy, and in a day's time he has learned to handle his silver with great dexterity."

"But what about the drooling?"

"It will soon stop," I promised gently, "but even if it doesn't, won't he have to learn to face people? That is a part of his recovery, Mrs. Kennedy, so shouldn't it begin with his family?"

"Oh, I don't know. I just don't know."

She pressed her hand to her brow, and I could feel her anxiety. She looked up at me obviously confused and said, "What shall I do, Nurse?"

"I know it's been an adjustment for you to make," I replied, "but believe me, Mrs. Kennedy, it is for his good, and I promise you he'll be all right."

"Well," she said, putting on her sunglasses, "if it will help him, of course I'll do anything I can. But nothing must go wrong. Absolutely nothing must go wrong. Nothing must disturb him in the slightest way. Nothing! He's been through too much."

"He's terribly excited about it," I went on. "He's already selected the clothes he will wear, and it's been wonderful to see his responses. You won't believe the difference."

"I hope so." She sighed painfully. "Oh, God, I hope so." I stepped away from the car, and they drove off.

The next morning everything went well for Mrs. Lester and me. Mr. Kennedy was beaming and cooperative, so the routine went like clockwork. As we dressed him, he was fanatically concerned that every detail be exactly right. He impatiently motioned for me to wheel him to the door mirror. He preened in front of it, critically studying himself and fussing with his dressing robe until every fold suited him. I made an attempt to brush his hair, but he was not satisfied and jerked the brush away from me. I held a hand mirror while he brushed and combed diligently with his left hand until every strand was in place. He kept looking at his watch, obviously impatient for his wife to return from mass. Usually, it was her custom to remain for two services, but on this morning she arrived home earlier than usual.

Louella had been posted as a lookout and came bouncing into the room, bubbling, "She's here, Mr. Kennedy. She's here."

He motioned for me to stand in front of his chair, his eyes squinting as he inspected me up and down. Then he indicated that I should turn around for a complete inspection. I waited for his approval. Finally, he reached out to flick a small speck of powder off my uniform. That done, he nodded his head in final approval and regally signaled us to wheel him through the door.

Ann met us in the hall with a wide smile and said, "Oh, Uncle Joe, you do look great. You really do look great. Aunt Rose is in the dining room waiting, so I'll take you to her."

I stepped aside for her to wheel him but followed close behind. I assumed that as his personal nurse I would be expected to eat with him, but when we reached the dining room I saw that only three places had been set.

As Ann wheeled him in, I slipped discreetly into the library, which was only a few feet from the dining area. From a chair, which I pulled up to the doorway, I was able to keep a close watch on him. I had to be able to see if he was swallowing his food easily.

Later that morning I learned that Mrs. Kennedy never allowed a "paid" person to share her table. This dictum went so far as to include some of the most highly respected doctors and specialists in this country. The rest of the family—Teddy, Bobby, the First Lady and the President, Eunice, Pat, Jean— had no such rule, and when we were together, meals were always shared.

This had been the arrangement with any patient I had nursed, but Mrs. Kennedy had a staunch rule and kept to it. Later Dora told me that Mr. Kennedy, prior to his illness, had always asked for, and expected, everyone to be in his dining room—governesses, nurses, everyone. She said that when they were in London during his term as ambassador, he made a great point of instructing his daughters to watch how the "nanny" acted. "See," he said, "she has manners. So pay attention. All of you. Pay attention and maybe you can become ladies, too."

I was told Mr. Kennedy had the highest regard for working people, but after his illness many changes were to occur in his household. As it stood, Mrs. Kennedy was the mistress, and I was pleased to consider her wishes, so long as it did not hamper my patient.

The meal began, and everything was going exceptionally well, especially for Mr. and Mrs. Kennedy. She talked to her husband and made a great effort to keep him at ease. Mr. Kennedy was very pleased with himself, and despite his problems, he was still an imposing and handsome figure.

He was eating heartily when without provocation or warning Ann suddenly decided to put on a show for him.

I stared in disbelief while she slipped out of her chair, dropped down on her hands and knees, and started crawling around under the table to "Uncle Joe." Mrs. Kennedy, oblivious to what was happening, was tucked behind the paper reading bits of news to her husband. Ann crawled up to her uncle and began making all sorts of wild faces, mimicking the mannerisms and facial expressions of Mrs. Kennedy peering over her glasses. She kept wagging her tongue and yanking at his pajama leg in order to hold his attention. All this time Mrs. Kennedy was completely unaware of what was going on. She was concentrating on her reading.

Mr. Kennedy succeeded in ignoring Ann until she began tickling his foot and leg, and talking baby talk. Suddenly Mr. Kennedy lost control and burst out laughing. Mrs. Kennedy dropped her paper, overturning her water glass, and stared at him, shocked by this sudden interruption. She was confused by his unexpected outburst, and seeing that he was not himself, she was frightened. She looked at him as if to say, "What have I done?" Dora, trembling, tried to wipe up the spilled water, but Mrs. Kennedy brushed her aside. Mr. Kennedy's laughter began to get out of control.

When a patient who has suffered a stroke is hit by a strong emotion, he is often unable to regulate his reaction the way a healthy person can. This will often result in fits of laughing or crying. Sometimes both the laughter and the crying take place at the same time, and this is what was happening to Mr. Kennedy. His laughter got wilder and wilder, and he was completely unable to explain to his wife why he was acting in such a way. Under more normal conditions, he might have looked at Ann, and perhaps thought her antics amusing, but he would certainly have ignored the matter and not have reacted to it in such a startling manner. He was completely victimized by the incident, for his illness prevented a normal reaction. Often, after a victim gets past the initial stages of a stroke, control will return, but this incident was too soon after his stroke and I saw that he had worked himself into the throes of an attack. I ran to help him, but Ann, frightened into tears by the scene she had caused, blocked my way by throwing her arms around his neck. Mrs. Kennedy sat transfixed.

Her husband was crying and laughing, beating on the table with his good hand.

"Yaaaaa," he screamed, "yaaaaa, yaaaaa."

His anxiety and confusion mounted to such a peak that he began swiping the dishes off the table.

"What have I done?" Mrs. Kennedy cried, almost out of control herself. "Oh, Joe, please God, tell me what I've done."

He screamed at her incoherently, ripping the air with wild bellows. Matilda, the cook, came running in from the kitchen.

Louella, who had been in the back of the house, heard the commotion and streaked down the hall. Mr. Kennedy tried to push himself away from the table, but his wheelchair had been locked in position for reasons of safety, and he found himself trapped. I was trying to maintain calm, but he was surrounded by a herd of sobbing, hysterical women, and he was utterly helpless to explain himself. He kept beating on the table with such force that the few dishes that remained on it bounced off.

Mrs. Kennedy, shattered and emotionally drained, ran from the room with her face buried in a napkin.

"Gaaaaa, gaaaaa, gaaaaa," he wailed after her, then slumped back in his chair, dropped his head on his chest, and started sobbing.

In the course of those few moments, he had run the gamut of emotions. From laughter to confusion to anger to tears.

It was imperative to get him back to his room, but Ann still blocked the way by tying her arms around his neck, hugging him tightly.

"Oh, Uncle Joe," she cried over and over. "You'll never have to go through anything like this again. I promise you. You're a Kennedy, and you don't have to do anything you don't want to do."

He appeared not to hear her, or if he did, he could not make sense of it. He was salivating profusely. Ann stayed bent over him and continued making devoted promises. Finally, Mr. Kennedy subsided to a quiet whimper.

The breakfast was a disaster. He had entered the room erect and proud, but he left slumped forward, shoulders trembling and crying like an infant.

I have always respected family wishes, but at that moment, it was important he be put to bed immediately and be given professional attention. I actually forced Ann aside in order to get him to his bed.

We were engrossed for several minutes, checking his heart and blood pressure. He needed a quieting medication, and I sternly ordered Ann, prior to the injection, not to disturb him.

We canceled the remainder of the day's schedule, and within thirty minutes, he became calm and stable.

An hour or so later Mrs. Kennedy called me to her room. She had made a valiant effort to compose herself, but she seemed harassed and apprehensive. She was not critical of the attempt we had made to bring her husband to the table, but she was adamant that we should not try it again.

"I've upset him terribly," she moaned. "And I don't even know what I did. It won't work, Nurse. I was afraid it wouldn't! My niece warned me that it wouldn't! I just can't put him through another experience like that!"

I tried to reassure her by explaining that the incident could not have a drastic or a lasting effect on him. He would probably be puzzled and even more upset if this new privilege was taken away. In his condition, problems were quickly forgotten.

I suggested that she come to his room later in the day and ask him what he wanted to do, ask him if he would like to make a regular practice of their dining together. I explained to her that she could learn to communicate with him and to understand what he was saying as well. This seemed startling to her, but she was very anxious to do anything she could for her husband.

"I feel so helpless," she said.

Later that afternoon she visited with him. When she cautiously posed the question, he smiled warmly and said, "Yaaaaa." From that time on he was able to share almost every meal with his family, and although he would often puzzle and concern his wife with his behavior, he was, to some extent, a functioning resident of his own home.

I assumed, after realizing the turmoil she had innocently created, Ann would explain what she had done to her aunt. It would have eased Mrs. Kennedy to know that she had not been the cause of the outburst, for she thought it had been her fault; but apparently Ann said nothing, and as was the Kennedy custom, the past gave way to the present.

Step by step I found myself gradually accepting the strange rhythms of life in the Kennedy household. There were always surprises and interruptions. The case was highly complicated, and the personalities involved often created deep frustration.

As time passed, I attempted to instigate many rehabilitative changes. Some of my efforts were thwarted. Others took hold.

As I came into closer contact with other members of the family, I learned their idiosyncrasies and eventually understood what it meant to function "the Kennedy way."

4

Wherever there was a Kennedy, there were children and animals, in gay, wild profusion. Mrs. Kennedy adored the children, but the animals, running around inside her house, were a great cross for her to bear. So much so that she finally issued a tight-lipped ultimatum. Dogs, cats, goldfish, gerbils, parrots, white mice, rabbits, snakes, falcons, ponies, or anything else that was not immediately recognizable as *homo sapiens* would never again be allowed inside her domain.

After this, it became a round-robin sport to elude the order. In Palm Beach everyone arrived with his own particular pet, and there was a constant and gleeful shuffling to keep them clear of "Grandma."

Mr. Kennedy was aware of the cloak-and-dagger escapades, and since he enjoyed animals, he found the shenanigans quite amusing. There was one incident I shall never forget.

Ann had acquired a Great Dane puppy, not quite a year old, and when Mrs. Kennedy was not about, he was allowed freedom of the house. On this particular day, he was brought in to Mr. Kennedy's room for his usual romp. Mrs. Kennedy was at mass, and the pup was having a wonderful time running in and out of the Ambassador's room, tearing across to the living room, jumping over sofas, then racing back again, slipping and sliding across the tile floors to a sprawling halt. Mr. Kennedy delighted in watching him, for he was a charming puppy who seemed already to have outgrown his skin. We were all involved in watching him and equally guilty of urging him on. Ann kept saying, "For heaven's sake, we've got to be careful and not let Aunt Rose find out." But we all felt safe because she was back to her routine of attending two masses, and there was still some time to go before her return.

Suddenly, through the window, I spotted the chauffeur coming across the lawn, and I gasped, "Lord help us, Mrs. Kennedy is home."

Everyone scattered. Ann! Louella! The aides! No one was left to face the music, except me, the puppy, who had no idea of what was in store for him, and Mr. Kennedy, who was thoroughly enjoying himself.

I am a slight woman, and the dog and I would probably have weighed in about the same. Even so, it was a mismatched tug-of-war that ensued. He was overpowering! I pushed, and he pranced. I pleaded, and he romped. I shoved, and he rolled over. Nothing was happening, except to Mr. Kennedy, who was rocking his bed with laughter. As for me, I definitely wasn't laughing. I knew if Mrs. Kennedy found the dog, he'd be on the next plane out and I would probably share the crate with him! I was about to give up hope when he suddenly stood up on his hind legs and put his paws over my shoulders. I staggered, wet-faced with his kisses, and held on for dear life. He barked gleefully as we danced, cheek to cheek, through the door, down the hall, and out the side entrance. Not a moment too soon, he galloped away across the lawn, and I slammed the door just as Mrs. Kennedy came into view.

"How's Mr. Kennedy?" she asked.

Secretly I crossed myself, raised my eyes to heaven, and lied through my teeth.

"Oh, fine! Doing quite well, Mrs. Kennedy. As a matter of fact, he's sleeping now, I think."

"Then I'll look in on him later."

St. Francis was standing near us all that day. I knew if she went in and found Mr. Kennedy doubled over with laughter, she would eventually pump the truth out of me. He had enjoyed the pup's antics so much that I couldn't bear to see the dog sent away. That is a weak justification for a lie, venial though it was, but I somehow felt that St. Francis understood.

As Mrs. Kennedy disappeared into the living room, I let out a long sigh of relief and then headed straight for Ann and Louella. Irish temper flew, but at least the dog remained.

At the compound, where everyone had his own home, animals romped in great, yelping waves, but never, never, were they allowed inside Mrs. Kennedy's house. If any unfortunate creature happened to go through the wrong door and she spotted it, her cries of "Out, out, out" would send it careening through the nearest exit.

Mrs. Kennedy adored her grandchildren, but she was never the kind of grandmother to bounce a baby on her knee. As a result, the countless little hordes of youngsters always put on the brakes and approached her with respect and curiosity. She would correct their grammar, the way they walked, or their lack of tidiness, yet it was always done with love. "Children," she often said, "are meant to inherit the earth and should be fit for it."

And they came, in great waves, laughing, biting, throwing up, falling out of trees, choking on gumdrops, breaking legs, stepping on bees, hugging, kissing, getting and giving black eyes, knocking out front teeth.

They were all marvelous little creatures, each with his own particular and individual charm, and were delightful comfort to both grandparents. They were special treats for Mr. Kennedy during his illness.

Whenever any of his family would arrive for their visits, they would race across the patio into the house, shouting, "Dad! Dad! We're home! We're here!" Always, he was the first to be greeted, and it was a miraculous medication for him.

There would be the President, bronze and handsome. He seemed to eat up space as he strode across the ground, waving and calling when he spotted his father watching him from the window.

To see the First Lady move, from a distance, was to see a woman of great style and composure. She always glided into view, tall, lean, unhurried, smiling, as Caroline broke loose from her hand to run past her father and catapult through the door into her grandpa's arms. Shrieking, kissing, "Oh, Grandpa, Grandpa."

John and Jacqueline Kennedy envisioned a daughter of studied charm and elegance, and as a toddler Caroline had already developed quite a flair. I think this is one of the traits that made her so special to Mr. Kennedy. She had an early toehold on being a lady, and he would swell with pride when she put on her "company manners" for him.

I remember Bobby and his family as altogether different from the President's. He and his brood would rip the air and ignite it with all the fantasy and excitement of a roadside carnival. He was rearing his children to be free, competitive, and natural.

"Bobby, Incorporated," as I thought of him and his family, exuded energy. He was a wiry, quick man, and there always seemed to be a child riding on his shoulders, swinging on an arm, or hugging a leg as he tried to walk. His wife, Ethel, had very little luck at discipline, but all Bobby had to do was quietly reprimand a child and he was miraculously obeyed.

Children never seemed to annoy him. He could be on the telephone holding an important conference while a youngster (not necessarily one of his own) would shinny up the back of his chair, twisting ten busy fingers in his stubborn hair. Another would be poking in his ears, while still another tried to pluck out his eyelashes or count his teeth. Through it all, he never lost his train of thought.

Teddy always sang around the house, and his favorite expression was: "Let's make it fun time." The boys would roughhouse with each other and their father, but they were especially tender to their mother. It was almost as if there were two sets of children, one related to the father, the other to the mother.

The Kennedys were amazingly considerate of each other, and during all the years I was with them I never heard one gossip about another. I never heard one criticize another or make an unkind remark. If they fought, it was kept to themselves and never shown in public. This trait alone could well set them apart from the norm. They were, in many ways, extraordinary.

Of all the Kennedys, with the exception of my patient, the one I had the most contact with on a day-to-day basis was Mrs. Kennedy. She is a complex woman full of inconsistencies which often generated crises around the household; but she is also a wonderful woman with a deep concern for others, and over the years I grew to care for her deeply.

Mrs. Kennedy had spent her entire married life in the role of protected mother and wife. Her husband and sons were the celebrities, and Mr. Kennedy's personal manager from the New York office once told me that there had been a standing order from the Ambassador: Never, under any circumstances, was his wife to be disturbed or upset about business or household matters. She was to have what suited her, without hesitation or questioning.

Prior to her husband's illness, she had never been involved in any managerial capacity in the household. He handled all the hiring and training, and everyone employed by him, whether at the home or the office, fitted perfectly in his assigned position. But after his illness, it became a divided house. His servants had always been accustomed to doing things in a particular way and never crossed over to another's job. Most of his personnel had been in his service for years and were highly qualified in their specific duties.

The old help stubbornly refused to change any custom Mr. Kennedy had established, and Mrs. Kennedy in an apparent effort to build her own staff and gain her own loyalties, began bringing in personnel of her choosing. Since she was not experienced at hiring, many unfair advantages were taken of her. Often she would hire a person simply because he agreed to work at a cheaper salary, and as a result, there were some disastrous situations with unqualified personnel who skimmed over their jobs or were simply incompetent.

Mrs. Kennedy was a woman who spoke her mind and made her demands felt. If she believed a person was responsible for a particular situation, she would tackle him directly with her complaint. She was brusque to the menial workers, and often her manner created ill feelings and dissatisfaction among the help. Although Mr. Kennedy had the reputation of being a ruthless businessman, he was supposed to have been an exceptionally benevolent and generous employer who took special delight in spoiling "his people." I think many of them resented having to take orders from Mrs. Kennedy especially because she was often so blunt. As a result, there was a rapid turnover, and the household existed in a constant state of turmoil. Nothing was ever finished. During the week, when only Mrs. Kennedy, Ann, the nurses, and the household staff were around, it was often calamity and chaos, with Mrs. Kennedy in the center trying to adjust to her new role as mistress of the house. But when the children came for weekends, somehow, meals were miraculously served on time, and all members of the staff seemed to exert a special effort to make things run smoothly.

Mrs. Kennedy was a woman who guarded time with a passion, and she believed that once a person finished his job, he should be put to work on something else. She abhorred idleness. She was also a stickler on money matters, and the thought of anyone taking coffee breaks made no sense at all to her. One morning she came into the kitchen to find me sitting at a table relaxing. I had just finished a very difficult shift with her husband. She looked around the room, giving it a rapid inspection, and then said to me, "Mrs. Dallas, how many times a day do you come in here and have coffee?"

Before I could reply, she continued, "It isn't that I mind, my dear, but coffee does keep going up and expenses can get out of hand, if we're not careful. So would you post a note on the bulletin board to the effect that I would appreciate it if the nurses would please confine themselves to, say, one cup of coffee a shift? Or perhaps it might be a good idea if they would fix themselves a little thermos at home."

She patted my hand, smiled, and hurried off.

Nurses, especially those working a night shift, survive on coffee, and I simply could not bring myself to issue such a stringent order. The problem was solved when we discovered that Dora had an electric hot plate, and rather than create more hostilities than already existed with the available nursing staff, we set it up in the nurses' room next to Mr. Kennedy's bedroom. With our own pot perking nobody had to go to the kitchen, and everyone was happy.

Mechanical instruments absolutely overpowered Mrs. Kennedy. The telephone, with its many push buttons, always confounded her, and she was notorious for punching the wrong one and making a disconnection. Her children and friends understood this, but it would infuriate her. She would come racing through the house, red-faced, shouting, "Who cut me off? I want to know. Who cut me off?" The person closest got the full brunt of her frustration, but no one took personal offense, for all of us were aware of her desperate battle with anything mechanical.

She kept a sheaf of notes written to herself pinned on the front of her dress with a huge diaper safety pin, and in the morning she looked as if she were wearing a large paper corsage. As she finished with one reminder, she would tear it off and go on to the next. By the end of the day her corsage had been plucked clean. She would be very proud of herself because she had systematically accomplished everything she had set out to do. Once she suggested that since I had so many things to remember, I should try her method. Of course I couldn't, for I could not imagine a nurse reporting for duty with notes to herself pinned on her uniform. I think it would tend to shake her patient's confidence.

She was always full of ideas for self-improvement and constantly urging them on whoever happened to be nearby. She often gave me what she believed was sound advice about all kinds of things, and often she was right. For example, she felt it was very wrong for women to bake themselves in the sun. "Look at those girls," she'd scold, seeing her brood sunbathing on the beach. "I keep telling them they'll have the hide of an alligator before they're fifty, but they won't listen to a word I say."

Then she'd turn to me and state, firmly, "Dear heart, don't ever let me see you in the sun unless you're wearing a large hat. You take my advice and protect yourself."

One day she bought me a package of her frownies, and for several weeks she carefully examined my face regularly to see if any new creases or wrinkles had appeared.

"Are you wearing them?" she'd inquire, with motherly concern.

"When I think of it," I always replied.

As a nurse, I was professionally adjusted to, and impersonal toward, the human body in all its sundry shapes and conditions. But, as a resident of the Kennedy household, my nursing decorum was frequently to totter on a blushing precipice.

One morning after breakfast I was in Mr. Kennedy's bedroom checking some things when Mrs. Kennedy came in to ask if I would take some towels out to the sauna for the Senator and some of his friends. I had nothing else to do at the moment and since Mr. Kennedy was napping I agreed to do it for her. As we walked to the linen closet, she made a statement which seemed strange at the time. "Mr. Kennedy brought up our children to be natural, and, since you're a nurse, it shouldn't bother you, should it?"

"I don't suppose it should," I answered, puzzled.

"Teddy and his friends are here," she went on a little vaguely, "and it's ridiculous that I should have to ask you to help out, but my maid simply won't do it. Even though she's Swedish, she won't do it. Can you imagine that?"

Loading a high stack of towels in my arms, she patted my shoulder and said, "But you'll be just fine, my dear. Just fine." Then she added suspiciously, "You're not Swedish, are you?"

"No, Mrs. Kennedy," I said from behind my stack of towels. "I'm Irish."

We started off to the sauna, with her leading the way, and she chuckled. "Thank heavens. The Irish I can understand." Cocking one eyebrow, she hastily queried, "Irish? Oh, dear, are you Catholic, too?"

"Yes, I am," I replied.

She pressed her hand to her forehead and gave a long sigh. "Oh, no, not another one."

"I beg your pardon?"

"No personal offense, Mrs. Dallas," she answered quickly, patting my arm again. "Dear, no. It's just that Protestants are so much less trouble."

"Pardon?"

"Scheduling masses, I mean. Have you ever tried to schedule masses for a houseful of people, and all of them wanting to go at the same time. Well, I'll tell you this much, there's no such trouble with Protestants. Once a week or not at all, for them. Life is so much simpler that way. So much simpler."

"Mrs. Kennedy, I was born and raised in the church, and it's never yet interfered with my work. Nor has my work interfered with it. Somehow, I've been able to handle both."

"I'm sure you have, dear heart," she smiled. "Yes, I'm sure you have. But then, nurses are supposed to be competent, aren't they? They have to be, don't they?"

At that point she left me and I continued out to the sauna, still wondering about her comment, "You're a nurse, and it shouldn't bother you."

I arrived at the sauna, stepped inside, and came face to face with Teddy and his friends, milling around, stark naked.

After the first shock wore off I tried to shrink into the stack of towels, but the men kept peeling them away while I hunched lower and lower behind the dwindling pile. In no time, there was nothing left between me and nature in its most masculine state.

The men were unconcerned and made no attempt to cover themselves. They tossed their towels onto the cots and chairs and stood chatting as though they were in Times Square.

Teddy apparently had been told that his father had a new nurse, and I guess I had been described to him, because he spoke to me by name.

He was prancing around jovially full of fun and laughter. Draping his arm around my shoulder, which was stiff with shock, he made a flamboyant point of introducing me to his friends. Never before, nor ever since, have I been introduced to a naked man. Propriety of such nature is seldom called upon.

Muttering, "How do you do," under my breath, I made a

quick exit, backing out of the sauna. With a mad dash, I was in the house. I bumped into Louella on the stairs. My mouth agape, I sputtered out what had happened. "Ah, yes," she nodded knowingly, and went her way.

Rather sheepishly, it seemed, Mrs. Kennedy showed up in the nurses' station a few minutes later and chatted a bit too gaily. I was in no mental state, at that moment, to listen to her, for I was too absorbed in fanning my flaming cheeks. She was scrutinizing me carefully, and although nothing was said about the incident, I knew that she knew, and she knew that I knew she knew. But what was there to say?

Mrs. Kennedy had a number of idiosyncrasies, and one of the strangest was a great concern to her chauffeur. Whenever she would go on a short automobile trip, she would wear her black sleeping mask, and you could see her settling down in the back seat of the car, her tiny figure almost lost in its immenseness. Before they moved from the drive she would have her rosary in her hand and her mask covering her eyes. But once they were on the highway, she would remove the mask just long enough to spot a hitchhiker. Her routine was always the same. The first boy in uniform they passed, she would insist that the chauffeur slam on the brakes and pick him up. The hitchhiker would sit up front with the chauffeur, and after they had ridden for a while Mrs. Kennedy would tap him on the shoulder and ask, "Do you know who I am?"

Usually the boy answered no, for she was not that well known in person. She would jokingly tease him then. "Make a guess," she'd urge. The young man, thinking he'd been picked up by some eccentric millionaire, usually slouched down in the seat and pulled his hat over his eyes. Not easily discouraged, she would keep prodding him to guess until, almost coquettishly, she would state, "What do you think your friends at camp will say when you tell them that you've been riding with the President's mother?" What the poor boys must have thought would be hard to imagine.

Working with the Kennedy family was always hectic, and there was little opportunity to relax; but one afternoon Mrs.

Kennedy invited me to play golf with her. It was impossible for me to accept the invitation since I was on duty, but I added, "Mrs. Kennedy, there is no way I could afford the fee at the country club."

"What do you mean, afford?" she said. "I don't pay a thing." Her eyes twinkled as she whispered, "I slip in on the fifth hole and play through the eighth or so, then I slip back off. You could do it, too."

"Mrs. Kennedy"—I laughed—"if you get caught, it would be chalked up to charming eccentricity, but I don't think the club would take the same outlook if they caught me doing it."

She left then, shaking her head, and called back over her shoulder, "Sure you won't change your mind? I'll bet we could get away with it."

I often have to laugh remembering these idiosyncrasies of hers, but at the same time I was constantly aware of the bewildering pain that her husband's illness caused her to feel.

Only a wife who has gone through the trauma of having a husband suffer a stroke could possibly understand the desperate frustration of seeing a loved one in such a helpless condition. The children felt that it was best for their father to continue his life in as normal a way as possible, and the doctors agreed wholeheartedly, so his private secretary remained on the job. She was so devoted to the Ambassador that she did everything she could to assist in his rehabilitation. In lay terms it would be difficult to describe his garbled speech. Sentences that he felt were clear usually came out as though he were chattering in a foreign tongue. Nevertheless, every morning his secretary would come to his room with her notebook and appear to take dictation from him. He would sit propped up in his bed and dictate for almost an hour without one understandable word. She never let on but would pretend to take notes in shorthand.

Often he would break his dictation and point to the phone, which she would hand to him. He would dial his office on the direct line and speak into the phone in this same garbled tongue. The New York office had been alerted by Stephen Smith, Jean's husband, so that whoever answered always satisfied him in their response. They usually said, "Whatever you say, Mr. Kennedy." Or "It will be taken care of your way, Mr. Kennedy." Or "You always come up with the right decision, Chief."

He was a man obviously addicted to doing business over the telephone, and these morning sessions with his secretary were spent dialing, jabbering, and issuing orders that could not possibly be understood. Mrs. Kennedy would sometimes stand in the doorway watching the pretense, and pain would spread all over her face. Her eyes would droop heavily in grief, and if I happened to be standing close to her, I would hear her sighing painfully.

Her husband was so involved and intent on handling his business affairs during this period that he seldom noticed her standing there. If he chanced to look up, he would smile briefly, then resume his work. Her reflexes were so quick that before his eyes found her face, she was able to wipe away the misery and put a twinkle in her eyes, especially for him.

I never saw her, during a time of crisis, give in under the strain. She would take a walk, or go swimming, or play golf, instead. She was not one to rip apart at the seams. She worked off, with physical exertion, any emotions that might have caused hysteria in another. She was isolated and self-sufficient, and she had a dread of anything or anyone penetrating her armor. When she had surgery in a Boston hospital, not one of her immediate family knew of it until after the operation. She believed it was her personal business, and went about it in her own way.

She had the reputation of being a globe-trotter, which was not true at all. The public was led to believe that she spent very little time with her husband, but she made only two trips a year to Paris to view the new fashions, and to retreat to a beauty and health spa. Regardless of whether she was planning a trip to Europe or a day or two in Boston, she always made a point of asking me, "Should I go? Is it safe to leave him?"

This routine never varied. She would call me to her room and say, "Mrs. Dallas, I've conferred with the doctors, and with

Ann, and I'm assured by them that it's safe for me to be away. But I want you to tell me what you think. How is my husband? Be honest."

I usually gave her the same answer. Her husband could go at any time. We all knew that. But if his condition was stable, I would urge her to take the opportunity to be away for a while.

There was a lot of the old sod in her, regarding her preparation for death. She had her mourning dress hanging in the closet in the event her husband died. Back and forth it was carried between Palm Beach and Cape Cod. She was prepared.

I had been a nurse for many years, but there was one thing about Mrs. Kennedy and Ann that was different from all the patients' families I had nursed. Families and friends never use the word "die" when they refer to a loved one's condition. They will say, "Will she make it?" or "How long will he have?" Such things as that. Ann and Mrs. Kennedy never spoke indirectly, and I always shuddered when either of them would say the word "die."

Mrs. Kennedy would say, in a general conversation, such things as "When Mr. Kennedy dies, I'm going to sell this big house and get an apartment." Ann would say, "When Uncle Joe dies, I don't think I'll ever set foot in Florida again. I hate the place."

In contrast, his children never referred to it in so brusque a way. Each one of them lived with the knowledge that his illness was severe, but they never talked about his dying.

It was during the first season at Palm Beach that vicious letters began pouring in, all threatening Mr. Kennedy for siring so despicable a clan. The letters never reached him, and we tried to screen them from Mrs. Kennedy as well. Often I was assigned to open the mail, and as soon as I would spot a poison-pen letter, I would put it in the large envelope to await the arrival of the Attorney General. It was when the letters became frighteningly vicious and numerous that Ham Brown was assigned as Mr. Kennedy's Secret Service agent.

Whenever one of these letters happened accidentally to fall into Mrs. Kennedy's hands, she would rush to her room and hang a "Do Not Disturb" sign on her door. She never cried in front of us, but we could see, when she finally came downstairs, that she had been weeping. This woman lived under a constant cloud of hatred and realized that, despite the adoration showered on her family, there were many fanatics who hated the very name of Kennedy.

Under these pressures, as the months passed, she became critical and on edge. Nothing seemed to please her, and she would take petty attitudes with her staff.

There was one aspect of Mrs. Kennedy that was difficult for anyone to rationalize. She was extremely devout about attending mass. The staff and domestics admired this, but no one could understand how she could come right from taking communion, step out of her car, and severely reprimand the first person she saw, for no apparent reason at all. A reprimand from Mrs. Kennedy could be shocking.

I think the explanation is that while she was at church she was at peace, but when she returned home, she knew that she was going into a house of sickness, responsibility, sorrow, turmoil, and tragedy. She was secure during those brief moments of worship, but when she stepped out of her car onto her home grounds, she had to face stark reality.

Although Mrs. Kennedy had not been prepared for this role and was often confused or exasperated by it, she eventually became the center of strength for her whole family. I had nothing but admiration for her strength in the midst of all the tragedy that surrounded her over the years.

5

I HAD BEEN attending Mr. Kennedy for more than two months and, as his nurse, felt highly rewarded, for his basic therapy began to take shape.

He responded with gusto to exercising, and soon he could prop himself up on his left elbow and push his body erect. The motion of being able to swing his leg out of bed, unassisted, was an achievement for a man in his condition.

After these elementary physical accomplishments, he became receptive to the routine of speech therapy and began to respond systematically. In short order, he could say "good morning," or, "yes," or, "no," or "I don't want to," rather clearly, and with each lesson he improved.

Soon he was able to perform more complex activities, such as buttoning and unbuttoning his shirt. As he perfected one function, others, more complicated, followed.

In the beginning, it was I who dressed him, and this I did as his nurse, with professional consideration for the patient's dignity, permitting him to handle the things he could do for himself. Often Ann assumed the dressing task, and when she did, he would arrogantly lie quite passive. He seemed to expect her to do everything for him, which she did. This provided him with the personal attention he was prone to demand, but it did nothing to spur his rehabilitation. Influencing muscles requires time, routine, and repetition, but the tearing down of what has been accomplished, unfortunately, takes only a little while. Every time a routine is broken, it means two steps back for the patient. Often I wished that he had remained in the hospital, where he would have recuperated more rapidly under disciplined care.

However, despite these problems, he made exceptional progress, and I was full of hope for him.

Finally in early April, 1962, Dr. Howard Rusk, founder of the New York Institute of Rehabilitation, invited Mr. Kennedy to take up residence in the newly built Horizon House located at the institute. Dr. Rusk and Mr. Kennedy were longtime friends. Before his stroke Mr. Kennedy had a deep interest in therapy and had spent a lot of time with Dr. Rusk discussing therapy and rehabilitation. He planned to back up his interest with large financial support. Horizon House was a dream come true for Dr. Rusk. It was a small bungalow in which the patient could live and learn how to function in everyday surroundings within a disciplined therapeutic structure. Mr. Kennedy's progress had been evaluated, and it was felt that he was making remarkable progress. Horizon House seemed like the ideal next step for him.

Those of us in the medical profession knew that Mr. Kennedy could serve as a stimulating incentive for others. When he was told that he had responded sufficiently to the limited therapy that had been available to him in his home and that he was strong enough to handle the more advanced therapy available at Horizon House, he was radiant.

The encouragement his children gave him was enough to spur on even the weakest of men, and Mr. Kennedy, in even his most desperate hours, was never weak.

Originally, I had planned to take the Kennedy case only through the end of the season, but the Attorney General made a special trip to Palm Beach to ask me if I would continue on the case and go with his father to Horizon House. The doctor also impressed upon me the necessity for Mr. Kennedy to have someone familiar with him, other than his family, during his initial indoctrination period.

I had been widowed some fifteen years, and my son, Vincent, was just starting college, so I was free to make the trip. I told the doctors and the family that I would stay with Mr. Kennedy until he finished his first sessions at the institute. I did not want to commit myself any further because I usually preferred not to take home cases at all, but I was anxious to give the Ambassador as much of an advantage as I could, if it would help him. These arrangements were satisfactory with everyone, and I made my plans by boarding my dog and closing up my small house in West Palm Beach.

Mr. Kennedy's plane, the *Caroline*, was coming down to pick us up, and I was introduced to a complex routine that would persist for years to come. The doctor asked that I contact Captain Baird, Mr. Kennedy's pilot, to discuss the flight with him. I had flown with many patients when they returned to their homes, so traveling with Mr. Kennedy did not seem to pose any special problems.

I phoned Captain Baird and introduced myself. He assured me that the plane was quite comfortable and well equipped for emergencies. I was in no way apprehensive about the flight, especially since Dr. Rusk planned to make the flight with us. This fact, in itself, was a new experience for me, for regardless of the wealth of the patient, none of them had ever flown with a doctor in attendance. Once again I was to learn that there is the Kennedy way of doing things.

In due time the day and hour finally arrived for our departure. Mr. Kennedy was put in his car to be driven to the airport. As we passed through Palm Beach, people recognized him, and all up and down the sidewalks they would call out, "Good luck." It struck home that this man had a large following and was well respected among those who knew him.

When we arrived at the airport, it was swarming with photographers and friends, all there to wish him well. This, I must admit, was a new experience for me, for I had never been with the Kennedys off their home ground. When I saw the throngs of people, I had my first real understanding of what it meant to be a Kennedy. It was overpowering to me, but Mr. Kennedy took it all in stride.

He was transferred from the car onto a narrow, straight-back chair that had two small wheels on the back legs. This kind of chair is always available in airports for the handicapped. All went well until the co-pilot began strapping him in. Mr. Kennedy stopped him with a firm clamp on his arm and jerked his head toward me, indicating that he wanted me involved. I had always relied on the pilot or co-pilot to handle the safety factors in transporting a patient, so I waited until the belt was secured; then, to satisfy Mr. Kennedy, I went through the routine of checking things over. While I did this, I said to him, "Mr. Kennedy, shouldn't Captain Baird check it, too? Don't you think it's better if a man checks to see if you're securely buckled?" Mr. Kennedy nodded seriously. This was a new experience for him, and he had a right to be apprehensive.

During the procedure, Ann was offering her instructions on how everything should be done, and before long, we were involved in a madcap mishmash. Dr. Rusk stood elegantly on the sidelines, looking dignified and remote. He, too, must have been wondering, "What's all the hullabaloo about?" The medical profession is accustomed to the routine of preparing patients for flight, but it was Mr. Kennedy's first trip since his illness, so he and his family had reason to be concerned and protective.

Captain Baird and his co-pilot were doing an excellent job, one in front, one in back, lifting Mr. Kennedy up the ramp to the plane, when all of a sudden Mr. Kennedy began bellowing and pointing at me. Again he seemed to want me involved, so to quiet him, I came up and put my hand on the side of his chair. He never once took his eyes off me. I kept telling him everything was going to be fine. When they got him to the doorway, I had to step aside, for it was necessary that the chair be tipped back in order to wheel it into the plane. When this happened, Mr. Kennedy let out another roar, and Ann began to scream. I shouted to the captain, "Please tell him exactly what you are doing. Don't tilt him back that way, he's frightened. He thinks he's going to fall backwards. Just tell him what's going on, and he'll be satisfied."

Captain Baird quickly squatted down in front of Mr. Kennedy and, looking directly in his eyes, explained exactly what was happening: "Mr. Ambassador, we're going to have to tip your chair backwards in order to maneuver it through the door. But Mrs. Dallas will be right here, and nothing is going to happen. Just hang on, and we'll soon get you to your compartment."

This seemed to satisfy Mr. Kennedy, for he quieted down. He seldom put up a battle if a new situation was first explained to him, but woe to anyone who sprung a surprise.

So, without further incident, he was taken into the plane and wheeled down the aisle to his compartment. Captain Baird lifted him into his chair and secured the seat belt. Dr. Rusk and I followed him in. The doctor sat near him and began talking about some of the good times they had shared together. I was exhausted, so I slipped out of the compartment, took the seat opposite it, and kicked off my shoes.

We were airborne only a few minutes when I noticed Mr. Kennedy was being waited on hand and foot. No one questioned what he wanted to eat or drink. Everything was brought in and placed in front of him. He had two stewardesses and many attendants on board. All he had to do was point to a glass on the table, and it was held for him while he drank. I knew Dr. Rusk was observing all these details, and on that flight it became evident what a tremendous job we had ahead of us.

It amazed me to see Mr. Kennedy in these new surroundings. He was the indisputable master, and I realized that this man must have always demanded complete attention. On his own plane he was king and was treated as royalty.

I knew he would have an abrupt awakening in store at Horizon House, but I felt he could take it, for in addition to being proud, he was a strong and intelligent man. But we faced a constant struggle between self-sufficiency and overindulgence by those who simply wanted to make him comfortable.

When we arrived at LaGuardia Airport I watched our landing from his compartment window, and when we stopped on the runway, I saw what was to me a thrilling scene. The apron was swarming with dignitaries, and a parade was standing by to escort the Ambassador into New York.

It must have been frightening to Mr. Kennedy, for when he realized what was awaiting him, he reacted violently. He did not want to be carried off the plane before all the people. It was different from the crowd in Palm Beach. Those who met him in New York were high officials, famous financiers, important sports figures, top law enforcement officers, men whose families ruled society, and many others. He simply could not face them as a cripple.

He yelled. He stomped his foot. He shook his fist. He swung at anyone who got near him. He bellowed, "Nooooo, nooooo, nooooo."

Dr. Rusk said, "We have to go."

"Nooooo."

He began throwing anything near him. His face was on fire. He was shaking all over. He would calm down for a moment or two and then look out the window, and seeing the hordes of people, television cameras, and news photographers, he would begin yelling all over again.

This went on for nearly an hour. Ann would get on her knees, dodge blows, and plead with him to get off the plane and meet his friends. He would shout "noooo."

The co-pilot pushed his way into the compartment and tried to question Captain Baird about what he should do. The crowd and the reporters were getting restless, for they had not received any information. The plane had landed, but the door had not been opened. There was nothing we could do to influence Mr. Kennedy.

Finally Dr. Rusk broke in, first as a friend and then, finally, as a doctor. "It's now or never, Mr. Ambassador," he said. "You're going to have to face this sooner or later."

Mr. Kennedy was furious.

Realizing that we were all exhausted, Dr. Rusk whispered to me, "I'm going to take a gamble. I've never done anything like this before, and it hurts me to do it to him; but it's worth a try."

He got as close as he dared to Mr. Kennedy, and in a firm voice said, "As sorry as I am, I have to leave. I have other patients waiting to have their cases evaluated, but if you need me, tell your nurse, and she'll see that I get the message. I'm sorry it has to be this way, but I can't wait around here any longer."

We were all taken aback by this maneuver, especially Mr. Kennedy. As Dr. Rusk left the compartment, he turned to me and said, "If he gives any indication that he wants to leave the plane, have the captain call me." With that he left.

Mr. Kennedy watched through the window as his doctor walked briskly toward the car that was parked for him on the apron. He looked as if he couldn't believe what was happening, couldn't believe that Dr. Rusk was actually walking away from him. He scowled at me over his glasses and pointed his finger toward the doctor.

This man could let anyone know by a lift of his eyebrow or a look or a movement of his hand exactly what he wanted. He could also tell you how much he thought of a person or how little he thought of that person simply by a gesture or an attitude. I knew that he wanted Dr. Rusk to return, and I immediately passed the word on to Captain Baird to stop the doctor at his automobile. Mr. Kennedy kept a sharp eye on the scene through the window. Dr. Rusk looked up and gave a faint smile. He lifted his hand in a brief wave, signaling to Mr. Kennedy that he understood his orders. When he reentered the compartment, the only thing he said was: "Are you ready to leave now?" Mr. Kennedy nodded his head quietly.

The plan had succeeded. Mr. Kennedy had made up his own mind, and that was the first step in rehabilitation. Therapy cannot be forced upon a patient. The decision must come from within. It was important that Mr. Kennedy not be coerced into beginning his rehabilitation program at Horizon House. He had the right to decide whether to go on to Hyannis Port or to remain in New York. He chose to remain.

I bent down to loosen the seat belt and whisper in his ear, "You keep your head up high and smile, if you want to. Or if you don't want to, just look dignified, like you do around the house. Remember, it's however you want to play it."

I put my hand under his chin and raised his face a little to me. "You keep that head up, so your friends out there will know you're Joseph P. Kennedy."

He set his lip and gave me a slight nod. When Captain Baird and the co-pilot carried him down the ramp, he sat very straight and solemn. I was misty-eyed with pride. All the dignitaries stood in a long line waiting until Mr. Kennedy was settled. Car after car in the motorcade had American flags on the fenders. There was a full escort of motorcycle policemen. Photographers were everywhere. Through it all, Mr. Kennedy was beautifully composed. His chair was wheeled to his limousine, and he sat straight and erect as the most important people of New York came by to welcome him. He did not try to speak but acknowledged each person with a nod of his head. He greeted everyone, posed patiently for the photographers, then signaled that he was ready to begin the drive to Horizon House. It was an exciting moment for those of us who knew the courage it had taken for him, strapped in a wheelchair, to face the city that he had conquered roughshod.

We arrived at Horizon House speeding behind the motorcycle escort and found that a group of Secret Service men had already been assigned to guard Mr. Kennedy. The press had given heavy coverage to his arrival at the center, and the threatening calls that had come in against him were too numerous to ignore.

Mr. Kennedy's personal entourage had a briefing by the chief of staff, informing us that all telephone calls were to be monitored at the switchboard. The switchboard had been alerted to this effect but there was always the chance that a prank call, well disguised, could get through. So to further punctuate this order, there was a personal phone message from the Attorney General, who made it absolutely clear that every call that came in to his father's bungalow had to be monitored by the nurse on duty. There was to be no exception. Every call, regardless of who it was from, was to be monitored from beginning to end.

He would take no chances on a vicious call reaching Mr. Kennedy.

If Mr. Kennedy was concerned about the full posting of guards, he never questioned or balked at this added invasion of privacy.

There was a great deal of excitement that first day. Each member of the family was accustomed to giving orders. From some, they came in an abrupt fashion. From others, the requests were quite polite. However, none of them ever asked. They told. And when they spoke, they spoke with authority.

The only one to say "please" or "would you mind" or "thank you" was the First Lady. For that matter, on thinking back, she was the only one who ever introduced herself to me. I remember the First Lady quietly entering Mr. Kennedy's room at Palm Beach, kissing him and then turning to me with a slight smile to say, "I'm Jacqueline Kennedy, Mrs. Dallas, and I'm so happy that you'll be taking care of Grandpa. We waited for you, you know." After that first visit and from then on, she never left without kissing me on the cheek and saying, "Thank you for taking such good care of Grandpa." She left no doubt with anyone that she loved and respected her father-in-law and was grateful for any help he received.

During those first few hours at Horizon House, there was even more confusion than usual. In the midst of unpacking and getting Mr. Kennedy settled in his new home, his daughters and Mrs. Kennedy arrived. The girls spent an hour or so reassuring their father that he was really going to get help. Pat and Peter Lawford came. Eunice and Jean. Each one radiated confidence to him, and always, when his children were around, Mr. Kennedy took on new vigor. Energy showed in his face and eyes. Eunice, who was deeply interested in all phases of rehabilitation and who had already toured the center, was full of technical explanations of the advantages of the center and how he was going to be helped by being there. Eunice was extremely impressive, and in many ways she was one of the most capable and competent women I have ever met.

Pat and Jean were shy women, and to watch them with

their father, one knew that they were "daddy's girls." They
were gentle ladies. Peter Lawford was a most pleasant man,
and everyone was drawn to him. He was positive, at all times, in
his attitude toward his father-in-law. Every statement was
prefaced with, "As soon as Grandpa gets well, we'll do so-and-
so." He never questioned the outcome, and his charm and easy-
going manner were quite refreshing. He always seemed to have
a drink in his hand, and when he'd pop in on Mr. Kennedy,
he'd grin in contrition and say, "I know, Grandpa, it's too early
in the day, but you know how I am." Peter was the only one
Mr. Kennedy tolerated drinking in such a manner, and after a
visit from him, he always seemed relaxed and amused. This son-
in-law was very good medicine.

One by one they filled the house that day to see their father
safely ensconced. The Attorney General and Ethel came, and
they made a great to-do about the charm of the tiny bungalow
and how well he had stood the trip. Mrs. Kennedy was fretting
about the cramped quarters, especially about the size of the
small Pullman kitchen. Over and over her children tried to
reassure her that everything would be fine, but she was still
not satisfied.

Ann was in full agreement with her aunt and decided that
someone should sleep at the house with him, so that he
wouldn't be left alone. Mrs. Kennedy, however, was more concerned about his meals, and it was finally concluded that a
conference with the doctors was necessary in order to discuss
the situation in detail.

I stood on the sidelines, in bemused disbelief. In Palm Beach
I had met the family one unit at a time, but to see them all
packed together in this small house, each yelling at the top of
his voice, was another matter. Ethel kept opening and slamming cabinet doors, peeking in the stove, and scouting the refrigerator. The Attorney General was busy checking out
the bathroom, flushing the toilet over and over, running the
shower and calling out, "Everything works, Dad." Pat and Jean
stayed close to their father, cooing encouragement to him.
Peter Lawford was draped comfortably in a chair, taking it all

in, and Mrs. Kennedy, with Ann hot on her heels, kept cluck-
ing that her husband could not possibly recuperate in a place
like this. Eunice, bristling with energy, went from one to another, thoroughly explaining the whys and wherefores and
doing everything she could to get things in order. But it was
impossible. A doctors' conference was indeed necessary.

Eunice put in the call, and it seemed to me that half the
doctors registered at the institute arrived for the consultation.
Mrs. Kennedy, whose grievances were coming across loud and
clear, was insistent that her husband would never function
properly without the food to which he was accustomed. Despite
the reassurances that every doctor gave her to the effect that
the hospital kitchen could furnish anything he liked, she decided, then and there, to send the *Caroline* for Matilda, his
personal cook at Hyannis Port, and Dora, his waitress. This
decision set in motion an amazing comedy of errors. With one
phone call from the Attorney General, the *Caroline* was dispatched. Everyone waited until Matilda and Dora finally arrived, bewildered but ready for work.

When Matilda saw the kitchen, she was as horrified as Mrs.
Kennedy. This woman was a highly trained chef, who simply
"could not be expected to cope with a few pots and pans." It
would be akin to asking Lily Pons to sing with Spike Jones.
The kitchen was quite narrow and had been designed with low
cabinet heights. It was built in this way so that any resident
who had to learn to cook from a wheelchair could find everything within reach. It was not prepared for Matilda, nor she
for it.

Matilda is Norwegian, and Dora is French, and there resulted an international crisis. The room was not large enough
for the two of them.

Matilda was beside herself. "I don't know what to do," she
moaned to first one and then the other. "I'm a trained chef.
I've spent years as an apprentice to become a chef. How can I
work in this?" She waved at the kitchen in despair. "How can I
work with no condiments? I don't even have knives. What
must I do? What must I do?"

Mrs. Kennedy joined in the melee. The doctors and her children kept insisting that everything would work out. Suddenly, Mrs. Kennedy threw everyone into shock by flatly stating that she intended to have supper with her husband that night. Dora and Matilda went to the kitchen and collapsed. The Kennedy girls saw immediately that it was an impossible arrangement, and so they convinced their mother to have dinner sent over from the Caravelle, Mr. Kennedy's favorite French restaurant in New York.

Louella, who had been standing by during this time, as had I, was immediately commandeered by the girls and "volunteered" into cooking breakfast and lunch for Mr. Kennedy. Louella tried to explain that she was there to assist in nursing, but the girls would not hear of it, especially since Mrs. Kennedy seemed satisfied with the arrangement. It did not matter that Louella had never worked as a cook before. She was a part of the family, and it was taken for granted that she would pitch in and help settle what was fast becoming an Irish Donnybrook.

Mr. Kennedy, who had evidently been enjoying the Mack Sennett comedy, decided, suddenly, that he'd had enough and began stomping his foot and yelling. A blanket of silence spread through the house, and every head spun to him. The doctors insisted that he had had enough excitement for one day and prevailed on the girls to take their mother back to the apartment. The Attorney General and his wife left. Peter Lawford shook hands with Mr. Kennedy and cuffed him good-naturedly on the chin. Ann left with her aunt and cousins. As we watched them leave, waving back toward Mr. Kennedy, giving him last-minute words of encouragement, Louella looked at me and shrugged her shoulders as if to say, "What can we do?"

The Irish whirlwind spun out of sight, leaving us numb in its wake. The Secret Service men, suppressing grins, excused themselves and went to the patio to sit down. Matilda and Dora grabbed their suitcases and disappeared.

The house was suddenly very quiet. Mr. Kennedy chuckled and signaled that it was his turn to tour the house. Until that moment it had been overstuffed with fourteen Irishmen, one Norwegian, one Frenchman, one Englishman, consulting doctors, two nurses, two guards, and one highly amused patient. He had loved every boisterous moment, but now he wanted to inspect his new home for himself.

Louella and I wheeled him through each room. He scrutinized everything, and when he was satisfied, he motioned for us to take him back to the living room. I was trying to convince him to take a nap when we heard a soft knock on the front door.

It opened, cautiously, and the First Lady peeked in. She had come, alone, to welcome him. Her timing was exquisite. She made no undue comments about the house but sat on a footstool in front of her father-in-law and whispered, "I'm praying for you every day, Grandpa, so you work hard while you're here." He nodded his head and placed his hand on her cheek in a gentle caress. She rested her head in his lap for a moment, then kissed his hand and stood up to kiss his cheek. One thing that I always admired about the First Lady was that she completely accepted Mr. Kennedy's condition. While the others pretended not to notice the side of his body that was affected by the paralysis, she always held his deformed hand and kissed the affected side of his face.

I will never forget a time shortly after I took the case when I found that someone had wrapped his stricken hand in a scarf in an attempt to hide it. It took a great deal of intense persuasion before the scarf was removed. One of the most damaging things to a victim of paralysis is to make him feel he is less acceptable because of any deformities. This can be a tremendous blow to his self-confidence and often makes rehabilitation impossible. The First Lady was trying to help Mr. Kennedy accept himself and not be ashamed of his condition. Perhaps that's one of the reasons he loved her so much. Her lack of fear helped him overcome his.

She had brought the afternoon paper with her and offered to read it to Mr. Kennedy. She concentrated on the front page, sensing that he would be interested in the news of the day.

Then she went on to chat about other things. She told him about the children and talked to him about the President, telling him the little blunders the President would make while he was at home. They both laughed and chuckled over the incidents.

Then she asked me if they could have a cola. I tried to find some glasses, but I realized that nothing had been sent over from the hospital, so I told her that we didn't have a glass or a cup or anything for them to drink out of. She patted Mr. Kennedy's hand and laughed, "There's nothing wrong with us drinking out of a bottle, is there, Grandpa?" He grinned and shook his head, so I opened the two bottles and put them on the table by Mr. Kennedy. The First Lady, still sitting on the little stool, waited until he served her. Then she lifted the bottle in a salute and drank from it as if it were a fine glass of hand-blown crystal.

Her visit with Mr. Kennedy was done in a whisper, and when she left, he was completely calm and receptive to a nap.

He had slept about a half hour when a call came informing us that the President was on his way. He was due to arrive within the hour. Louella and I had hoped the Ambassador would have had a chance to rest until just before his dinner with Mrs. Kennedy. As it was, we had no choice but to get him up. He was grumpy at first, but when he learned that his son was coming, his mood turned to pure excitement. He motioned that he wanted to get out of bed immediately. He then surprised us by pointing to his leg brace and signaling that he wanted to put it on. This was rare, for he often waged a desperate battle against wearing it. He then insisted on wearing his finest suit. He was highly nervous and impatient with us as we dressed him, fussing and yelling about the way I combed his hair, and grumbling over the knot in his tie. At last, he was grudgingly satisfied, and he motioned for us to wheel him onto the patio. The President was not due yet, but he insisted on waiting outside for his arrival. He maneuvered his chair until it was adjacent to a supporting pole and settled down expectantly.

When his son came bursting through the door of the institute and began the long walk toward the patio, with his full entourage surrounding him, Mr. Kennedy suddenly grabbed the pole and pulled himself to his feet, balancing himself perfectly, without assistance.

His son, seeing this, ran toward him. There were tears in the President's eyes on seeing his father stand alone. Mr. Kennedy, with great pride, raised his hand in a silent salute. When he reached his father, the President stood very straight and applauded him. Mr. Kennedy stood erect and proud accepting his son's acknowledgment. He was greeting him not as his son, but as the President of the United States. This was a man who had never stood without help or assistance, but at the sight of his President, he grabbed the pole, held onto it, and rose to his feet.

The President then came to him, wrapped both arms around his shoulders in a tight embrace, and kissed him. He cupped his hands under his father's elbow and gently helped him back to his chair. Neither man made an effort to hide his emotions. Speaking for the first time, the President choked, "Oh, Dad."

Probably a hundred people witnessed the scene, but these two men were truly alone with each other in that wonderful moment of love and pride between father and son. Then the President himself wheeled Mr. Kennedy into the house. We all knew they wanted privacy for a few moments. The Secret Service men made a tight circle around the house, and the staff and entourage waited quietly while father and son had a solitary visit together.

The two men stayed inside for several minutes; then the President wheeled his father back onto the patio. He pulled up a chair alongside his father and talked with him about his trip up, about Jackie's visit, and about the comforts of Horizon House. His schedule was hurried, and he told his father that this would be a short visit, but that when he came back in a week or ten days, he wanted to tour the institute and meet as many of the other patients as he could. He asked his father if he would go with him on the tour. Mr. Kennedy readily agreed.

When it was time for the President to go, Louella wheeled

Mr. Kennedy back into the house. The President then wanted to have a serious talk regarding his father's condition with the doctors and then with me, as the attending nurse. He focused on every question and answer with the same piercing eyes his father had.

The President was very emphatic about the information he wanted, especially to what extent his father was improving.

When he was satisfied with the information he had received from the doctors, he took me by the arm and led me back into the house. He wanted one more word with his father. He had evidently heard reports of the afternoon Donnybrook and brought it up to Louella with a boyish grin on his face. She filled him in with more details, and he and Mr. Kennedy roared with laughter. But once more he became serious and called me into the kitchen to double-check his father's condition. It surprised me that he would ask, having discussed it with the doctors, but that's the way the family operated. They double-checked everything.

Finally the visit was over, and after kissing his father again, the President left.

The three of us were alone again, but Mr. Kennedy was a rejuvenated man. He was in control of everything and everyone. He decided that he wanted to watch television and spent a very pleasant hour just relaxing. When Mrs. Kennedy arrived to have dinner with him, it was beautifully served from the Caravelle, and he assumed the role of a gracious host bent on entertaining a very special welcome guest. His wife was ecstatic, and she left after dinner more relaxed than I had seen her since taking the case.

When we put him to bed that night, there was no struggle. He went to bed like a man and slept like a baby.

Louella and I were exhausted by that time, and when Dr. Rusk phoned and assured us that one of his best nurses had been assigned to the night shift, we could not wait to get to our hotel.

Ann had won her point that some member of the family should live on the premises with Mr. Kennedy, and since she was the only one free to do it, she had moved into the extra bedroom. This arrangement made it necessary for the nurses on duty to use the living room as a station. With everything finally settled Louella and I headed for our hotel.

We said a quick good-night and went to our respective rooms. I fell across the bed and was immediately asleep, but in the middle of the night the phone jarred me awake. The night nurse, who had been assigned to the graveyard detail, was screaming in my ear, "Mrs. Dallas, can you hear me? If you can hear me, Mrs. Dallas, I'm resigning from this case."

Half-asleep, I tried to make sense out of her conversation, but she was so furious that I was having difficulty understanding her.

"What kind of people are they?" she screamed. "I won't work when I'm not allowed in the room to do a simple routine check on my patient."

"What do you mean?" I interrupted.

"His niece won't let me in. She's in there right now sleeping on the floor by his bed, and I won't put up with it."

"I'm a paraplegic nurse, not a baby-sitter," she boomed.

Nothing I could do would pacify her or convince her at least to give it another try. She would not finish the shift.

"In no way," she said flatly. "I quit."

There was nothing for me to do except dress quickly, pick up a cab, and head back to Horizon House.

The next morning the doctors assigned Pat Moran, one of the main nurses in rehabilitation, to be the night nurse. Pat, though young, could not be intimidated by anyone and took complete control of her shift. The third shift was relatively light in duties, so we finally found a nurse who would assume charge of it, and at least for a while, the situation was eased.

6

At Horizon House, I saw a whole new vital energy emerge in Mr. Kennedy. He was raring to go. Everything had to snap like clockwork. He had a job to do, and he seemed to be saying to himself, "By God, I'll do it."

He shouted and pounded his fist, but in a new and different way. It was not a tantrum; now he hammered and screamed in full-blown authority. Louella and I were overwhelmed at his new approach to life. When the doctors came to discuss his schedule with him, he listened intently, stopped them when something was not made clear, then nodded his head firmly, after he understood.

He wanted to get well. He was willing to do anything in order to assure his recovery. He was becoming part of a new world. He nodded pleasantly to all the other patients in the cafeteria and was very proud of himself.

He became a fanatic on punctuality. If a nurse or even his children happened to be a minute or so late from the time they said they would be there, he would fly into a rage.

I learned from one of his men in the New York office that when he was working, if he had an appointment and the person was one minute late for it, regardless of who it was, that appointment was automatically canceled and never rescheduled. He had run his life and business on punctuality, and this exacting habit was now carried over into his new life. The only one who ever got away with being tardy was the First Lady. She would sweep breathlessly into the house, stoop down, kiss him, and whisper in her soft voice, "I'm sorry, Grandpa, but here I am, late again."

He apparently loved her so deeply that he never once scolded her for it. Perhaps he sensed in her the same independence that he had developed in himself, but for anyone else his fetish for punctuality often reached absurd proportions.

The speech therapist who had been assigned to him was, of course, the finest and, therefore, one of the most overworked women in the institute. She made every effort to be on time for her appointment with Mr. Kennedy, but she usually showed up a few minutes behind schedule. When she would come for his therapy sessions, he would not cooperate in any way. It went so far as his refusing to even look at her. We tried to explain that she was late, not because she was lax in her work, but because she was trying to assist as many people as possible during the day.

It was finally decided, since his lessons were at a standstill, that he would go to speech therapy class instead of having a therapist come down to Horizon House. This was explained to Mr. Kennedy and seemed satisfactory.

The first day we reported to the class, he looked into the room, and seeing all the people sitting there, he swung his leg out of the wheelchair and signaled for us to stop. He looked startled. The therapist came out to greet him, and as he was trying to wheel him into the classroom, Mr. Kennedy began screaming and shaking his fist.

He went into an uncontrollable rage. There were people sitting in the waiting room, waiting for their husbands or wives or friends to come out of the various classes. I leaned down to whisper to him that we would take him back to Horizon House and discuss the situation there, and as I did, I got in the way of a sledgehammer fist.

Mr. Kennedy's flailing arm hit me full in the eye. The blow stunned me, and the look of horror that came over his face when his fist connected was as painful to me as the blow I had received.

I thought I was going to pass out, but his agent, Ham Brown,

(Photo: Edward F. Carr)

Mr. Kennedy with Cardinal Cushing, Rita Dallas, Dick Segura, and
Ann Gargan

Palm Beach —
the Kennedy estate

Hyannis Port —
Bobby Kennedy's
house

Horizon House

Mr. Kennedy with
Pat Kennedy and
Patrick Kennedy

The President and
Mrs. Kennedy

Mr. Kennedy
. and Caroline

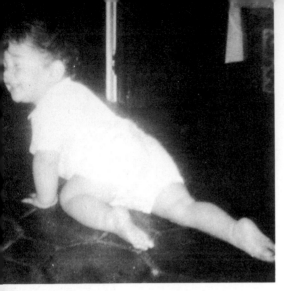

President Kennedy's
son, John

Sam, one of the many beloved pets

Caroline and her
brother, John, with
young Steve Smith

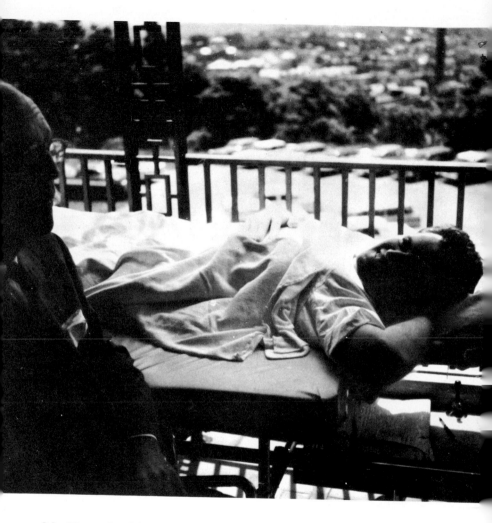

Mr. Kennedy visiting Teddy during his recuperation from the plane crash

(Photo: Bob Davidoff)

Hyannis Port – the "walk" to the beach taken so often by all the Kennedys

ran to me, put his arm around my waist and led me to a chair.

Everyone in the room was watching me, and I knew that I could not let them see me cry or faint.

"Ham," I said, "get me out of here without drawing any more attention to us. Let one of the therapists take Mr. Kennedy back."

A male therapist came over to see how I was, and through his teeth, he said, "If he was standing on his feet, I'd knock the hell out of him."

I knew that if I gave any indication that I was injured, word would spread and the rumors would enlarge completely out of proportion, so I managed to laugh and say, "There's no problem. It was my fault. I walked right into it."

I went back to Mr. Kennedy and tried to tell him that everything was all right. When he saw me, he started sobbing, and then he reached up and patted my face. He took my hand and put it to his cheek and began crying harder. The people in the room turned their heads and looked away, for they were sympathetic to this man, who could not say the words "I'm sorry," and, yet, had found a way to offer an apology.

I wanted to get us out of there before my eye began to swell, and with the help of the agent and another therapist, we returned to Horizon House.

Dr. Betts, who had been put in charge of his case, was at Horizon House when we arrived. He gave Mr. Kennedy his attention and told him that he would not have to attend classes again, but that another therapist had been assigned to him. She would report once a day to Horizon House.

After Mr. Kennedy was settled, the doctor examined my eye and asked if I thought I could finish out my shift. The eye had started to swell, so Louella went to the commissary and bought a pair of dark glasses for me. In that way I was able to finish the shift and not cause too much embarrassment for Mr. Kennedy, but by the time Louella and I had arrived at the hotel that evening I had a shiner.

I knew it would not be possible for me to report to work the next day, so I called Dr. Rusk and explained what had happened. Arrangements were made for the nurses to double up, and for the first time since I had come on the case, I had a day off. I spent it soaking my eye in ice cubes and answering the telephone, for the nurses and Ann were constantly calling, most generally to find out when I was returning to work. I remained away two days, and then, still wearing the dark glasses, I reported back to Mr. Kennedy.

When I walked into his room, he looked at me for a long moment and then started weeping. He put out his hand, and when I took it, he pressed it to his cheek. With that, all was forgiven and forgotten.

The new therapist always arrived at least five minutes ahead of time, and although Mr. Kennedy had nothing to do, other than wait for his speech lesson to begin, he would deliberately stall until the exact moment arrived for his lesson. Then he would motion like a king for us to let her in. Overall, he was pleased and satisfied with the new arrangement.

His lessons were progressing well, but there was the usual frustration. When the therapist would give him a word to work with and he was unable to master it immediately, he would become angry and start to thunder. Ann would rush in the room and order the therapist to leave. "If my Uncle Joe doesn't want to do it," she'd say, "he doesn't have to do it." After such a scene, Mr. Kennedy would completely turn off, and there would be nothing more the therapist could do.

There was so much interference of this sort that the doctors finally held a meeting with the family and said, in so many words, that Mr. Kennedy stood a better chance of being rehabilitated without any member of his family around, except during specified visiting hours. These, too, were to be curtailed. The doctors explained that none of the other patients had their families living with them, for it was a detriment to recuperation, rather than an asset.

The next day Mrs. Kennedy told Ann that she thought it would be nice if she visited her sister in Detroit, but Ann was reluctant to leave. Nevertheless, someone obviously took control, and in a day or two, Ann was off on her vacation.

With only professionals attending him, Mr. Kennedy buckled down, and before too many days had passed, he began to treat Horizon House as though it were his personal residence. He was very much at home in the small bungalow, and there was nothing or no one to hamper his progress.

Eunice was fanatically faithful to her father during this time. She would come every day and encourage him in his work. In the evening Mrs. Kennedy would join him for dinner. It was a settled, productive period. You could feel a change taking place.

In the beginning, Mrs. Kennedy, hardly daring to hope, showed heavy strain, but as the days wore on, she began to relax and would enjoy watching her husband exercising in the pool or listening to him in his speech therapy. We could see a new kind of happiness shine through for both of them. When his children came, we could tell by their actions and by the sounds of their voices that their hopes were running high.

One morning, when we were on our way for a medical examination in the main building, Mr. Kennedy began pointing his finger until it became evident that he wanted a tour of the center.

I was not familiar with the institute, so I stopped at a desk phone and called the main office. His doctor came immediately to where we were, and together, we covered the complete project. Mr. Kennedy saw men his own age walking, exercising, and doing almost impossible things in spite of their handicaps. He watched everyone intently. When we had made a full circle of the building and had returned to Horizon House, he seemed to take on an even greater incentive.

He was a complete and prime subject for rehabilitation. He dug into his exercises without ever complaining, and his progress was so rapid that finally the day was fast approaching when he would be able to walk unassisted with his brace.

This is a major achievement for a handicapped person. This is the thing they work for. This is what the pain and suffering is all about—the chance to walk, unassisted.

Mr. Kennedy had been fitted for a full leg brace in Florida, but examination at the institute revealed that, due to the lack of regimented therapy and exercising, there had been atrophy in the left leg muscle. This meant, unfortunately, that the alert muscles, still functioning in the leg, had become emaciated and weak.

Once a muscle has lost its nerve supply from the brain, it never comes back. It actually disappears. The stroke had hit his leg hard and it was considerably paralyzed, but an evaluation of his case, and his general progress since residing at Horizon House, prompted a major effort to strengthen and develop the remaining muscles.

The first reason for rehabilitation is to utilize the muscles that are left, strengthening them to their fullest extent. The second reason is to prevent the strong muscles from deforming. The damage had already been done to his wrist. It was no longer flexible. It was drawn and permanently deformed, but there was still good reason to concentrate on the rest of his body.

Since the leg had shrunk, it was necessary for him to be measured and fitted for a new brace and surgical shoe. Minute attention is given to proper fitting, for the slightest misfit can cause a patient severe discomfort. A poor fitting has a tendency to discourage him. Learning how to wear the new brace and going through the difficult process of developing walking skill with the brace are difficult enough without the added pain of an improper fit.

A surgical shoe is a strange-looking contraption. It is high-topped and laces from the tip of the toe up. It is designed in such a way that, by lacing, it can be tightened to give a contour fit from the toe to three or four inches above the ankle. It also enables the shoe to be put on with ease, for it completely opens up. In advanced paralysis the foot has a tendency to deform and the surgical shoe is crucial in preventing this deformity. Gradually, if a patient is faithful in exercising and walks constantly, this kind of corrective measure can be dispensed with.

Dr. Betts personally brought the new shoe and brace to Horizon House early one morning. He laid the shoe in Mr.

Kennedy's lap. Mr. Kennedy stared at it, critically, then abruptly threw it off his lap.

His reaction to the surgical shoe was understandable. It requires an adjustment for anyone, because when worn, it accentuates the abnormality of the handicap. Also, Mr. Kennedy was a man of superb style and taste. Everything he wore was exquisitely tailored and crafted, so it was especially disconcerting for him to accept the heavy and cumbersome shoe.

He glared at Dr. Betts over his glasses and shook his head emphatically no.

The doctor studied him thoughtfully, then tossed the shoe back in his lap.

A look of amazement came over Mr. Kennedy's face.

"Look, Mr. Kennedy," Dr. Betts said, "it's not my shoe, it's yours—if you want to walk, that is. It's all up to you."

In explicit language he went on to explain the purpose of the shoe, and why it was necessary. Little by little Mr. Kennedy became absorbed, and by the time Dr. Betts was finished with his explanation, Mr. Kennedy was nodding his head in agreement.

Dr. Betts said to me, "It's all right, put it on him."

I took the shoe from Mr. Kennedy's lap and knelt down, lifting his leg. I laid his foot in the shoe and began lacing it up. I could feel his eyes on me, studying every move.

Dr. Betts supervised the lacing, making sure that it was properly tied, and explained everything to Mr. Kennedy as we went along. When we had finished, Mr. Kennedy peered at his foot and commented with a shrug and a dismal shake of his head.

The shoe had been built with a slight elevation on the sole, and a new brace was required. The next task we had was to get him into the brace. We were gratified and relieved when he did not object, and it confirmed our belief that this man really wanted to walk.

A week or so passed after this incident, and one morning Dr. Rusk came to Horizon House filled with great excitement.

"This is the day we've been waiting for, Mr. Kennedy," he said. "This is the day. Are you ready to walk?"

Mr. Kennedy puffed out his chest and nodded.

He was ready.

Dr. Rusk carefully explained what he wanted him to do. He was to walk, unassisted, using only a cane. When he was sure Mr. Kennedy understood, he handed the Ambassador a regulation hook-handled cane that was issued to all the patients by the center. When the Ambassador saw it, his face grew red and he began to scream, "No. No. No." He grabbed it and threw it across the room. It bounced against the wall, barely missing the patio doors. He had grudgingly accepted the ugliness of the surgical shoe, because it was necessary, but he would have no part of such a cane. He made faces at it and filled the room with sounds of mock gagging. He was telling us that it was ugly. It was ordinary, and in his mind, if he had to use a cane, he would at least carry one befitting his taste.

Dr. Rusk hastily promised that if he would use it that day and not disrupt his therapy schedule, he would personally get him the finest cane in New York.

It took a great deal of diplomacy and persuasion to influence him, and for nearly an hour we stood by while Dr. Rusk did what he could to pacify his patient. Time and time again the cane was handed to Mr. Kennedy, only to be tossed away, until, finally, with a distasteful grumble, he took it.

Before he could change his mind, we wheeled him from Horizon House, up the ramp, into the main building of the center. The walking and exercise areas used by the patients were the long halls that stretched throughout the rehabilitation center. It was assumed that for his first effort Mr. Kennedy would take a few modest steps.

Being who he was, Mr. Kennedy invariably drew attention and curiosity. This was part of the game, so to speak, for with a regiment of famous sons and daughters it was natural that he received more attention than the average person.

There was quite an entourage on hand. His two attending physicians, several of the staff doctors, and many patients were standing around, waiting to see how he would do. Louella and I were joined by the other nurses who contributed to his care.

It seemed to me that most of the therapists in the hospital were also clustered around us. The doctors decided that it would be best to work on the second floor, for it offered more privacy, so the group separated and went up in different elevators. I was growing concerned, for I knew Mr. Kennedy resented crowds of people staring at him, but my fears were soon calmed. He ignored everyone. He seemed settled and anxious to be on with it.

I had taken his cane when we started out for the center, and I was quite apprehensive about giving it back to him. I had visions of another outburst, but when his agent, Ham Brown, wheeled him out of the elevator and I handed him the cane, he accepted it with a slight twinkle in his eye.

At last, everything was ready. He had been wheeled down the hall and listened again to the doctor's instructions. He nodded that he was ready to go.

He was just attempting to push himself up from the wheelchair, when the First Lady, flanked on either side by Secret Service men, came running down the hall toward us.

"Wait a minute, Grandpa," she called out breathlessly. "Wait just a minute."

Mr. Kennedy, surprised at seeing her, dropped back in his chair.

"I heard you were going to walk today," she said, after kissing him, "and I just had to come. Oh, Grandpa, I'm so happy for you."

Mr. Kennedy smiled up at her. She knelt down in front of him, and with his left arm he gently embraced her. He blinked his eyes to keep back the tears.

She took his face in her hands and whispered, "Oh, Grandpa, do you have any idea how proud I am of you? How very proud?"

Seeing his tears, she brought a handkerchief from her purse and wiped his eyes and then her own.

"Aren't we foolish?" she laughed, coaxing him out of his tears.

"I have something for you," she went on, motioning to one

of the agents. She stood up, put her arm around his shoulders, and smiled. "Something especially for you, Grandpa."

The agent handed her a package that looked like a long, thin mailing tube. She was all smiles.

"Can you guess what this is, Grandpa?"

He shook his head in delight, for he loved gifts and surprises.

From the tube she withdrew the most beautiful walking stick I have ever seen. Glistening black, with a heavy silver head. And on the band was engraved, "To Grandpa, with love, Jackie."

"Can you read what it says, Grandpa?"

In response, he took it, ran his hand up and down it, in a caress, read the inscription. He then handed the hospital cane to an aide.

Holding his elegant new walking stick proudly, he braced himself and miraculously stood up alone. His therapist, caught off guard by the sudden and unexpected move, tried to catch him, for he wavered briefly. The First Lady shook her head no. She kissed the afflicted side of his face and hooked her arm, gently, through his paralyzed arm.

"Come on, Grandpa," she said. "Let's take a walk."

With her at his side, there was no way to stop him. He began walking down the hall, shoulders back, head high, using his cane. He swung his leg wide, with her praising his every step. Whenever he faltered, she moved slightly in front of him, looked up in his face, held out her arms, and said, "Come on, Grandpa. You can do it, you can do it."

He walked! And walked! And walked!

He walked the full length of the hall and back again. We could see the effort it was taking, but she encouraged every step, and it was a remarkable thing to see a man his age struggling so hard to accomplish an almost impossible feat. He insisted that they keep on walking. We turned corners time and again.

Dr. Rusk was growing concerned and thought he'd had enough. He didn't want him to overtire, but when he tried to stop him, Mr. Kennedy shook his head, leaned on his cane, and took a full step, as if to say, "I'm going back to the starting line and do it all over again."

I asked Ham Brown to bring his wheelchair, and he and I hurried down the hall ahead of the party. We were waiting for Mr. Kennedy when he walked back toward us. He looked at the wheelchair, and despite the doctor's urging him, he refused to get in it. He pointed to the elevator, and the First Lady laughed. "Are you going to see me to the door, Grandpa?" He nodded his head and grinned.

He was concentrating on two things: the coordination it required for him to walk and his daughter-in-law. Nothing else concerned him.

On the elevator, to the first floor, the First Lady could not contain her elation. She kept saying over and over, "Wait till I tell Jack, Grandpa. He won't believe it. Wait till I tell him what's happened."

Mr. Kennedy stood erect with his shoulders back and his eyes straight ahead, leaning on his cane, in a most debonair manner.

When we got off the elevator, he motioned for her to follow him. He surprised us all by heading for the ramp that led to Horizon House. It was quite difficult for him to maneuver the ramp, but step by step, with her arm still linked through his, he made it to the patio. I had been following close on his heels with the wheelchair, for we fully expected him to collapse at any moment. When he finally reached the patio, I moved it in position behind him, and he sat down, exhausted.

Once more, the First Lady knelt in front of him and cupped his hands in hers.

"Grandpa," she said, "remember when you told us that you didn't believe in coming out in second place?" He nodded. "You told us over and over always to go for first. You told us to lose well, but to try for victory. Do you remember?"

She kissed his hands.

"You came out first today, Grandpa. You had yourself a victory."

Her voice was tight in her throat, and not wanting to give way to her emotions in front of him, she added quickly, "I have to go now, Grandpa."

She stood up, and he bent forward for her embrace. With

her cheek against his, she cried, "You are a magnificent man."

She left quickly, nodding her good-byes, too emotional to speak.

Mr. Kennedy watched her out of sight, then let out a long sigh and motioned that he wanted to go to bed. Louella and I quickly undressed him and massaged his foot and leg. Neither of us spoke. We wanted nothing to dispel the memory of Jacqueline Kennedy. It was something for all of us to savor.

He was so exhausted that he fell asleep immediately. Louella and I tiptoed out of the room and found ourselves the closest chairs. We were also on the verge of collapse. Our patient had surpassed our furthest expectations. He was determined to outshine any record that had gone before him. He had sensed that the First Lady would immediately report his phenomenal feat to the rest of his family, and he wanted them to know it was a job well done. He had justified their faith. He had once again shown them the impossible was obtainable.

That night Dr. Rusk ordered that we keep a very close watch on him. The doctors were concerned that he might have serious side effects from his exhaustion, but to our relief, he showed no adverse reaction and slept through the night.

He gave us a gift that day. He let us know he was a fighter. Those of us who knew him only as a stroke victim saw the man that once had been. Tough. Determined. Victorious. He had showed us that incentive in any undertaking is the most important ingredient. All the frustration and defeat that he had suffered the past months melted away in the presence of that willowy and beautiful young woman.

Jacqueline Kennedy had come at his most crucial moment and brought with her a gift selected with deep insight. Her faith in him had told her that someday he would walk, and long before it happened, she had found the perfect gift to commemorate it.

She had said over and over, "I am so proud, so very proud," and these words, coupled with her deep devotion, provided Mr. Kennedy with the spirit to accomplish the impossible.

7

THE MIRACLE WALK—and it had been that—sparked
the Kennedys anew. The doctors were equally exuberant, and
no one seemed to doubt that Mr. Kennedy was on the threshold
of a better life. A life with new meaning.

He had radically changed his previous hit-and-miss attitude
toward therapy, and had reaped results. The shoe and brace
continued to bother him, and he was always relieved when he
could take them off, but for the most part, he was responding,
mentally, physically, and emotionally.

We had decided that it was important to get him involved in
class therapy. The doctors felt that when he saw how other
patients were working with similar or more severe handicaps he
would gain confidence. Seeing their progress and learning to
work and compete with them in groups was an important step
in his rehabilitation. He agreed with the idea, but at first he
was shy in open class work and held back. But when he realized
that other people were too busy helping themselves to stare at
him, he relaxed and fell into a productive pattern of work.

Finally, it was decided that he had gained enough self-
confidence to learn how to take a shower alone. This is a very
important step in therapy, almost as important as walking, because it means that the patient is no longer intimately dependent on another person to care for him. The privacy and luxury
of taking a shower by himself can be a great morale boost and is
a big step in restoring his sense of personal dignity and self-
sufficiency.

It was also a big step because it would be the first time Mr.

Kennedy had tried something without Louella or me there to give him direct assistance or encouragement.

We took him up to the specially equipped shower room, which was in the institute, for his instructions. The therapist met us and explained to Mr. Kennedy what they were going to teach him to do. He got out of the wheelchair, unassisted, and went into the shower room with the therapist. Louella and I waited for him outside, for what seemed to us to be a very long time, but when he finally came out of the shower, he was well scrubbed, beaming, and a bit frisky.

Another victory!

Mr. Kennedy had been taught, in one lesson, how to take a shower for himself. He had learned how to stand and move about in the stall, how to use all the physical safety bars and rings that were installed for his protection, and in one lesson he had grasped the precautionary measures that were necessary to assure his physical security. A proud therapist reported that Mr. Kennedy had been spectacularly observant and alert and had completed his shower without any need for assistance.

Mr. Kennedy had every right to be elated that day.

We took him back to Horizon House, and he had a short nap. Then, without any argument, he went back to the institute for further therapy in the massage and whirlpool.

The daily momentum of his schedule kept building. He was quick, and he knew how to listen, how to learn, and, most important, how to apply what he had learned. Day by day, he continued to make major accomplishments.

His family, cooperating fully with the doctors, kept to the suggested visiting routine, so as not to interfere with his therapy work. Eunice and her sisters came every day. Eunice was always on the run. Her hair tossed, her purse stuffed with papers for one project or another, she would dash into the room, throw her arms around her father's neck, and let out a marvelous, gusty laugh. "Oh, Daddy, Daddy," she'd say. "You're a real whopper!"

Mr. Kennedy would rear back in his chair and beam at this girl who was, every inch, a Kennedy.

She never came to see him without first getting a progress report from the doctor. This she did every day, and she let her father know that she was keeping a watchful eye on him.

"You can do anything you want to do," she'd say with encouragement. "Anything at all."

Eunice is a brilliant woman with a vibrant philosophy toward life, and she never stopped trying to encourage her father.

Pat and Jean would come, and their visits were quiet and restful for him, in contrast to Eunice's. Hers were fast and exhilarating. Pat and Jean, on the other hand, usually talked to him about a show they had seen the night before or a special news feature on the President or other members of the family. They spoke of general, uncomplicated things—things that he also needed to hear.

Mrs. Kennedy's disposition was rapidly smoothing out. She no longer gave the impression that she was mentally wringing her hands, and the sense of fear that her husband would fly into a rage or scream at her was almost gone. They enjoyed each other's company, and every evening she would come to Horizon House to have dinner with him.

His personal waiter from the Caravelle would arrive ahead of time, with glistening silver and gleaming linen. He would light the candles on the intimate table for two, and there, in that small, simply furnished bungalow, one of the world's richest men would dine alone with his wife.

His days were so full and productive, and his nights so restful and healing, that I felt my time on the case was nearing an end. My understanding had been that I would remain at Horizon House until his condition was reevaluated, and since we were all sure of his progress, I met little resistance when I approached Robert Kennedy with my thoughts about returning to hospital work in Florida.

He was generous in expressing his gratitude, and we agreed that I could leave the case when I was ready by giving them a month's notice. When he told his father that I would be returning to Florida, Mr. Kennedy grumbled and frowned, but he was not actually discontented. This was a most healthy sign, for often the patient becomes too dependent on one person, and this is one of the worst things that can happen.

When a patient is dependent, he becomes vulnerable to the moods of the other person. There are pitiful cases where patients actually freeze in their progress, owing to abnormal dependency. Their lives become dull and restricted in scope. Everything revolves around this dependency, and they become powerless to control their own destiny. Time and again, I have seen patients almost destroyed by their dependency on one person. So when Mr. Kennedy took the news that I would be leaving without any discontent, I felt he was on safe ground.

My next days passed quickly, and as Mr. Kennedy improved, his disposition followed suit, but there were exceptions.

One afternoon the President and Bobby came to visit Horizon House together. They had been in New York on an unexpected trip and decided to stop over and spend time with their father. It was not the best day for a visit, for Mr. Kennedy had been out of sorts. Perhaps he was trying too hard in his therapy program, but he would not slow down.

When the boys phoned and told him they'd be over in an hour, he was all excited. Once again he made a special point of dressing and carefully selected a handsome pair of slacks and a sport shirt. We wanted him to put on his leg brace, but he became quite angry with us and threw it across the room. It was his intention to wear his own shoes, and when he was that determined, there was no changing his mind.

I wheeled him onto the patio and noticed he was clutching his cane in a tight fist, as though he thought someone might try to take it away from him.

I was coming to know my patient well enough to realize that he was up to something. I could tell when a scheme was brewing in his mind, so I watched him carefully.

The boys arrived, and they talked with their father for quite a while. One of the doctors from the center had accompanied them to Horizon House and was going over Mr. Kennedy's rapid progress. He absorbed it all, nodding his head, answering back and, even though there were only occasional clear words, the boys listened intently. At this point in his illness, Mr. Kennedy was not consciously aware that he could not be understood. I'm sure he realized his speech was halting and, thus, needed therapy, but he was not aware that he was "jabbering."

The President, Bobby, and the doctor listened attentively when he spoke, and the more the doctor talked about his progress and praised his efforts, the more Mr. Kennedy talked.

Suddenly without any kind of warning, he started to get out of his wheelchair alone. He had evidently become so carried away on a crest of enthusiasm that he thought he could walk without his brace. The doctor dashed over to prevent him, but with a powerful left Mr. Kennedy brushed him back. He pushed himself up, stood for a moment, then began to stagger.

In a lightning move, Bobby grabbed his father. Mr. Kennedy tried to struggle loose and began swatting at him with his cane.

We were horrified! The Secret Service men sprung to attention and moved in. The President wisely refrained from getting involved in the fracas. Even though he was ducking blows, Bobby gradually succeeded in easing the tension by starting to laugh and tease his father.

The doctor intervened and got Mr. Kennedy back in his chair. He was screaming and shaking his fist at his son. Despite this, Bobby leaned down, rested both hands on the arms of his chair and said, "Dad, if you want to get up, give me your arm and I'll hold you till you get your balance. That's all I'm trying to do."

He gambled a blow to the face and kissed his father. "That's what I'm here for, Dad." He smiled. "Just to give you a hand when you need it. You've done that for me all my life, so why can't I do the same for you now?"

He talked on and on, soothing, pacifying, until, finally, his father became calm.

When the tension was over, the President joked that Bobby was still not too big for his dad to whip. Mr. Kennedy grinned, and the crisis had run its course.

Bobby made a pretense of going to the kitchen for a Coke, and motioned for me to follow him. He fumbled with the bottle opener and cleared his throat several times before he spoke. Then, unashamed, he turned to me and with tears in his eyes, said, "How is my dad, Mrs. Dallas? How is he, really?"

"He's very much better," I said. "It's only that he's tired. He just wanted to show you and your brother that he could do something without anyone's help."

Bobby leaned against the refrigerator and stared intently at me. He had the same steel eyes of his father. The same ability to cut and slash with a glance, but once that shield was removed, they were the eyes of a truly gentle man.

Mr. Kennedy, his condition being what it was, had forgotten the incident by the time we returned to the patio. He was fully enjoying himself listening to the President fill him in on White House anecdotes. Bobby, pulling up a chair, entered into the conversation in a modest, guarded way.

The Secret Service men later told me that they had been placed in a terrible position. If Mr. Kennedy had swung on the President, they would have had to repel the attack in the quickest, most effective way—even if it had meant throwing Mr. Kennedy back in his chair and twisting the cane out of his hand. Their job was to protect the body of the President, and they all agreed it would have been a disastrous situation to face. Had he picked on the President instead of Bobby, it could have resulted in a free-for-all, for none of us believed that either son would have allowed their father to be manhandled regardless of his behavior.

It was during that meeting that the boys told their father he would soon be well enough to visit the White House. The President said that it would be his biggest day since he had taken office. He told his father that the pool was finished—a pool Mr. Kennedy had personally given to the White House—and he and Bobby explained every detail of it.

Construction had begun prior to his illness, and Mr. Kennedy had commissioned the artist to paint murals on the wall, depicting Nantucket Sound. He had personally supervised the design and lighting system but had yet to see the finished product. It was then that I realized Mr. Kennedy had not been to the White House since his son had taken office.

"You'll come, won't you, Dad?" the President asked. "Just as soon as the doctors give their okay, you'll come, won't you?"

Mr. Kennedy nodded his head emphatically yes.

"Now this is one promise you're not going to break." The President laughed. "You've stalled me long enough."

"Wait till you see him in the office, Dad," Bobby added proudly. "He really fits it."

When they finally left, Mr. Kennedy was full of pride and excitement.

One of the most endearing memories I have of my years on the Kennedy case occurred at Horizon House.

It was Father's Day, and all morning long calls had come in from his children, wishing him well. With each call, he grew more saddened, for none of the children had been able to come to Horizon House. No one would be there to celebrate his day, and he spent most of the afternoon slumped in his chair, staring moodily into space.

Mrs. Kennedy arrived to have dinner with him as usual, and she was spritely and lively, but nothing she could do would pull him out of his doldrums.

Just before dark, and without any warning, his children arrived in a group and came bursting into Horizon House laughing, teasing, and bulging with gifts of every description for him.

They had made their visit a surprise, and Mr. Kennedy was overjoyed. It was the custom, I learned, that on his birthdays his grandchildren conducted an entertainment program for him. But on Father's Day, it was his own children who did the entertaining. Each year they made up a play, and they all acted parts in it.

So there they were. The President and Eunice, Bobby and Teddy, Jean and Pat. With their spouses on the sidelines, they presented a little skit, reminiscent of incidents of their childhood.

Mr. and Mrs. Kennedy were weak with laughter. The in-laws were gathered around his chair, hissing and booing the performance, and when something particularly sentimental touched Mrs. Kennedy, she clapped her hands and, being Irish, wiped a few tears from her eyes.

When the imaginary curtain fell on the little skit, they stood in front of Mr. Kennedy and applauded him.

First the President applauded. Then he was joined by Bobby. Next Eunice. Then Teddy. Then Pat. Then Jean. One by one, until they were applauding together. Then the boys bowed at the waist, and the girls curtsied, first to their father, then to their mother.

The room was stacked high with gifts for him. There were exquisite things, beautifully wrapped. But the gifts that meant the most to him were the trinkets they brought. He loved stuffed animals and toys. The boys took special delight in finding the most garish pillows with quaint and occasionally risqué quotations or pictures printed on them. These he adored, and as time went on, his room abounded in toys and pillows—gifts from his children.

After the packages were opened, the refrigerator was raided. Then, one by one, each couple drifted off to the patio. They had arrived as a unit, but they slipped away singly, so as not to leave him suddenly alone in an empty room. They waited for each other on the dimly lighted patio.

When it was all over, he was a tired, happy man, and Mrs. Kennedy sat by her husband with her hand resting on his, talking quietly—remembering.

Later that evening Ann phoned from Detroit to wish him happy Father's Day. She spoke at length to her aunt and then talked, gaily, to Mr. Kennedy—or so it was assumed.

When the conversation was finished, Mr. Kennedy was very upset. He began yelling at his wife without any apparent provocation. I could see the old look of sadness come back on her face. A perfect day had been suddenly spoiled.

She pressed her fingers to her temples and hurried from the

house. I knew she was badly upset, so I walked to the center with her.

"I don't understand, Mrs. Dallas," she wept. "I simply don't understand. I thought he was getting along so well, but now, this. It's like it used to be."

"He's tired, Mrs. Kennedy," I said. "And it's the only way he knows to react. He'll be all right in the morning."

"I wonder if he misses Ann that much," she mused.

"I don't understand," I said.

"The call upset him," she replied. "He was fine until then. So I think talking with Ann made him lonesome for her."

"Perhaps," I said.

I left her at the entrance to the center. She patted my arm good-night, and then said, "I'll have to talk this over with the girls."

I walked slowly back to Horizon House, despondent that her evening with him had ended badly. The nurse and I had a very difficult time putting him to bed. He was extremely irritable, and during one of the wrestling matches we had with him, the nurse muttered, "Wait till I tell you what happened."

Finally, he fell asleep, and the nurse and I settled down in the living room to collect ourselves, for we had had a long, exhausting day.

It was then she related the gist of Ann's call, and she wanted my advice. She had overheard the conversation because we were still under strict orders from the Attorney General to monitor every call. According to the nurse, Ann had broken down during the conversation and had wept profusely. She begged Mr. Kennedy to let her come back. The nurse said that the more Ann cried, the more upset Mr. Kennedy became until he ended up shouting over the phone in angry confusion.

I advised her not to make a special report on the incident— just to enter it in the log and comment briefly on what had happened. I felt that he would be fine by morning.

When the night shift came on, I went to my hotel. I slept soundly that night, hoping Mr. Kennedy was also at rest, but the next morning, the night report read that for the first time in several weeks, the patient had been difficult.

All that day he could not concentrate on therapy. He picked at his food and wanted to stay in bed. We felt he had earned some time off, so we devoted ourselves to making him as comfortable as possible and enjoyed spoiling him a little.

Late that night, the next day, and for the next week, Mr. Kennedy received up to three and four phone calls a day from Detroit. Since all these calls had to be monitored, all the nurses on duty were keenly aware of what was happening. Ann cried and pleaded, for she was pathetically homesick, and since Mr. Kennedy's speech was so limited that he had no way of responding to her, he became more deeply disturbed and extremely difficult to handle. He would slouch in his chair and rock back and forth, fretfully, for hours at a time. His fist stayed in a tight clenched ball, and day and night he seemed restless and filled with frustration.

I knew of his genuine concern for Ann, for during this period one of the men from his New York office recounted a day when Mr. Kennedy had said, "Make her rich." An investment portfolio had been set up in her behalf, and in a matter of a few years, she would come into high profits. But for the time being she had no other security than to be with him. The desperation of her calls left us not only sad, but extremely embarrassed for having heard them. We also became greatly concerned over our patient's setback. The doctors did everything in their power to cope with the situation without bringing the family into it. We all thought he could work himself out of the problem. But it finally reached the point where Mrs. Kennedy and his children were becoming panicked about his retarding condition, so the doctors had a consultation with them and explained the calls were causing his severe reaction.

The doctors recommended that Ann not be permitted to return to Horizon House. He was at a crucial point in his rehabilitation program, and they wanted nothing to interfere with it. Nevertheless, it was decided to bring her back, and Mrs.

Kennedy, hoping to please him, told him of the family's decision.

He reacted adversely, shaking his head and saying, "No, no, no."

She tried to explain that she would be leaving in a couple of days to open the house at Hyannis Port for the summer and since she would not be able to visit, Ann could take her place in keeping him company. But he kept shouting at her and stomping his foot.

She told him the doctors had promised he could come home for a couple of weeks during the Fourth of July celebration, but even this did not quiet him down. The veins in his neck bulged, and he was almost hoarse from screaming at her.

"Oh, Joe," she groaned. "Oh, Joe! Joe! We're trying to do what's best, and you know we have to take care of Ann."

For the first time in weeks, he started swinging his arm, trying to strike her. I quickly walked her out of the house. We could hear him throwing things after us.

There were tears in her eyes as she said to me, "Oh, Mrs. Dallas, if you could only have known him when he was well. He never once raised his voice at me. And to strike out at a woman would never have entered his mind. He's a good man," she cried. "And, oh, Mrs. Dallas, I'm so sorry you never had a chance to know him as he was."

"Please! Please! Don't worry about it," I said. "It's frustration, nothing more."

Mrs. Kennedy, however, was never able to adjust to this kind of violence, and as she left that day, she took my hand and held it tightly for a moment.

"I don't know what to do," she cried. "I just don't know what to do."

The next afternoon Ann returned from Detroit, and she was genuinely thrilled to be with her uncle once again. She had a great vitality, and for the first few days, she kept him amused by telling him of incidents that had happened on her vacation.

When one of his staff predicted that if "Miss Ann" went to the Cape, Mr. Kennedy would not return to Horizon House, I shrugged it off. It never occurred to me that the old pattern would be taken up so quickly. Unfortunately, it was. But in respect to all concerned, I cannot place the responsibility solely upon Ann.

What happened had to be a family decision, and knowing the Kennedys, I realized that bringing her back was not done in a casual manner. They thought things out. They always discussed a situation in minute detail, and not one of them ever went off half-cocked when an important decision was to be made. They were too sure of themselves and their positions ever to be coerced or unduly influenced. No one ever pressured a Kennedy into anything. In this case they simply overruled the doctors' recommendations.

It was to be my last week on the case, and things were in total confusion. Mr. Kennedy was balking at everything we tried to do. He was impossible to handle, and I was not too surprised when the Attorney General phoned to set up an appointment with me. At the meeting he asked that I stay on the case for a few more weeks and go to Hyannis Port with Mr. Kennedy for the July celebration. "Just until he levels off a little," Bobby said.

I could see that Mr. Kennedy was almost back to where he started when he had come to Horizon House, and I was in a quandary about what I should do. Bobby did not high pressure; he simply stated, "We need you, Mrs. Dallas, and you know that Dad needs you." In good conscience, I had no choice but to remain on the case.

That evening Mrs. Kennedy arrived for dinner and asked to speak to me privately.

She said, "My son told me that you've agreed to go to the Cape with us, and I want to thank you. I also want to tell you that we consider you the head nurse. Louella is going to be the liaison between the doctors and the family, and Ann will be in charge of my husband."

It had all been settled. Fate had not decreed his destiny—his family had.

The next day Cardinal Cushing came to visit the Ambassador. The cardinal had been quite ill, but when he heard about his friend's setback, he had gotten out of a sickbed to come down from Boston. He was quite pale and very unsteady on his feet.

It had been reported that he was undergoing radium treatments, but even so, I was shocked by his pallor and condition.

He walked slowly, and there was a great throng of people around him that had congregated from the institute. Everyone of the faith was anxious to kiss his ring and be blessed by him.

When he was finally able to work his way into the house, he was breathing hard.

"Your Excellency," I said, "since you've just come out of the hospital, perhaps you would like to sit down."

He nodded his head, and I found a chair and put it beside him. He sat down directly across from Mr. Kennedy.

His shadowy face broke into a mischievous smile, and he regaled his friend with wild stories about the nuns in the hospital and the jokes he had played on them. He made very light of his own illness, and before long, they were both laughing together.

The cardinal never acted as though Mr. Kennedy could not talk, and he had a long involved conversation with his friend, each of them, at times, trying to outshout the other.

As he started to leave, he shook his finger at Mr. Kennedy and invoked him to "be good."

"I don't want any more bad reports about you, Joe," he teased. But there was a ring of admonition in his voice.

The rest of the day Mr. Kennedy was in excellent spirits.

That evening Ann came to dinner with her aunt and decided to move back into Horizon House.

8

ANN'S DECISION to move back into Horizon House and the family's acceptance of this stirred very mixed emotions in me and still does. As a nurse with my patient's welfare at heart I could not feel that it was going to benefit Mr. Kennedy. Although I had an obligation to remain objective and not be affected by the decisions of the family, I had grown very attached to Mr. Kennedy. This man was a patriarch. He had molded an empire and given his family the drive and ability to fulfill their roles in history. At the same time he had become tremendously vulnerable after his stroke, and his struggle to overcome the serious handicaps he was afflicted with was incredible. I never saw a man fight so hard to stay vital and alive. I became devoted to him because of his spirit and his unwillingness ever to give up.

Mr. Kennedy's spirit had been instilled in the whole family, and they all wanted to see him win his battle with rehabilitation. But there was another overriding motivation in all the activities of the Kennedys, and that was the desire to project an image of unity, an image in which Mr. Kennedy was an integral part and yet not a part. As the aging patriarch he fitted in well, but as a figure of influence and political wisdom he had to be faded into the background.

After he was stricken he could reemerge as part of the total family image, and at his side was Ann, his niece, the devoted companion. Mr. Kennedy was in the care of a member of his family, and no one could accuse the Kennedys of having abandoned him. With Ann there the picture of family unity was complete, even though she was not a real "Kennedy." So effective was her place in the image that the public soon accepted her as Mr. Kennedy's nurse. Wherever he went she was at his side. The family turned Mr. Kennedy over to Ann when they let her move into Horizon House with him, and after that point the two became inseparable.

Not only was Ann Mr. Kennedy's companion, but she also took a position of authority regarding his care and welfare. The family did not oppose this, and it often put me, as his nurse, in a position of conflict with her.

The key to the problems presented by Ann's position with Mr. Kennedy is revealed in her statement about nursing in the *Ladies' Home Journal* when she said, "I had no interest in science, but I was drawn to the human part of nursing." Her devotion to Mr. Kennedy cannot be questioned, but when the family would take Ann's recommendation regarding Mr. Kennedy's welfare in spite of what the doctors urged to the contrary, I could not agree with them as a professional nurse.

His life, or, for that matter, the life of any ill person, should be under the direction and supervision of the medical profession. The finest doctors in America attended Mr. Kennedy, but their decisions were usually circumvented. I would not deny that physicians are fallible, but I also know that they are the only mortal healers we have to rely on.

In minor situations, everyone, at one time or another, will find himself disregarding "doctors' orders," but it's usually at a personal, physical expense. Few of us will risk another person's well-being. We might not take our own medicine, but let a member of the family come down sick, and everyone usually directs his attention to getting that person well. We call a doctor for a loved one and do what he tells us to do for him.

But the complicated life-style that results from a stroke is like the legendary Chinese water torture—it gradually drives a family mad with worry, confusion, and grief.

Mention "stroke" and the invariable response is that the patient is going to die. With that belief hanging over a family, it is logical that they want their loved one to be as comfortable and as happy as possible, during the time that he has left.

Mr. Kennedy's family functioned under the apparent belief that he lived on a day-to-day basis. I'm sure they believed he would "go" at any time. But they forgot to reckon with his will to survive. This man was a born fighter.

During the years he did have many low periods. He had innumerable cardiac arrests, and I had to administer emergency resuscitation to him, but somehow, from the depths of his soul, he would struggle back. He wanted to live. And he did.

Had he been a lesser man, perhaps he would have terminated in a few weeks or months. Instead, he lasted nearly a decade.

Once Mrs. Kennedy said that if she had known he would last so long, things would have been different.

As it turned out, he would not give up. Despite everything, he would not give up.

And the family fought along with him in their own way. They gave him the best doctors, they were willing to spare no expense, but they were caught because no one of them except Ann was free to give him constant time and attention. But this was the way it had to be, because not one member of his family was free to disentangle himself from his political and public commitments. Not one could be expected to give his full attention to the routine problems of caring for him. And Mr. Kennedy would not have wanted any of them to do this. It is ironic in a way, but Mr. Kennedy had created a family so filled with drive and ambition, so dedicated to taking their place in history, that when he suddenly was in a dependent position, they were so committed to carrying out the roles he had prepared them for that they could not give full attention to his needs. This is not to say they didn't love him, because he was surrounded by love. And in truth, Mr. Kennedy often had great fun with Ann. She could be a marvelous companion for him, and the family saw this.

But in allowing her to assume so much authority, they were often allowing a lay opinion to take precedence over professional diagnoses. As a nurse I could not agree with this, but I cannot honestly say that I would not have acted in the same way if I had faced a similar situation without the knowledge of my experience and training.

His stroke was frightening, and they thought he was dying. Therapy was painful and slow, and they wanted him happy and comfortable. But he had taught them always to win—to fight and not to lose—and although he himself continued to fight, his battle was erratic. It was not conducted under the professional guidance and discipline that could have brought him greater success over his handicaps.

As the years passed, I would see pain cloud his eyes, and fear take hold. I would see him watch and wait for his children, sorrowed that time was passing him by. I saw his strong body finally wither, but I never saw him give up. He would fail and fall back, but his drive for survival invariably forced him forward again—and I knew that so long as he tried, I would do everything in my power to help him.

Once, after a severe cardiac arrest, a member of the staff said to me, "Why don't you let him die? Why work to keep him alive? He'd be so much better off if you'd let him go."

I was so angry that I shouted, "So long as that man tries, so will I. He'll know when he's ready. When he gives up, nothing I or anyone else can do will save him—but as long as he fights, so help me God, I'll fight with him!"

Mr. Kennedy taught me so much—almost taught me what life is all about, and I carry his memory in a very special place in my heart. He would sink, only to rise again, and my admiration and devotion almost matched his determination.

It was during those last few days we had at Horizon House that I knew that I was committed to him for as long as he lived. I made a pact with myself that so long as I could, I would help him.

Ann was in charge, and I realized that, by alienating her, I could not do the best for my patient. As a woman, I liked her immensely, but she had power entrusted to her that surpassed her capabilities.

The family allowed her this role and whenever conditions

regarding him were questioned by any of his children, Mrs. Kennedy, who was the undisputed head of the family, would answer each with: "Can you come and take care of him?"

Each child, at one time or other, sadly turned away and said, "No."

As his nurse I came to know his children, his friends, and his wife. They were the spokes of a great wheel—a wheel, with Mr. Kennedy as the silent, dying hub.

9

WHEN ANN MOVED BACK into the small bungalow in order to be near Mr. Kennedy, it was only a matter of time before she began exerting her newly authorized position. She was overconfident and strong-willed, even toward the doctors in charge of his case.

A day or two after she moved back, she said to him, "Uncle Joe, the family has put me in charge of you, and you'll have to do as I say from now on." He had a wild look in his eyes for a moment, and then he slumped in his chair and all the wind left his sails. It was evident, by the expression on his face, that he had not been brought into the family's decision, and this cut his spirit to the bone.

From then on, it became more and more complicated to care for him, and the joy and spark that had once filled his family with expectation now diminished and sagged. They still visited him with the same regularity, but in their opinion, Mr. Kennedy was having a serious and, perhaps, final setback.

He became a most trying patient. He would become irritated and scream at the slightest provocation. When it was time for him to exercise or go to the pool for therapy, he would roar and shake his fist. "Naaaaa. Naaaaa. Naaaaa."

We all walked in a wide circle at these times, for he would strike anyone who got near him. Anyone except Ann. He screamed at her, threateningly, but never struck her.

Mrs. Kennedy had left for the Cape, and I was glad that she was not around to see his behavior. Under the circumstances, I doubt if she could have faced up to a daily visit and still retained her composure. Before she left, she informed me that if any purchases had to be made for Mr. Kennedy or if he needed clothing or anything else, I was to speak to Ann about it, and she, in turn, would discuss it with the New York office.

"I have given Ann my permission and notified the office that I want things handled this way," she said.

After Ann informed him that she was in charge, she was the only one able to settle him down, and she would do so by coddling him, as one would a child. He responded sullenly. Whatever he wanted, she provided.

It was decided by the professional staff that if there could be some way to turn her into a properly trained therapist, Mr. Kennedy's rehabilitation would take an upward swing again. When the doctors recommended that she go into therapist training, they received unanimous and enthusiastic approval from the family.

One of the main doctors of the institute invited her to his office for the purpose of discussing this possibility, and I know he sincerely hoped to interest her into taking a special training course.

In reality, she was a woman without a profession, and this made her totally dependent on the family for her security. Not only would this training have given her a sense of independence, but its benefit to Mr. Kennedy would have been unlimited. As it turned out, she was extremely hostile to the proposition and was adamant to the doctor in her refusal ever to consider it.

She was furious when she returned from the meeting with him and shouted at us, "I'll never be away from Uncle Joe, and I don't need any so-called training to take care of him. And you'd better remember it."

Her decision was obviously accepted by the family, for Ann remained in charge but also retained her amateur standing.

Mr. Kennedy had been under the care of the most talented doctors available, and the results had been evident, but soon all their efforts were weakened. He was being spoiled again, and there was no longer any challenge for him to meet.

If he grumbled about his brace, he didn't have to wear it. If he grew bored in speech therapy, he'd let out a yelp, and the lesson was over. If a meal displeased him, he shoved the dishes on the floor. If his massage seemed too rough, he would throw out his arm or kick up his leg and land the therapist a solid blow.

He was cross and easily antagonized. He continued the habit of rocking back and forth, groaning, or pounding his fists together.

The many productive hours of disciplined therapy were lost, and the elation we all felt over his walk with the First Lady became a sad memory.

Once again, owing to the drastic situation, the doctors requested that Ann be restricted from interfering with the treatment. The Kennedy daughters tried to alleviate the situation by promising to do what they could to keep her occupied.

They invited her to the theater and to lunch, and took her out to dinner with them as often as she would go, but she was not willing to leave Mr. Kennedy for any long period. Whenever she returned from being away she would come to him saying, "Oh, Uncle Joe, I missed you so much." Kneeling by his chair, she would lay her head in his lap, often crying. After this, her mood would change, and she would entertain and amuse him with stories about where she had been and what she had been doing. She could indeed be charming, and he enjoyed her at these times; but it was difficult for him to see her when she cried.

The situation did not alter, even after the second request, and for the third time, the doctors met with the family and asked that she not have the authority to overrule therapy. Once again, nothing changed.

It broke my heart to see him so confused that his eyes would dart, like a panicked animal, caught in a trap. I knew my patient well enough to know that, given half a chance, he could swing back, but I was afraid it would soon be too late.

One afternoon, while Ann was out with a cousin, I decided to ask Mr. Kennedy if he would like to meet some of the other men in the center. In therapy classes, patients have very little opportunity to make personal contacts, for it is a hard work session and they have to concentrate on their own tasks. We had developed nodding acquaintances with some of the men at the institute, but that was as far as it had gone. I felt that, perhaps, some personal contact might be a great boost to him and revitalize the drive he had seemingly lost. Also, it seemed important to me because Mr. Kennedy was almost constantly surrounded by women except when his sons came to visit. This had been true in Palm Beach, and it was still the case at Horizon House. I felt he needed some male companionship so he could relax outside the hard and frustrating work of his therapy.

When I asked him if he would like to meet some of the other men, his eyes lit up, and he nodded his head, vigorously. I phoned the doctor, and he was so pleased at the idea that, very soon, four men, near his age, arrived in wheelchairs. There were no nurses or attendants with them. They came on their own—and Mr. Kennedy took all this in and watched how they handled themselves.

Each man was in a more serious condition than he, but they had such vitality and determination that you could see they were strong contenders for rehabilitation.

Two of the men were stroke victims. One had been in an accident that had cost him both legs and one arm. Another had fallen and was paralyzed from the waist down.

They sat on the patio with Mr. Kennedy and visited. The two men who could talk clearly kept up a running conversation, and it was remarkable to see the other men, including Mr. Kennedy, communicate by sign or expression.

After what seemed like a short visit they got ready to leave. Evidently the doctor had advised them not to stay too long to avoid tiring Mr. Kennedy. As they were leaving, one of the men said, "Mr. Ambassador, we're having a cookout tonight and we'd like to have you come. We have a lot of fun, you know."

Mr. Kennedy quickly put out his hand and said, clearly, "Yes."

When the doctors heard of this, they were walking on air. Here was an important breakthrough, and they wanted to hang onto it.

Mr. Kennedy was almost his old self. We kept building up the cookout during the afternoon, and he grew more excited about it. He kept saying, "Yes. Yes. Yes."

When Ann returned, we were exuberant—but it was easy to see that she was quite tense when she heard of the plan.

The afternoon aide said to her, "Once Mr. Kennedy gets involved with the boys, we'll see some changes take place."

The cookout was scheduled for six thirty, and since things appeared to be going well, or at least I thought so, I decided that I would go back to my hotel and take the evening off. The doctor said that since he would personally escort Mr. Kennedy, I could sign off duty.

All evening long, I kept thinking about him, and I felt great relief and happiness in knowing that he was having another chance.

I retired early and fell into an untroubled sleep.

About eleven thirty, my phone rang. It was the night nurse, brokenhearted.

"What's wrong?" I asked.

"Oh, Mrs. Dallas," she cried. "I waited until now to call, until everyone was asleep."

"What's the matter?" I repeated. "Is something wrong with Mr. Kennedy?"

"Well," she sighed, "you can judge that for yourself."

Then she related the happenings of the evening.

She had dressed Mr. Kennedy in a special sports outfit. He had carefully selected something simple to wear, obviously feeling that he did not want to overdress with the other patients. She said he was really excited, and when the doctor came for him, he was all smiles and ready to go.

Just as they were leaving, Ann became agitated and said that there was no way her uncle could possibly enjoy spending an evening with "such men." She argued hotly with the doctor and threatened to call the President, if necessary. Mr. Kennedy sat wide-eyed, taking it all in, and the nurse said that she thought the argument might have come to blows if Ann had not grabbed her uncle's wheelchair and raced with him to the bedroom.

He was screaming, "No. No. No." But there was nothing anyone could do.

After that, it was all over.

Although the doctors and the staff never gave up on Mr. Kennedy, it was apparent that he could not deal with all the conflict going on around him. He became more and more difficult, and the only thing that would cheer him up was the coming visit to Hyannis Port for the Fourth of July celebration. As preparations got under way for his departure, it was decided that Patricia Moran, one of the instructors in therapy, and Elinor Noble, one of the nurses who had worked with Mr. Kennedy at Horizon House, would go with us. Pat Moran and I had discussed the situation, and we both felt we should do all we could to try to keep up his therapy program even though he was going to be away from the professional staff of therapists at the institute.

Originally the plan was that Mr. Kennedy was to return to Horizon House after a couple of weeks in Hyannis Port, but as things developed, he never went back. Dr. Rusk constantly tried to get him to come back, but somehow the family never could make the decision to return him to the institute. Horizon House stood empty waiting for him and, eventually was made available to other private patients. It is also used now as a showcase house, an example of the most fully equipped environment for a patient in rehabilitation.

During the last days before his departure I think Mr. Kennedy realized that he had lost his greatest chance, for he was sluggish and listless. The spunk was gone out of him, even though Ann did everything in her power to keep him cheered.

The morning we left, she wheeled him onto the patio and

started with him up the ramp. Halfway to the center he put his foot out and stopped her.

Slowly, he twisted around in his chair and, for a long moment, looked lingeringly over his shoulder at Horizon House.

It had been his, and he had lost it. He was leaving, never again to return.

10

THE LIFE-STYLE AT Hyannis Port was in direct contrast with what it had been at Palm Beach, for Cape Cod was home to the Kennedys, and they congregated there as one bulging unit.

In Palm Beach the main estate was enclosed, and the other Kennedys rented nearby when they came for the winter season. But at the compound all the houses were close by, and there were no fences in between. It was a "compound" only in the figurative sense, and all the children and grandchildren roamed freely from house to house. Also, during the winter season the family visited only on weekends, and they were unable to be there as often. The grandchildren were in school, and the big Palm Beach estate was often empty during the week. But in the summer the grandchildren were there almost all the time, and the families were constantly popping in and out of the Ambassador's house. It was a free-flowing atmosphere all during the summer. Hyannis Port was truly home for the Kennedys.

The main Kennedy house was on Scudder Avenue, a picturesque street, typical of any that can be found in exclusive resort areas. The first house in the compound was the Ambassador's. Next to it was the President's, and back to back with it, was the Attorney General's. Jean and Steve Smith's house was just below the big house. The Shrivers at that time rented a place a short distance away, and Teddy and Joan had a home on Squaw Island, which was about fifteen minutes from his father's place.

There was a long drive that circled around the main house.

In front of it, swooping down to the sound, was a wide span of grass.

It was on Mr. Kennedy's front lawn that the Presidential helicopters always landed, for there was not enough space in any other area to handle them. Also on Mr. Kennedy's property were the tennis courts and swimming pool, used by all the family.

The big house was a large conglomeration of rooms. It was comfortable, though not elegantly furnished, and had a bright, sunny disposition about it. It was painted white, as were all the others, and a long porch ran across the front and around the sides. It was not the largest or most impressive house on Scudder Avenue, but it was sturdy and very much at home in its Cape Cod atmosphere.

That first season a small house had been rented for me down the street from the President's house, for I was adamant that I did not want to live on the premises with my patient. I knew I would have long hours wherever I was, and I needed a private place of my own in order to relax. The New York office took care of the arrangements, and I found the little house comfortable and charming.

Mr. Kennedy's spirits had picked up when we reached the Cape. As soon as we arrived at the house, he had us take him on a tour, so he could inspect everything carefully. Dora and Matilda greeted him with affectionate squeals, and the rest of his staff lined up, for their annual first inspection and welcoming.

The Fourth of July had long been a traditional week of family celebration. This was always the first weekend that the whole family was together, and it was the real beginning of summer for the Kennedys. The horses had been shipped up from their winter stables in Maryland and had been settled on a farm, annually rented by Mr. Kennedy. All the grandchildren were out of school. The boats had been serviced and were anchored at the dock in front of the main house, and by the Fourth everyone had arrived.

The magnificence of the Kennedys struck me full force as the celebration got under way.

Early on the afternoon of the third, everyone came to the big house to await the arrival of the President. I would judge nearly two hundred people were on hand—brothers and sisters, grandchildren, in-laws, servants, staff, gardeners, guests, sports directors, tutors, governesses, stable hands, agents, and nurses. Everyone.

The immediate family stayed on the porch, beside Mr. Kennedy. The grandchildren and their governesses stood in loose formation on the lawn, just in front of us, while the household staff lined up along the side drive.

Clustered around in an informal group were the guests: actors, writers, TV stars, singers, politicians, statesmen, ballerinas, nobility.

Throngs of tourists were held back at the foot of the street, and pleasure crafts and sight-seeing boats darted among the Coast Guard cutters that were patrolling the waters in front of the house.

Everyone was there except Mrs. Kennedy. It was her custom to wait in her room until her son came to her.

As head of the family, Mr. Kennedy sat on the porch and had every reason to be proud. One son was the President, another a Senator, another the Attorney General. One son-in-law directed the Peace Corps, another was a well-established motion-picture star, and another was credited as one of the leading businessmen in the country. They were gathered around him to observe the most important holiday in American history—and to pay honor to his son, the President of the United States.

Every eye was peeled on the sky until, at last, breaking into view, came the three Presidential helicopters. As soon as he saw them, Mr. Kennedy sat very straight in his chair at attention. We all followed suit.

There was a wonderful moment of hushed anticipation as the helicopters swooped down, hovered for a moment, and then, one by one, landed, with the grace of a butterfly. From the first two planes came the high government aides and the

chiefs of staff. Generals and admirals, Cabinet members and
their aides, Secret Service agents, and an array of special guests.

According to the chain of command, the officers and aides
lined up at the third helicopter, making an honor guard. The
guests stood to one side.

And then—there he was.

He stood in the doorway, his crisp hair tossed, his wide shoulders almost cramped in the narrow opening. His eyes swept the
ground, finding first his father, then lifting to the second floor,
where his mother was watching from her bedroom window.
The President trotted briskly down the steps and turned to
await the First Lady and his daughter, Caroline. A governess
followed them with young John.

He gathered his family and walked through the honor guard.
He stopped and waved to the tourists and then acknowledged
the people on the boats. With that, whistles began to blow in a
wild salute, and the tourists shouted and cheered. On the porch
his family applauded and the staff stood at attention. Then
the children broke loose and swooped down across the lawn,
screaming, jumping, cheering.

Somehow he managed to touch and kiss each one.

Caroline and her mother held back politely, allowing the
children to have their moment. Young John, however, was
straining to get down, but his governess held him in a firm
grip.

The President finally pulled away from the youngsters. Then,
with his arm around his wife and holding Caroline with his
other hand, he came toward us. Once more, his brothers and
sisters applauded as he approached. He walked across the porch,
stood in front of his father, laid both hands on his shoulders,
and stooped to kiss him.

Caroline, no longer able to restrain her excitement, broke
into gales of giggles and tried to jump into Mr. Kennedy's lap,
but her mother gently held her back.

Then, with the President's hand still on his father's shoulder,
the First Lady dropped to her knees in front of him, rested

her hand on his arm, and whispered, "Hi, Grandpa. We're home."

Mr. Kennedy gave a quick, emotional nod, then motioned for them to greet the rest of the family.

One by one, they greeted Sargent and Eunice Shriver, Steven and Jean Smith, Peter and Patricia Lawford, Robert and Ethel Kennedy, Edward and Joan Kennedy.

John Kennedy shook hands with each one, not as a brother, but as the President of the United States. It was a serious and proud ceremonial moment.

Then he went back to Bobby and Teddy and said, "Let's find Mother."

Bobby grinned and replied, "She's in her room, waiting."

The three sons left the porch, arm in arm.

With that, the weekend was under way, and it was bursting at the seams with activities.

I had seen the President countless times, at Palm Beach and at Horizon House, but it was not until the welcoming ceremony at his home in Hyannis Port that I had the full impact of John Kennedy as the President of the United States. This ceremony of the President and the First Lady holding court with their family took place every time they arrived or departed, and it never failed to move me. The ritual was always the same. It was the family's chance to give John Kennedy the accolades they felt he and his office justly deserved, and every time I saw it I knew that Camelot was real.

One thing I noticed in particular during that first weekend in Hyannis Port was that Mr. Kennedy's children, regardless of how many guests they were entertaining, always sought each other out. The compound could be alive with celebrities and dignitaries, but you would never see a Kennedy alone. There was always another one nearby. At large gatherings, sooner or later, they would invariably huddle together and tend to cut out everyone else, including in-laws. Many times I've seen Teddy raise his head from the circle and look around the room for his wife, Joan. When he found her, he would flash her a smile and motion for her to join him.

"Come on over, Joansie," he'd call, and occasionally she would, but it took courage to invade the Kennedy circle—for, united, they were a formidable group.

The big house was always open to the children and grandchildren, but guests were never brought there unless specifically invited by Mrs. Kennedy. With her husband unable to talk, it was usually only the family who visited him. The exceptions were his old and personal friends, but even these men had to make specific arrangements to see him before arriving.

We had two seasons with the President at Hyannis Port, and they seem to blend together in my memory. They were gay, carefree months, for the Kennedy bandwagon was rolling in high gear.

I think back on the events that happened, and I remember them as generally being good for Mr. Kennedy. He managed to hold his own, despite several serious setbacks. Perhaps he weathered these because his family was always near him, and it was an easier way of life.

It was home.

I I

When we got to Hyannis Port I had been on the Kennedy case since January. I had seen a lot of the family during those months, but it wasn't until we got to Hyannis Port that I really got to know what each of the Kennedy brothers was like.

Teddy was the youngest, and although he had won election to the Senate, he was the baby of the family. He had tremendous energy and was always racing around filling the house with warmth and laughter. The family responded to his exuberance and seemed to treat him a little like a lovable puppy who was not quite housebroken.

When Teddy was around, there was always a flood of laughter. He was cute, and he knew it. He would flirt outrageously with everyone like a college boy, and his charm was completely disarming.

He boiled over with health and energy. His mother often said, "I feel better when Teddy is at home, for he has so much joy about him. It's always been like that. Even as a little boy, no matter how troubled things were, Teddy lightened my load."

He never seemed to have a care in the world. Life to him was "fun time," and to some, he might have acted like the spoiled son of a rich man, but as I came to know him, there were times when his ever-present smile didn't quite reach his eyes. To me, they were often clouded. They twinkled mischievously, but there was still a sadness in them at off moments.

He idolized his older brothers. It was a pure and simple case of hero worship, and he made no pretense about it. The President humored him at this and would tease him unmercifully at times about it. Teddy would be expounding on some new idea, and the President would peer behind his ears and grin.

"Hmmmmmm, still wet, I see."

"Aw, Jack," Teddy would mumble, then bounce off to something else.

Whenever Teddy saw his brothers together, he would bolster himself up and go bounding to them. They would look at him, their eyes mischievous but would invariably turn off the serious matters at hand and start to roughhouse with him. I commented on his exuberance one day to Louella, and she said, "Teddy is one of the most loyal men you'll ever meet. It's just that he's a little taken up with the excitement of being a Kennedy, and he's yet to come into his own. But when the chips are down, you can count on Teddy."

I thought about Louella's words at great length and realized that Teddy was a man who had a lot to live up to, for he was surrounded by opulence and fame. It was little wonder that he made boisterous efforts in order to be heard and noticed.

I can remember seeing him and his wife, Joan, on a tandem bicycle, with him in front pedaling hard and his youngest child tucked in the handlebar basket. Seeing his father in the sun room watching him, he'd whiz by and wave broadly.

"Hi, hi, hi," he'd yell, and then start his daredevil antics by throwing his hands in the air and sticking out both legs. He'd wiggle the handlebars until I thought they would all go tumbling. Mr. Kennedy would sigh and shake his head, but he always waved back. Teddy always tried hard to keep his father in a light mood and usually succeeded.

He was like a small boy full of the thrill and excitement of having a brother who was the President, and when the helicopter would land at the Cape, he would actually jump up and down for joy. He would crane his neck until he spotted his brother alighting and then shout, "There's the President! Everybody, look, there he is!"

Teddy always took personal delight in calling him "The"

President and did so at every opportunity—even when speaking to his brothers and sisters. They indulged him in this, for I'm sure they secretly enjoyed his adulation and high-stepping antics.

The President and Bobby had a very special relationship. They constantly communicated by sight even when they were not talking together. And whenever they were together, it was impossible not to watch them. They would sit facing each other, hunched over in deep conversation. Bobby would talk earnestly at great length, and the President would listen. Seeing them this way, one realized that these two men could not leave their business at the office. There was a devoted tie between them that confirmed love and intelligence.

Both men were unique. Whenever I think of Bobby, I can see him racing up the stairs at the White House in Washington very late at night. He never took the elevator but swallowed the steps two at a time. Without fail he would end the day with his brother, checking again to see if there were any last-minute details that needed attention.

The main lights in the White House would be out, the tourists would be long gone, the last guest had departed, and the air was hung in silence. It was a time, they said, when the ghosts of the past walked. And then there would be Bobby, his tie loosened, a coat hung over his shoulder, his shirt blousing behind him, and his face worn in serious thought. He was the President's closest, if not his only, confidant.

It was during that first summer that my affection for Bobby came into full bloom. At first, it hurt me whenever Mr. Kennedy treated him roughly. It seemed that he yelled at him constantly, but as time went on, I realized it was almost as though he were trying to urge him on to accomplish greater and greater things. They were so much alike in many ways it was like two firecrackers exploding themselves when they were together.

It was a running joke with the family that when they were growing up, Bobby always took the blame for everything, and I think his tough reputation came as a result of this. It took time to get to know him, but once you gained his confidence and the steel left his eyes, you knew he was a warm, compassionate, and dependable man. The other two boys were robust and would tend to swagger, while Bobby had a fast, clipped gait that some called cocky. Perhaps it was his way of keeping up with them.

I saw him once when his son David was being ruthlessly picked on by his older brothers. David had taken some severe thumpings and a lot of ridicule because of his small build. That day Bobby took his son aside and told him, "Don't let anyone buffalo you. Learn how to fight back and learn how to win."

He then took his son to the sports director and told him to teach the boy how to win a fight. For the next few weeks I could see the small boy practicing, and Bobby would praise him and urge him on. Finally, the great day came, and I was cheering for David.

The Ambassador and I watched the fight through the window. David put up his mitts and won hands down. From that time on the bullying stopped. I imagine Bobby had gone through the same thing as a child, and he saw in this youngster a remembrance of himself.

One hot summer day, an excursion was planned on Mr. Kennedy's boat, the *Marlin*. It started out to be a small party, but before too long everyone had decided to go along, and "everyone," when all in tow, could well have populated a small town. So many people were involved that the President decided to take some of them on the Presidential yacht, the *Honey Fitz*.

The *Marlin* was overloaded as usual with children, pets, sons, and daughters. Mr. Kennedy was enjoying the day, especially when a friendly race developed between the two boats that had been sailing side by side. Of course, there was no contest, for the *Marlin* could have been set in one corner of the Presidential yacht. But it was fun, and everyone shouted and cheered.

The President's dog, Charlie, who was some sort of half-and-half Airedale, had somehow gotten aboard the *Marlin*, and he was very fretful. He kept watching his master on the other boat and whimpering. No one was paying too much attention to the dog, for we were all busy keeping an eye on the children, who romped and ran and rolled and hung over the sides. Bobby was on our boat and doing his best to keep order. There were probably a half a dozen other animals on board, as well as young Bobby's current favorite, a falcon that rode on his arm wherever he went.

The President spotted his dog and shouted across to him, "How's it going with you, Charlie?" With that, the dog let out a bark and jumped overboard! He began to swim toward the larger boat. We watched in horror, for there was no way that the tiny animal could avoid being pulled under by the propellers.

Without any hesitation, Bobby jumped overboard and swam as hard as he could to the dog. Suddenly, a hush fell on both boats, for we knew that at any moment the animal would be sucked down and destroyed by the propellers. We also thought that Bobby couldn't possibly reach him in time—but he kept right on swimming, apparently oblivious to the fact that he also was heading straight into the propellers.

It had happened so rapidly that the captains on both boats had not slowed down. They were obviously unaware of what was going on. The dog was within inches of his death, fighting now to keep himself from being drawn under. He and Bobby went down at the same time. Someone yelled, "Stop the engines! For God's sake! Stop the engines," and for what seemed like an eternity we held our breaths.

Finally, Bobby surfaced with the dog in his arms. He treaded water, showing Charlie first to the President, then to us! A wild cheer went up! The children screamed and yelled! The adults clapped and whistled! Some of us wept. Charlie was hauled on board, his tail wagging, and when Bobby was helped up, the two brothers ran to each other and embraced. I was standing by Mr. Kennedy, and I heard him shudder when it was over. He closed his eyes in relief and slumped forward, exhausted from the strain.

Bobby was often impulsive, and although he usually thought things out, he was always ready to throw himself into something if he was needed. I had to admire him for this. The President was not as spontaneous as his brother, but he always had a great sense of humor. He often joked and kidded with his father, and one of their favorite games was when the President would go to his father's bathroom and say, "Boy, Dad, you've got some pretty fancy towels in here, and I could sure do with some." He would always come out with one or two draped over his arm, and his father would chuckle and wave him on his way.

One Sunday morning the President was watching a weekly television news program with his father, and a certain politician was being interviewed. The man was an extremely high-ranking Democrat, but he apparently did not set well with Mr. Kennedy. He suddenly shook his fist at the television set and said in absolute clarity, "You son of a bitch."

The President threw back his head and roared. I did not want to laugh in front of Mr. Kennedy, so I ducked out of the room to keep him from seeing me. The President realized his father was dead serious, so he came to the nurses' station wiping his eyes.

"Dad always has disliked the guy"—he chuckled—"and did you hear what he called him and how clear he said it?"

The President was still laughing when he rejoined his father.

He never seemed to tire of being with Mr. Kennedy. Perhaps, suffering from his own physical handicap gave him a deeper and more compassionate understanding for his father's illness. Suffering with his back as he did required that he use a cane a great deal of the time, and he never wanted his father to see him walking with it. He knew this would worry him.

He would walk across the yard, leaning heavily on the cane, but when he would start into his father's room, he would stand outside and motion for me. He would hand me the cane to put aside, so his father would not know that he had to use it. I don't think he realized that his father was watching out his window and would see him. Always after he would leave, Mr. Kennedy would keep his eye glued to the window, and when his son would pass by, limping and leaning on a cane, he would watch him out of sight and shake his head in sorrow.

John Kennedy was the eldest living son, and when his father was stricken, the President had to take the role of the masculine head of the family. But it always seemed clear that he felt he was nothing more than an acting figurehead. The respect he gave his father confirmed this.

For instance, if any added expenditures for the family had to be made or if drastic changes in plans had to take place, the President invariably conferred with Mr. Kennedy about them. He would dash in and out, sometimes several times a day and often only for a moment or two, to tell him of a new problem or to ask his advice. Mr. Kennedy would listen to him, thoughtfully, then respond with a yes or no.

The President once said, "Even if my Dad had only ten percent of his brain working, I'd still feel he had more sense than anyone else I know."

Each of his children had the same attitude toward their father, and it often caused me to ask myself how they could have agreed to the decision of removing him from Horizon House. They must have seen his progress there, and it didn't make sense that they would allow this alert, intelligent man to miss the chance for more complete rehabilitation.

Many times I would see his children bend down to kiss his hand and say, "I'm sorry, Dad."

His daughter Jean was so sensitive that she usually cut her visits short, for she would have to leave the room to keep her father from knowing that she was crying. A little later she'd return, having composed herself, and he would touch her cheek and smile, gently. He knew.

I was always impressed at the way the President responded to his father no matter what else was going on. I remember the time just before the Cuban crisis when the President had brought his Cabinet to the compound for a high-level conference. We all knew it had to be an important meeting, but none of us had any idea what was afoot. Mr. Kennedy also knew something special was going on, because the President and Bobby brought in the Cabinet members to meet him. This was the first time they had all convened at the compound.

Later the same day all the men were gathered in front of the big house, huddled in a circle around the flagpole, talking. Mr. Kennedy heard the President's voice and pointed outside. He motioned in such a way that I knew he wanted his son. To make sure, I asked, "Do you want the President, Mr. Kennedy?"

"Yaaaaa," he yelled emphatically and kept pointing with his finger.

We were on the second floor, so I went to the balcony and called down, "Mr. President, your father wants you."

He looked up from a heated discussion with Robert McNamara, flashed a wide smile, and said, "Tell him I'll be right there."

I relayed the message to Mr. Kennedy, but in just a few minutes he became impatient and started pounding on the chair with his fist. I dashed back out on the balcony and called again, "Mr. President, your father wants you. Now."

"I'll be right there," he repeated. Chuckling to the men, he said, "When Dad wants something, he wants it."

Mr. Kennedy and I listened for the elevator, and when the doors opened, the President rushed in, put his arms around his father's neck and kissed him.

"What's on your mind, Dad?" he said.

I pulled up a straight-back chair for him to use. He sat down with his chin propped in his hand and listened to a long dissertation from his father, which was almost completely garbled. The President took in every sound, nodding his head throughout, in agreement. When Mr. Kennedy finished, his son clasped his hand and said, "Thanks, Dad, I'll take care of it. I'll do it your way. Right now I'd better get back to the boys."

Mr. Kennedy was satisfied; but I watched as the President waited in front of the elevator, and during the private moment he was alone, his head was bowed and his shoulders slumped forward. As the door opened, he straightened up and walked briskly back to his meeting.

The next week, at the height of the Cuban missile crisis, it was announced that he would appear on television to speak to the nation. We then realized what the reason was for the high-level meeting at the compound. The next morning Mrs. Kennedy stopped me in the hall and said, "What did you think of Jack's—I mean, the President's speech?"

"Magnificent," I answered.

She covered her face with her hands and began crying. "My son, my poor, poor son, so much to bear, and there is no way now for his father to help him."

Somehow I could not agree with her because although most of his conversation was garbled, he radiated a strength and confidence to them that were invaluable. Although it was painful for them to face him and see his handicaps, I think they drew strength from his enormous will and vitality. They listened intently to him, and when a word did come out clearly, it meant a great deal to them. A word from their father was of more value to them than volumes from others.

12

MRS. KENNEDY changed a great deal after her husband left Horizon House—perhaps because a decision had been reached that not only relieved her, but also left her conscience intact. Whether it was a right or a wrong one was not the issue. Only the fact that a figurative sword was no longer hanging over her head, regarding her husband's care, seemed pertinent.

He was to be kept at home and made as comfortable as possible for as long as he lived, and this decision, once made, at least gave her a sense of "insecure security"—if such can be the case.

She was an aging woman, baffled by the brigade of nurses and doctors that infested her home. And to her, we were doing just that. She was nervous and uncomfortable around illness of any kind, and she had gone through severe shock in trying to cope with her husband's condition. The most heartbreaking task for her was to learn how to accept his disability as part of her way of life. She simply did not understand it. Perhaps there was a psychological fear seeing what she loved destroyed, for often she would leave Mr. Kennedy's room, shake her head, and say, "Oh, Mrs. Dallas, I don't understand. I simply don't understand. Why do these things have to happen?"

At such moments, she would talk about her daughter Rosemary and her son Joe, who had been killed during the war, and her daughter Kathleen, who had lost her life in a plane crash. "Why do these things have to happen?" she would repeat over and over, "and now Mr. Kennedy."

I believe she was sincere in feeling that she had made the right choice by putting Ann in a position of authority. It had been a difficult decision for her, but she knew she was neither physically nor emotionally able to take care of her husband. With Mr. Kennedy's incapacitation she became the head of the family, and her decisions were as ironclad and binding as his had been. In the public's eye she became the matriarch, and she made many decisions that were difficult and controversial, but she was a strong-willed woman, and when a decision was made, she expected to see it carried through.

Once early in the summer she called me to her room for a "chat."

"Mrs. Dallas," she said, "I simply can't stand all that whiteness of nursing uniforms. All of you make us so aware that there is sickness in the house, so from now on, will you and the rest of the nurses wear casual clothes while you are on duty? Just blend in, if you will, with the scenery. Please."

I wanted to explain that some of the nurses might not be receptive to her suggestion, but she was well into her dissertation.

"I sometimes wonder," she went on, "what my husband must think in seeing nurses all the time. And always in white. So please, we just can't cope with it."

Even though I was proud of my uniform, I was relieved not to have to fight the skirt while on the boat, and since we went out on it every day for lunch, casual clothes did seem more fitting.

The next day I showed up in a rose-colored slack suit, which I thought was quite nice. Once again I was called to Mrs. Kennedy's room. She said bluntly, "Mrs. Dallas, you're wearing *my* color."

I looked at her questioningly.

"Rose," she explained. "Rose is my color, you know, and it's usually worn by me. Rose is my flower. Rose is my name. Rose is my color."

"I understand, Mrs. Kennedy," I said. From then on I made a special point to inform nurses as they came on the case that they could wear any color except a shade of rose.

Mrs. Kennedy had an active aversion toward doctors, and, as

a result, treated her personal ailments with all sorts of old-fashioned home remedies. One day, when I saw her with a towel wrapped around her neck and the aroma of a patent chest medicine wafting behind her, I knew she was feeling bad. There was no mistaking Mrs. Kennedy's state of health. When she was not feeling up to par, her face sagged, her shoulders dropped, and her temper was invariably sharp.

"Are you ill, Mrs. Kennedy?" I asked.

She grumbled, hardly above a whisper, that her throat was bothering her "a little." I offered to look at it, but she would not allow me near her. The next morning, however, she could hardly speak and was really short-tempered. Nevertheless, I managed to get her to open her mouth and say "ah." Her throat was swollen nearly shut, and I saw immediately that she had painted it herself, with a purple throat dye.

"Mrs. Kennedy," I urged, quite concerned, "I really think you should have a doctor look at you."

When she agreed, I knew that she had to be sick. I phoned the local doctor immediately, and when he came to examine her, he was shocked. She was running a high temperature and had a severe streptococcus infection.

He was very sweet and gentle with her. With perfect manners, he convinced her that she had to stay in bed. She followed his orders completely except for one thing. During the run of the infection, she never missed mass. She would leave early in the morning, bundled up, attend service, and, upon returning home, go immediately to her room and remain in bed until the next morning.

Her recuperative powers were superb, and in near miraculous time, she was up and about again, giving all the credit to "that marvelous little bottle the druggist sent me."

She took care of her own ailments, but she wanted whatever was best for her husband. Mr. Kennedy began having dental trouble and so she decided to send for an oral specialist whom they had both used during their younger days in Boston.

Ann made the arrangements, and when the dentist came, he

was a dignified, but tottering, old gentleman, who had been retired for ten years.

Mrs. Kennedy was startled when she saw him and whispered to me, "My, my, how he has aged."

Mr. Kennedy did not recognize him, and it was apparent that he was not happy having a stranger in his room, for he began to set up a loud caterwaul.

"Joe, dear," Mrs. Kennedy explained patiently, "this is our dentist from Boston. Remember? He used to work on our teeth when we were first married, and he's come all the way up here to help you with your toothache now."

Mr. Kennedy's eyes bulged, and he began to shout, "No. No."

She patted the doctor's arm encouragingly. "He'll be fine," she cooed, and hurried out, with Mr. Kennedy screaming at the top of his voice.

The doctor majestically ignored his patient's behavior. Trembling with age, he went about preparing for the examination. He scrubbed up in Mr. Kennedy's bathroom and rummaged through his bag for a mirror and pick. Then, without any words to his patient, he came teetering to the bed, listing critically to one side.

The Ambassador hid under the covers.

"Let me explain it to him," I urged. "He'll be all right. He just wants to know what's going on."

"Of course, he'll be all right, young lady," the dentist squeaked. "I know what I'm doing, and I'll need no help from you."

"But, Doctor," Louella said, "you can't handle him alone."

Mr. Kennedy scrunched up, pulled the sheet tighter over his head, and screamed, "No, no, no."

"You just can't shove your finger into his mouth, Doctor," I explained. "He won't accept it."

The dentist was furious with me. He flung out his arm and, with palsied fingers, pointed to the door. "Go into that room and wait," he ordered.

"But, Doctor—"

"In that room! Now!"

"But, Doctor—"

"I don't want another word out of you," he commanded in a quavering voice. "Get in that room before I throw you in it."

Louella looked at me and shrugged. "Better do what he tells us."

"Now," he roared. "Right this minute!"

He tottered over to the door and yanked it open. Glaring at us, he trumpeted, "Now, get out."

"But, Doctor—"

"Don't say another word."

Louella and I did as we were told, and he slammed the door. We sank to the floor and burst out laughing.

He had put us in Mr. Kennedy's clothes closet!

We sat there with our fists shoved in our mouths because we were laughing so hard. Louella crawled over in the corner and buried her face in her lap. I hid my head in Mr. Kennedy's clothes.

"What if he locks us in?" she said, gasping for breath. "What will we say when they find us?"

All of a sudden, we heard a scream.

"That's the doctor," I said.

Wiping her eyes, Louella said, "What should we do?"

We both knew what had happened.

"He didn't call us," I giggled, "and he'd have our heads if we barged in, so let's stay out."

Just then another wild scream filled the room. "Nurse! Nurse! For God's sake, where are you?"

He yanked open the closet door.

"What the hell are you doing in there?" he gasped, shaking his finger in pain.

As elegantly as possible, Louella and I emerged from the closet. Under her breath, she kept repeating, "Don't you dare laugh, Rita Dallas. Don't you dare laugh."

Mr. Kennedy had disappeared back under the sheets. The doctor glared at him and stomped out of the room. I followed, offering to bandage his finger. "At least, let me stop the bleeding," I urged. He clutched it to his chest, like a purple heart. "I was called out of retirement," he wheezed, "called out to take care of Mr. Kennedy, and I almost had a heart attack in that room just now. He bit me. He actually bit me. Not once. Twice. So, will you notify the family that I am going back into retirement, just as fast as I can return to Boston!"

He raised himself to his full stature and added loftily, "Good day."

I have countless memories of humorous situations involving Mrs. Kennedy. For example, most wealthy women are called the mistress of the house, but Mrs. Kennedy pictured herself in quite a different light. Her old-world morality shuddered at the sound of the word. I discovered this one day when I referred to Mrs. Evelyn Jones as being the housekeeper, which, technically, she was.

"I am the only housekeeper in this house!" Mrs. Kennedy corrected me, emphatically.

"But you are the mistress, Mrs. Kennedy," I said.

"A housekeeper, I am," she said. "A mistress, I am not."

Another time she noticed that one of the aides was reading a book while Mr. Kennedy swam. I'm sure she intended to reprimand him for "idleness," but apparently the title of the book took her fancy. She was a great advocate of reading or, for that matter, of doing anything that stimulated the mind. She squinted through her glasses and said, "Young man, is that a good book you're reading?"

The aide hesitated before answering, "Well . . . yes," he hedged. "I'd say it's interesting."

"Is Portnoy a town?" she asked.

"No," the aide said, turning red. "It's a man's name."

"Well," she exclaimed, "I guess I'd better see what he's complaining about."

I learned the outcome of the story later. It seemed she phoned the bookstore without first identifying herself and inquired about the book. When they told her it was on the best-seller list, she gave her name and ordered it sent to her.

A few days later I was in the village, and the woman who owned the bookstore stopped me on the street and said, "Mrs. Dallas, who in the world recommended *Portnoy's Complaint* to Mrs. Kennedy?"

I laughed. "Why? Did she order it?"

"Didn't she. And I never saw a book come back so fast in my life."

For days I could not get the picture out of my mind of her settling down in bed, thinking perhaps she was going to read a book about a famous man, and turning ashen with the first page.

Her charming innocence was one of her most endearing qualities.

Shortly after, she pulled the coup of the year. She succeeded in hiring a personal maid away from one of the richest women in the world. This maid had traveled around the globe with her former mistress and was dripping in elegance and snobbery. It was a known fact that her past employer provided her servants with personal servants. In other words, the maid had her own maid. Also, much had been written about the exquisite servants' quarters on the woman's estate, so when the maid saw her tiny room at the Kennedys', she was aghast.

"*I* am expected to live in *this?*" she breathed painfully. "*I*, in *this?*"

Mrs. Kennedy patted her arm, muttered an endearment, and scampered away.

A day or two later the laundress became ill, but Mrs. Kennedy saw no cause for concern until dirty clothes began stacking up. Even then she was not terribly perplexed. She simply told her new maid to do the wash.

The maid was horrified.

"Madam," she hissed, "what possesses you? I am accustomed to having my laundry done, not doing it."

"Well, surely you can pitch in this one time."

The maid turned on her heel and stated that she would send for her luggage. She made a grand exit by commandeering Mrs. Kennedy's limousine and was whisked away by the chauffeur in response to a grand "drive-on" sweep of her elegant hand.

I was next.

Mrs. Kennedy came to the nurses' station and, using the beguile of a leprechaun, asked me if I would wash the clothes.

"Can you imagine," she said, "the maid just told me it was beneath her and quit! So you'll do it, won't you? At least, until the laundress comes back?"

With the schedule I had to keep, there was no way to take on any more duties. Also (and I venture that I shall sound like the maid), nurses do not do laundry.

"I won't be able to do it, Mrs. Kennedy," I said. "You see, I'm Mr. Kennedy's nurse and I . . . well . . . I just can't do it."

"But, Mrs. Dallas," she replied, baffled, "you'd do the wash if you were working for a poor family, wouldn't you?"

"Mrs. Kennedy," I said, "poor families do not have private nurses."

"Oh, dear"—she sighed—"there are so many things I have to learn."

She left me, scratching her head, and went in search of Mrs. Jones. Putting on her most brilliant smile, she asked, "Do you do laundry, Mrs. Jones?"

"No, Mrs. Kennedy," the housekeeper replied. "I don't do it either."

Mrs. Kennedy began to get very exasperated. "Well, *I* don't know *how* to do it, and it has to be done by somebody. The house is full of dirty clothes."

Just then her secretary came in, but before Mrs. Kennedy could tag her, she backed out of the room. "No, no," she said, "don't look at me, Mrs. Kennedy."

"Surely, in this house someone can wash clothes," she exclaimed, going from room to room, maid to maid. She went to everyone, but the staff was so overworked that no one could, or would, find the time to take on another full-time job. She was turned down flat.

She came back to the secretary and said, "Call the New York office and tell them I need someone down here right away to do the wash."

"Bravo!" I cheered to myself.

Even though the New York office was more adjusted to having Eunice call with the order to transfer a million dollars to a new foundation, they nonetheless sent up a temporary laundress.

Often her innocence regarding money sent the New York office into panic. She always thought she was "helping out" or "doing my share" when she would sell things she no longer used to the thrift shop. She would have the chauffeur load up the car with bundles of clothing, books, dishes, or anything else she could scavenge and call out, "Be sure to get a receipt," as he drove off. The chauffeur was quite embarrassed, but she would shush his objections and send him on his way.

She diligently sent the receipt to the tax department at Mr. Kennedy's office, and even though the accountant tried to explain to her that it caused a great deal of confusion to enter it on the returns and suggested that she should give the items away instead of selling them, she refused to do so. She could never understand how making a little money could be a problem, and kept right on selling things to the consternation of the New York office.

She came up with many other money-saving schemes through the years.

A light burning in an empty room could really set her off. She would storm through the house, shouting, "Cut off the lights. Cut off the lights!"

This would go on constantly, and no one seemed to pay any attention to her, or so she thought. So she finally devised a secret little scheme to catch the culprit.

During the day I usually made dozens of trips to the hall walk-in closets for linens and sickroom aids. One morning I was getting a fresh supply of tissues for Mr. Kennedy and had just closed the door on the closet when Mrs. Kennedy jumped out at me.

"Aha!" she squealed. "So you're the one!"

"Mrs. Kennedy," I gasped.

"I caught you, and there's no denying it!"

"Mrs. Kennedy."

"It's you! You're the one who leaves lights burning. I saw you! You walked right out of that closet and left the lights on. I've said over and over, 'Please turn out the lights.' You've heard me say it over and over! Over and over and over."

"Mrs. Kennedy," I stammered, "let me explain."

"There's nothing to explain," she said. "Nothing at all. There is simply no excuse for this kind of flagrant disregard for other people's money. It's a waste, a waste, and I won't have it!"

"Mrs. Kennedy," I sputtered, "I don't think you understand. The light goes off when you close the door and comes back on when you open it, just like in a refrigerator. It's automatic."

"You don't mean it?" she said in disbelief.

Not one to take anyone's word for anything, she tiptoed into the closet and closed the door after her. In a moment she came out, with a sheepish grin on her face, and said, "Isn't that perfectly marvelous!"

She was a great organizer and once decided that I wasn't getting enough fresh air and exercise. Apparently, it never occurred to her that I spent up to two hours a day on the boat with Mr. Kennedy and walked at least three miles a shift. One day I had been trying to get my lunch for hours; but some crisis or other kept coming up, and I kept missing it. By the time things settled down it was late afternoon, and I was sitting alone at the dining-room table waiting for Matilda to fix me a cup of tea and a sandwich. I was staring wistfully out the window when Mrs. Kennedy came in. Seeing me sitting there in such a contemplative mood must have given her the impression that I had extra time to idle away.

"Mrs. Dallas," she said, taking the chair beside me. "You simply sit around too much. It's hard on your circulation. So, every day, from now on, I want you to take a walk on the beach. Walk fast and take deep breaths. Get some of that fresh ocean air in your lungs. It will invigorate your system, and you don't feel like sitting around all the time."

She patted my arm as she got up to leave. "Now, every day I want to see you taking a brisk walk down the beach. You'll see, dear heart, you'll feel much better. Remember, deep breaths."

I had been with Mrs. Kennedy long enough to know that she would check up on me the next day to see if I'd carried out her orders, so that evening, after work, I started down the beach at a slow trot, inhaling per her instructions.

The next morning I could hardly breathe. I was fighting a losing battle with a suffocating head cold.

Mrs. Kennedy heard me sniffling when she came in to visit her husband and said, "Mrs. Dallas, if you'd taken my advice, you would have worked that cold right out of your system."

"That's the trouble, Mrs. Kennedy, your advice has just about done me in."

"Oh, you and Pat," she scolded, shaking her head. "The same thing happens to her every time I chase her out for some fresh air. But now I'll tell you what you must do. I want you to go to the sauna and sweat it out of your system. That will fix you right up. So go along; we can't have you sick, you know."

Obediently, I gathered up a supply of towels and, later that evening, went to the sauna. By morning I was on the verge of pneumonia.

I dragged myself into work, and when she came bouncing into the room after mass, she looked at me and gasped, "Mrs. Dallas, you sound perfectly horrible! Come to my room. I have something that will clear your head right up."

"No, thanks, Mrs. Kennedy," I replied, hardly able to breathe, "let's leave well enough alone."

She patted my hand and said to her husband, "She's such a frail little thing, isn't she, Joe?"

Mr. Kennedy looked at me over his glasses and just shook his head, as if to say, "Lord, help us."

She was delighted and endearingly smug when she was named to the best-dressed list, but she believed in total comfort around her house. She wore very stout arch-support shoes, and she had one false tooth that caused her no end of trouble. She had worn an ill-fitting bridge for years, and it caused her a great deal of discomfort; but she would never go to the dentist for a replacement.

"It's still as good as new," she'd say, rubbing her gums.

At home, the bridge was usually tucked in a drawer, and when there were no guests expected at the house, she would tramp around in her heavy shoes, her frownies stuck on her face, her tooth out, and a comfortable, well-worn robe wrapped around her. There were times when she would laugh at herself, saying, "How do you like my outfit? Here's what the best-dressed woman wears."

Around company, when it was cold or windy, she wore an old-fashioned snood on her head and her favorite black coat. No matter what the weather, she would always go for a walk. There could be a bitter gale, and she would brave it. Mr. Kennedy, on the other hand, hated wind, and when it would start to blow and howl around the house, we would close the windows tight so he could not hear it.

Ann told me that, when he was well, no matter where he was, if a wind started up, he would fly out of town. She explained that he simply could not stand the lonely and mournful sound.

So often I've thought of him when I heard the wind and of the long years when he was ill and lonely and mournful. Ill in his body. Lonely in his soul. Mournful in his spirit.

Whenever there were heavy storms to depress him, I would turn up the stereo to drown out the sound and draw the shades.

Mrs. Kennedy was very sensitive to her husband's moods and loneliness, but sometimes she would unwittingly create difficult and painful situations for him and for herself. One time when she had been having slight problems with her throat, she was taking her daily walk under the protection of the porch since it had been raining. In her left hand she was squeezing a soft rubber ball, for she was also having mild arthritic attacks. This was her way of keeping her fingers flexible.

When she finished her walk, she came in to visit with her husband and tossed me the ball playfully.

"You should use this, Mrs. Dallas," she said. "It's a great boon to keep your fingers from getting stiff. Boxers do it all the time, I understand."

She flexed the fingers on both her hands to show me how freely they moved.

"Why, I have friends so crippled with arthritis that their knuckles are actually gnarled," she said. "It's grotesque to have to look at them, and you can't tell me that exercise isn't the key to prevention."

While she was talking, she stooped down to kiss Mr. Kennedy, then drew away in embarrassment. Before her lay a man with a rigid useless hand, and she realized, immediately, how her words must have affected him.

"Oh, Joe," she moaned, "I'm so sorry. I didn't think. Who am I to complain about a little arthritis when you are so brave in your suffering?"

Mr. Kennedy raised his left hand to wave her away, and as she left his room, her shoulders drooped despondently.

Later in the day she stopped me and said plaintively, "Why do I speak without thinking? I know how deeply I must have hurt my husband this morning. Why do I do it?"

"I don't think you hurt him, exactly, Mrs. Kennedy," I replied gently. "I think he motioned you away because he knew you were upset. I might suggest one thing, however. You should never pretend that he has no problems. He's more aware of his difficulties than anyone else, and to act as though there is nothing wrong with him or to be embarrassed because there *is* something wrong with him will only create deeper frustrations on his part. It's best not to emphasize his handicaps, but don't dismiss them either . . . and don't let him feel they embarrass you. If he ever senses that his illness is an embarrassment to his family, then we have lost our battle."

"But"—she sighed—"I always say the wrong thing, and I don't mean to. Oh, I doubt if I'll ever learn."

"You're doing fine," I consoled, hoping my words would give her some reassurance. But, for the next few days, she and I both knew, judging from his attitude toward her, that he was more than slightly agitated.

A couple of days later she received an invitation to Truman Capote's *Black and White* to be held in New York. It was heralded as the social function of the year, and she was overjoyed at the prospects of attending the gala. Seeing her reacting like a young girl going to her first party, I realized that she was probably a woman who had never had what one could call a great deal of fun.

She had said so many times when she was feeling philosophical that she had had a good life but a plain one.

"I was awfully busy being a mother," she said, "but now that my son has become President, it's like starting all over again! Only let me tell you, Mrs. Dallas, it's much better the second time around. You reach a certain time in life when you think it's all over, and the only thing you have to look forward to are creaking bones and an aching back . . . but for me, life is just beginning, and it's all new and shining. I can hardly believe it. My husband was never one to socialize, you know. He was always working. But all my life I've adored parties and balls. When he took time off, Mr. Kennedy usually preferred to sit around and visit with his old, faithful companions. But once in a while, particularly when he was the Ambassador, we would have marvelous times."

The closer it got to the day of the ball, the more excited she became. She was very particular about the dress she selected to wear, and she decided to take her diamonds out of the vault and "outshine them all."

"After all," she said, "I am the President's mother."

She was going to New York with her daughters the day before the ball, so she decided to give Mr. Kennedy a special preview of her gown. She had her hair specially dressed and spent hours on makeup. When she came to his room, she was exquisite. I had never seen her so radiant. She twirled and danced around the room, modeling her dress and jewels and draping her fur over her shoulder in a stylishly casual way.

"What do you think, dear?" she asked her husband, beaming. "Do I pass inspection?"

Mr. Kennedy was very critical. He frowned and shouted, "No."

Her spirits fell. But on that occasion nothing could have dashed them for long. She shrugged slightly, bent to kiss him, and promised, "I'll phone you early this evening. I'm going into

New York with the girls, and I'll be staying overnight, but I'll phone you."

I walked out with her, and she said, "I shouldn't have shown my dress to Mr. Kennedy. I think it upsets him to see us all going places when he's not able to, so I mustn't do anything to make him feel left out."

"I'm sure he thought you were very beautiful, Mrs. Kennedy," I said, "but perhaps you're right."

After that, whenever she was invited to a particularly important function, she would always call me to her room and put on the clothing she was going to wear.

"Just in case," she said, "you'll be able to tell my husband if he should want to know how I looked."

Even though life was indeed glittering to Mrs. Kennedy, in retrospect, it was not complete, for she was edged with the knowledge that her husband was at home, lying helpless. This, I'm sure, left a great void in her existence.

13

AFTER WE REALIZED that Mr. Kennedy would not be going back to Horizon House, we tried hard to keep him involved in exercises and therapy, but it was difficult without the disciplined control of professionally trained therapists. I was pleased, therefore, when I learned that a physical therapist would be coming down every day from Boston to continue working with Mr. Kennedy.

She turned out to be an attractive young woman with a breathtakingly beautiful figure. There wasn't a man on the compound who failed to notice this, nor, I might add, a woman, for she was exquisite. She was also a superb therapist. She handled Mr. Kennedy in the pool with dignity and professional know-how. She was able to remove his wet suit without ever causing him any personal embarrassment, and Eunice, in particular, respected her talents and capabilities.

The young woman had everything that could be desired in a therapist, but I knew, judging from the side glances she was getting, that she would not last long—and she didn't. No reason was ever given for her dismissal or by whose orders. She simply faded away one day and never returned. Unfortunately, she was not replaced.

After that, Bobby told me that, whenever he was at home, he wanted to be at the pool when his father went in for exercises.

"Maybe," he said, "if some of us are there to encourage him, he'll keep it up."

I gave him the daily schedule which noted that Mr. Kennedy's pool period was set up for early in the morning. He stuffed it in his pocket and said, "I'll be there."

The next morning Ann moved the schedule up a half hour. I told her the Attorney General had requested that he be with his father during his exercise period, but she countermanded: "Uncle Joe wants to go into the pool! Now!"

"Why?" I asked. "How do you know? Why change his schedule?"

"Now!" she said.

Unfortunately, I could not tell Bobby of the last-minute change, for it required a concerted effort to get Mr. Kennedy into the pool, and there was no time to notify the Attorney General.

He had his swim, with Ann and one of the aides in the water to assist him. I sat on the side, watching him struggle to remember the exercises the therapist had taught him, but the whole thing was being botched up.

Just as he was getting out of the pool, Bobby came running across the yard. He was furious!

"Why wasn't I called?" he shouted. "You told me wrong, Mrs. Dallas. What's the matter with you? Can't you keep a schedule straight?"

Ann looked up and said sweetly, "Uncle Joe changed his mind. Why are you so excited?"

Bobby saw that his father was watching them, so he smiled at his cousin and said to Mr. Kennedy, "I am going to be here tomorrow, Dad, and watch you do your show."

Mr. Kennedy looked relieved, for I think he expected a confrontation between his son and Ann. I vowed that if the schedule went through a last-minute change again, I would somehow see that Bobby was notified of it.

Par for the course, the exercise time was pushed up to an even earlier hour the next morning, but as we were leaving the house, I caught one of the maids and said, "Call the Attorney General's home and tell him that Mrs. Dallas said his father is going into the pool now." In a matter of minutes Bobby came racing across the yard and dove head first into the water, waving for his father to join him.

After that, whenever he was in the compound, he never missed exercising with his father. The schedule was tinkered with, and we never knew exactly when Mr. Kennedy would "decide" to go swimming, especially when Bobby was at home, but I always sent word to him when we were on our way. I did this, for I doubted that Mr. Kennedy had anything to do with the fluctuating schedule. He was always happy to have Bobby in the pool with him, and at that time he needed all the encouragement he could get.

During the years that followed, I watched Bobby strengthen his father, laughing with him, praising him, then he would swim away. His eyes would fill with tears, and a look of deep sorrow would cloud his face, but he would quickly compose himself, swim back to his father, and begin once more doing what he could to assist him in therapy.

Sometimes he would sit on the edge of the pool and dangle his legs in the water. Mr. Kennedy liked to perform for Bobby, for his son would applaud loudly whenever he accomplished a particular exercise. "Attaboy, Dad," he'd call. "Keep it up and you'll be walking out of here in no time."

The most painful thing for Bobby was to watch his father being removed from the pool. The wheelchair would be rolled down the ramp into the water. Mr. Kennedy would be strapped into it and then an aide would haul him up. It was a picture of a completely helpless man. This phase of his therapy, conducted without a qualified therapist, always frightened me.

After Bobby took up the habit of watching his father, the other children pitched in when he wasn't at the compound. Eunice, in particular, was a true cheerleader. She never gave in to failure, to her one inch of progress was worth any cost. But no matter how devoted his children were in attending him, they were still unqualified to conduct his rehabilitation. They could give him love and praise, but they were not able to strengthen his muscles or train his body.

There were many problems on the Kennedy case, and one of

them revolved around the nurses' salaries. The Kennedys never gave raises. Any pay increase came only when the state approved an across-the-board hourly hike for nurses. When that happened, I usually had added problems with new nurses, for their check from the New York office would not include the state increase. I would tell Ann when a new hourly rate had gone into effect, and she would promise to report it to the office; but it never happened, and the nurses were furious when their pay was short.

Finally, I talked with Eunice about it. I told her it was very difficult to get and keep nurses on the case, and to make matters worse, word was getting out that the family did not pay scale rates.

"Why don't we?" she asked.

"I don't know. I've told Ann about it, and she's promised to notify the office; but the raises are not coming through on the checks."

"I'll take care of it," she promised. And did. Eunice was very much like the President. She was always in a hurry, but what she said she would do, she did.

As Mr. Kennedy's nurse, I earned the standard hourly rate, which amounted to $43 per day. Never more, regardless of the hours. But money had become almost an obsolete commodity to me, for I was never away from the compound or from the Florida estate, except to sleep. I worked seven days a week and often for as long as six or seven months, without taking a day off.

It was almost impossible for me to get away. Staff nurses never lasted too long on the job. They were compelled to work under nerve-racking conditions and one of the main reasons for their quitting was Ann's dictatorial supervision. This, plus the fact that they had to sit at the desk in the nurses' station and be treated as though they were invisible, was a humiliating situation. The family never noticed them or acknowledged their presence.

One incident I will never forget took place with a young nurse from the Midwest. She had signed on the staff at the

Cape Cod Hospital primarily in hopes of someday seeing a "real, live Kennedy." One evening she phoned my home and said breathlessly, "Oh, Mrs. Dallas, is there any way I can ever work as a relief nurse? I adore the Kennedys and I can't think of anything I'd rather do than help one of them."

She made the same request of the local doctor who was in charge of the case, and he called me the next afternoon, pleased that there was someone who would enable me to take some time off. He said she was an excellent nurse, and so I took his recommendation and made plans for my family to visit me the next weekend.

I called my sisters, Alice Minehan and Helen Murphy, and then asked my brother, John McNally, to bring my father to visit me. He is a marvelous man. Ninety-eight years old and as Irish as his name, Patrick McNally. He was delighted at the prospect of the trip, and it began to look as if I'd finally get a weekend off.

Neither Mr. nor Mrs. Kennedy liked the idea, but I stood my ground.

The day finally came, my family arrived, and I met the young nurse who had offered to relieve me. She was a young, bright-cheeked girl who was bubbling over with excitement at the thought of meeting a Kennedy. I went over the record book with her and was pleased with her professional knowledge. Under her "fan" exterior was an intelligent and competent nurse. She was quick and seemed capable.

I introduced her to Ann and Mr. Kennedy and left the house walking on clouds. Two whole days with my father. Two whole days away. Too good to be true . . . and it was.

Midafternoon the nurse called me in a fit of tears and frustration. It seems she had gone to the closet to get clean linen for Mr. Kennedy, and in the meantime Ann had come by to take him down to lunch. They had to wait about five minutes for the nurse to return, and this, according to Ann, had thrown their whole schedule off. Mr. Kennedy was also highly indignant and had yelled "horribly" at her.

I heard the rest of the story through tears and sobs. They

finally went down to lunch, and Ann refused to allow the nurse in the dining room. I had told her about observing Mr. Kennedy when he ate, and unfortunately at lunch something went down the wrong way. He started choking. Ann began screaming and shouting orders at the nurse. "Do this." "Do that." "Stupid! Stupid! Stupid!" Everything went to pieces. The young girl and half the staff were so upset by Ann's screaming that they forgot all about Mr. Kennedy choking.

He recovered on his own, but the nurse did not.

"I can't work in this place another minute, Mrs. Dallas," she sobbed. "I can't stand it. No one has ever yelled at me like that before. I'm sorry, I'm leaving."

I dashed out of the house, telling my sisters I would call them later. Later was seven thirty that evening. When I finally phoned, I told them that the relief nurse had quit and that I would have to stay on duty.

The whole weekend was lost, and I never did get to see them. They were amazed at the working conditions, and at other times when they came for a brief visit, they couldn't believe how the phone would ring at one or two o'clock in the morning, and I would have to rush off and replace another relief nurse who had just walked off the job. I always went because I knew it was too dangerous for Mr. Kennedy to be left without professional attention.

Oftentimes they would ask me, "Why don't you quit? Why are you putting up with all this?"

The only answer that I could give them was that I had become deeply attached to Mr. Kennedy. I could not simply abandon him, and I was having considerable trouble keeping satisfactory coverage as it was. I knew that if I quit, Mr. Kennedy would very quickly have no professional care at all because Ann was not qualified to handle the staff. Leaving Mr. Kennedy without professional nursing could have been fatal.

Also, although we had lost the therapist, I was determined to continue fighting with him as long as he was willing to fight. After we left Horizon House, I had encouraged him to keep moving the fingers on his spastic right hand. I told him that, maybe, just maybe, they would become flexible again. I first showed him how to take his left hand and move the fingers of his right hand. Then I taught him how to do a number of motion exercises with his arm. He would take his paralyzed right arm and with the left hand, move it up and over, bringing it across to his left shoulder and then back again.

He could not do as much as I hoped for, but at least it helped him pass the lonely hours in his room and kept his mind fixed to the idea that he was working on his muscles.

When we knew that no other therapists would be assigned to the case, I talked with him about it.

"Mr. Kennedy," I said, "you've been on top of the world, and you know what it's like. You've made a fortune with your mind and with your strength, but you've got something to achieve now that's worth more than money. If you can flex one toe, or bend your knee, or bring your leg out of bed, eventually your body will follow."

He listened carefully and nodded, as I talked.

"I'll make a pact with you, Mr. Kennedy," I promised. "I won't quit trying until you quit trying, and you know something? We're both Irish enough to make it work."

He held out his left hand for me to take, then drew my hand to his cheek and tried desperately to say the words "thank you."

It would have been impossible for me to desert him or to desert any other patient who tried as hard as he tried.

He wanted to live, and I never knew a man to give it a better fight.

Often I would see him sitting in his chair, working his fingers, grinding his teeth in an effort to make them move, and I remembered the misdirected decision, "Make him comfortable and happy for what time he has left."

Comfortable? Never! He was in anguish over his incapacity. Happy? Impossible!

I saw him weather the fatal blows that struck his family, and he would almost sink from grief. Then he would rally back, a little weaker and with a little less reason to meet the next challenge, but he never gave up.

14

ONE OF THE MOST important factors in Mr. Kennedy's will to live through so much was the great joy he got from his grandchildren. They were always around in Hyannis Port, and life was continually full of surprises with twenty-three growing youngsters flowing in and out of Mr. Kennedy's life. His eyes could be cold and penetrating, but whenever he saw his grandchildren, they would radiate with the warmth and love he felt for them. It wasn't long that first summer before an elevator was installed that opened directly into his room. Many times we would hear the elevator door open, and one or two of his younger grandchildren would be standing in it, all alone. They would peek out, take a shy, quick look at their grandfather, then quickly push the button, and down they would go.

They were a constant delight, and I particularly remember something that used to happen any time we were out on Mr. Kennedy's boat with the family. Lunch on the *Marlin* was always a supremely elegant affair. Ethel was justifiably proud of her cook, and great delicacies were prepared for her children. Jean and Pat had baskets packed with delightful things, and the First Lady usually sent along tea sandwiches and light desserts for her children. But the heroine of any boat trip was "Aunt Eunie." She was always running late, and she and her youngsters would be the last on board. Usually she carried a paper sack with their lunch in it, which consisted of a loaf of bread and jars of peanut butter and jelly.

When luncheon was served and the delicacies were spread

out, Eunice would rip open the loaf of bread, find a knife, and proceed to make peanut butter and jelly sandwiches. Then an auction would start, for all the other children would want to trade their lunches with the Shriver children for one of "Aunt Eunie's" sandwiches. She would sit on the deck with her legs crossed slapping peanut butter on slices of bread, then slopping jam over it until it ran off the side. She would often look over at me and wink, licking her fingers, while her children munched on the French delicacies they had traded in payment for one of "Aunt Eunie's specials."

Ethel Kennedy, of all the daughters-in-law, saw to it that her children stood in awe and respect of their grandfather, especially when they visited him in his sickroom. On the boat, the sky was the limit, but whenever they made a call at the house, she held them in tow.

I never heard her fail to tell them, just before they entered his room, "Everything we have, we owe to Grandpa. Everything! So when you go in to see him, remember that everything you have, every toy, every pet, the house we live in, everything we owe to Grandpa."

The Kennedy grandchildren were aware of their wealth, I'm sure, because it was so evident on all sides. They were also aware that they were a special breed of people.

Some of them had strong traces of their grandfather's eye for making money. One time in Palm Beach Caroline and the Lawford children decided to go in business for themselves. Their first day they made a large bucket of the most dreadful-tasting lemonade and proceeded to sell a glass to everyone in the house, including their grandfather. They charged three cents. None of us minded paying, but they would stand there waiting for our approval until we had emptied our glass. Evidently we convinced them with our exclamations and smacked lips that they were number one lemonade makers, for the next day, without anyone knowing it, they made another batch and set up a stand on the street in front of their grandfather's house.

No one realized they were doing this until the afternoon

nurse, Eleanor Wyman, came on duty, and reported that there was a real traffic jam in front of the house.

The President was visiting with his father, and when he heard Eleanor recounting the incident, he was delighted. It seemed the children had sold out their lemonade early and decided to stretch their profits even further by selling water. With the business they were doing, why waste money making lemonade? Of course, the tourists, who were constantly driving by, recognized the children, especially Caroline, and stopped to take pictures. Shortly, traffic was backed up far down the street. The young Lawford boy would dash back through the gates and fill up his water bucket, while Caroline and the other children sold the wares.

The President knew it could not go on, so he informed his agents to break up the thriving business, as well as the traffic jam. When Mr. Kennedy heard about it, he puffed out his chest and smiled.

"They did pretty well too, Dad," the President said. "Looks like they know how to turn a buck, just like you."

The grandchildren were always treated in a very special way. The Kennedys knew that the future rested in their hands. Each child was studied and provided with every opportunity to take advantage of his particular talent.

Young Bobby Kennedy had an inquisitive mind and was fascinated with insects and snakes. At a very early age he was a well-informed amateur botanist, but he had developed this talent as a secret project. All summer long he collected bugs and snakes and butterflies, and by the end of the season he had himself an impressive collection. Granted it was crudely put together, but he was justifiably proud of it.

He invited me to look at it one day, and I was genuinely impressed at his knowledge. He very seriously explained each specimen in great detail. I commented on how proud I knew his parents must be of his initiative. He looked a little shy, and said, "They don't know about it. I haven't shown this to anyone else."

I assumed that he would, so later, when I mentioned how

impressed I was with his collection of specimens, Ethel Kennedy was quite surprised. He still had not told them. I was troubled to think that I might have spoiled his plans, but Ethel came by later and said that when she had mentioned it to young Bobby, he told her his reason for not letting them in on his hobby was that he thought they might not feel it was good enough.

Ethel was extremely proud of him, and so was the Attorney General, because his son had done something on his own without any assistance or prompting.

On our next visit to Hickory Hill, Ethel urged her son to show me his new collection. He reluctantly took me to his hobby room, and there I saw an exquisitely framed collection of labeled specimens on display that would have been suitable for any topflight botany museum or laboratory.

He dismissed the room with a shrug, and when I asked, "Where are the things you collected last summer?" he muttered, "Oh, I guess they're around here somewhere."

Had Mr. Kennedy retained his faculties, it is doubtful that his grandchildren would ever have had their incentive pampered. But with his illness his power to mold the second generation was thwarted. He had seen to it that his heirs did not have to be ruthless in business in order to acquire wealth. He had freed them from that and instilled in them an even more potent drive: the drive to alter the face of history. I saw his children respond to this, but the grandchildren were brought up in a more flamboyant atmosphere, and some of them, quite naturally, suffered from the exaggerated attention that was showered on them wherever they went.

I have been asked, many times, if I had a favorite among the grandchildren, and as I think back, there is one who stands out in my mind. That is young Joseph Kennedy, the son of Bobby and Ethel. He was more like his grandfather than any of the others.

Perhaps I'm guilty of partiality toward boys. I have a son of my own, and had I not been widowed I would have hoped for at least six more just like my Vincent. I can see my husband so often in his face, and I believe that in young Joe I saw so much of Mr. Kennedy that I was naturally drawn to him.

Even when he was but a lad I realized that Joe possessed the potential to become the principal figurehead in the Kennedy panorama.

He was a long, lanky, bumbling sort of boy who would come in to visit with his grandfather and make a concerted effort to relate what he was doing in school or how he was progressing in sports—but he was awkward and ill at ease. I'm sure Mr. Kennedy made the boy uncomfortable, for he would squint at him over his eyeglasses with such intensity that young Joe would shuffle his feet and blush. He would nervously clear his throat and squirm, but this would never stop him from talking to his grandfather with great sincerity.

I would throw him a sentence or an idea that would help him build a conversation, and on his way out after visiting with his grandfather, he would always stop and say, "Thank you, Mrs. Dallas." When he was gone, Mr. Kennedy's eyes would twinkle, and he would get a big grin on his face as if to say, "There's one I've got under my thumb."

Young Joe had a courtesy that was inborn. His natural politeness was very much like Caroline's. They were the only two, of the lot, who would automatically say thank you for the least thing that was done for them. There was no need for parental prompting. Courtesy was natural to both of them, and they were a great pleasure to us all.

The time came when Joe was sent to school at Milton, and shortly after beginning he came home to spend a weekend with his father. Since it was after Labor Day the houses were closed, so he and Bobby stayed at the big house. This was a great treat for Mr. Kennedy, for it meant he would not have to share them with anyone.

It was a beautiful fall, and young Joe was sitting on the steps of the porch studying. Bobby and Mr. Kennedy were in the sun room talking, and Mr. Kennedy's eyes kept darting to his grandson. Finally, he snapped his fingers and signaled for Bobby to look at his son. Young Joe was sitting with his back against the wall, his long legs stretched out in front of him, a book facedown on his lap, staring out across the ocean dreaming dreams as boys of that age will.

Bobby went to the porch and told his son to move closer to the window. "Sit up here where Grandpa can keep an eye on you," he said.

Joe glanced at me and grinned, because we both knew that his grandfather was going to watch and see if he studied. Then Bobby said, "Well, Dad, I've got some work to do. But I guess you can keep an eye on Joe for me and see that he studies." Mr. Kennedy nodded, very seriously, and after his son left the room, his eyes really lit up. I could almost imagine him thinking of the times when he would make his own children study, pulling them away from their dreams, as it were.

Young Joe diligently kept his face buried in the books long into the afternoon, and finally, Mr. Kennedy indicated that he wanted me to bring him in. I went out on the porch and told him that his grandfather wanted to see him.

"Is he upset with me?" he asked.

"Not at all. I think he'll want to know how you're coming along and if you like school. But don't worry, he's very proud that you've studied this afternoon—especially since it's such beautiful weather."

"Oh, if he only knew how I hated it." He sighed.

"Well, tell him how you feel," I urged. "He'll like that, and he'll respect you for it. Remember, he'll know if you're being evasive with him, so talk freely and lead the conversation as you always do."

When he went in, he smiled at his grandfather and said, "I guess you caught me dreaming, Grandpa."

Mr. Kennedy nodded warmly and motioned for him to sit down.

Young Joe went on telling him that he was not caring for school too much. "I don't like the confinement, Grandpa. I like books and reading, and I like to study, but in my own time. Is that why I'm a dreamer, do you think?"

Mr. Kennedy nodded slowly, and with a wave of his hand he

pointed toward the beach and made a sweeping gesture. Young Joe and I both knew that he was dismissing him from his studies. There was no communication gap between the young boy and his grandfather. Joe was old enough, at the time, to admire the patriarch not because he was told to, but because of the instinctual ties that existed between them.

After his father was assassinated it was young Joe who went through the funeral train shaking hands with everyone, thanking each one and seeing to his comfort. He was, in all ways, a Kennedy, able to lay aside his own loss and grief to attend to the image. No one told him to do this. It was done by instinct.

I was saddened a year or two later when he came to me and said, rather glumly, "I just found out what being a Kennedy means. You know, Mrs. Dallas, I can get any girl to go out with me just because my name is Kennedy. But I don't like that. I don't like it at all." Then, with some bitterness, he added, "It either comes too easy to get what you want, or it comes too hard."

He pressed his lips together, in deep thought. "But I guess I'd better learn to get used to it. Once a Kennedy, always a Kennedy."

With those words, I realized that no special grooming would be necessary for young Joe to take his place. The identity and the image were already stamped in his mind. He had the same personal kindness I saw so often in his father—and I think he had a bit of the dream long cherished by his grandfather.

Young Joe was not terribly handsome. When his face was in repose it was quite serious, but when he smiled, his whole personality came to life. In it I saw the vitality and strength that would insure the significance of future generations.

Caroline had the same direct personality. Once, during a visit to the White House, we were standing together watching the ceremony to make Winston Churchill an honorary citizen of the United States. We were on the balcony overlooking the lawn where the ceremony was taking place. The governess kept repeating, "Caroline, keep your eyes on your father. See how well he handles himself. It's something for you to learn."

Finally, Caroline turned her pert little head and looked straight into the eyes of her governess.

"My father," she said, "has told me to always watch the other people, because they're the important ones. My father says that I should always keep my eyes open and see other things. My father says I can see him anytime, so today I think I'll watch Mr. Churchill."

This great sense of knowing their place in history was grasped by many of the grandchildren, and Mr. Kennedy instinctively recognized them as sharing his particular vision. He knew he would not see the completion of the tapestry he had started, but he was secure in the knowledge that there were others to come after him well equipped to carry on his name.

He provided the fortune, the influence, and the power. He paved so smooth a road for them that they owed no man a favor for anything they had, except him. He had established his empire in such a way that his children and their children could never be bought or tempted. This being so, their only goal was power . . . and influence. In his grandchildren he could see that there were heirs who were capable of carrying forward his dream for the Kennedy name in history.

15

THE FIRST AUTUMN we spent on the Cape was crisp and unseasonably cold. Mr. Kennedy had been ill a year, by then. He had had a strenuous summer, and his therapy had dwindled to a catch-as-catch-can program. He had had a tremendous adjustment to make during the year, and his life was entirely different from what he had ever dreamed it would be, but despite the obstacles created by his stroke, he had handled his first year under handicaps reasonably well.

I think Mrs. Kennedy breathed a sigh of relief when the Cape closed, for she said, "I always pictured that my life, when I grew older, would be peaceful and quiet, but instead, I'm surrounded by illness. It's also very trying to cope with people I've never met. They come and go as though we were running a hotel. Since my husband is out of the picture, I sometimes wonder what life is all about."

I imagine many of the Kennedys had similar thoughts that fall—thoughts about the long year past and the changes his illness had wrought. I'm sure they mulled over, in their most secret thoughts, how drastically their lives had changed because of his stroke.

I had accepted the family's decision when we left Horizon House, and when I did, I made up my mind that if I were to continue on the case, I would never run from one to the other with complaints or criticism. So long as Mr. Kennedy was alive, I could not allow myself to be placed in the position of carrying tales or trying to undermine or rebuke Mrs. Kennedy's right to decide what was best for her husband. My job with him was to make the best of whatever situation occurred. Of the ninety-three nurses who were on the case, I lasted, I think, primarily because I respected their right to say, "This is the way it has to be." Often I would lie awake at night, struggling with myself, and yet I knew that anything I or any of the doctors said could not affect or alter the situation—so in order to last I made the best of it.

The case, however, was so paradoxical that I lived in professional chaos. One incident that occurred late in the fall is a perfect example of all the chaos and disorder I had to face in trying to carry out my job.

Mr. Kennedy had suffered a perplexing kind of seizure that was never fully diagnosed. The President had been home for the weekend with only his official entourage, so everyone was staying at the big house. Early in the evening Mr. Kennedy turned pale and seemed to fall into an almost catatonic state. Ham Brown and I were in the room. We both saw that something strange was happening. There was only a slight change in his pulse, but he stared vacant-eyed, without any kind of response.

I sent out an alarm, and the President was in the room immediately. He saw his father and shot an order to Agent Brown, "Go get my doctor."

Admiral George G. Burkley, the President's physician, was at the Cape for the weekend, but in the short length of time it took the agent to bring him to the room, Mr. Kennedy was coming around. The President told the admiral to stay with his father until he could get the specialist down from New York, and he went downstairs to make the call personally.

Admiral Burkley was a little perturbed over the sparse emergency aids we had on hand and said that he would go to the White House trailer and gather up the supplies that were always kept in it. While he was gone, the President returned to check on his father. That was the only time I ever saw him "lose his cool," as they say. He was furious when he saw me sitting with his father and only Agent Brown with me.

"Where is the doctor?" he wanted to know.

"Dr. Burkley went to the trailer to check on emergency supplies," I answered.

"Oh, that's just great. Just great. When I say I want a doctor in here with my dad, that's damn well what I mean. So you go over there and tell him that I said he's to sit with my dad all the time, and I mean all the time, until the other doctors get here."

I started out, but he stopped me with: "Wait a minute, Mrs. Dallas, you stay here. Brown, you go—and make it snappy."

Agent Brown turned smartly on his heels to carry out the Chief Executive's orders.

The President looked at me with a very stern face and said, "I want my dad to get all the attention that money can buy. I don't intend to spare a dime. Look at him. How did it happen?"

His eyes swept to his father who was, by now, resting peacefully. The President clenched his fists in frustration and almost cried, "I'm sick of this. Surely there is something that can be done. We're not making any progress with him, and it can't keep up."

That evening I learned the power of the Presidency. Official planes had been dispatched to New York, and shortly doctors began arriving. Dr. Rusk arrived with Dr. Betts and Dr. Boles. The local physician from the Cape had also been called, and they all converged to examine Mr. Kennedy.

"What happened to him?" the President kept asking.

Finally the doctors reached a diagnosis of sorts, which was that he had had a slight seizure, possibly owing to emotional stress and disturbances. They assured the President that the electrocardiogram showed that all his responses were functioning orderly and their examination did not indicate cause for undue alarm, but the President was still far from satisfied.

Mr. Kennedy was resting peacefully, and there was nothing more the doctors could do. The President reluctantly accepted the decision that Dr. Rusk and Dr. Boles should go back to New York since Dr. Betts planned to stay at the Cape for a day or two, in order to observe the patient. Admiral Burkley urged the President to retire, reminding him that they were to leave first thing in the morning for Washington, but he brushed this aside and stayed with Dr. Betts and me until Bea Tripp, the night nurse, came on duty. Only when Dr. Betts decided we should all try to get some sleep did the President reluctantly leave his father.

I slipped over to my home, hoping I would be able to rest through the night. Mrs. Tripp was a fully capable nurse, and unless there was a critical emergency when she was on duty, she could take care of things.

Agent Brown also showed heavy strain as he went to his room at the Candlelight Motel for the rest of the night. As we expected, Mr. Kennedy slept through it without alarm.

The next day we had an adventure that would rank in the annals with the funniest antics of the Keystone Kops if it had been put on film. It was typical of life with the Kennedys: near tragedy one moment, pure comedy the next.

I reported to work about seven thirty that morning, and I saw that Mr. Kennedy was not only out of bed, which was unusual, but also sitting at the table eating breakfast. Even more astonishing, he was dressed in a woolen shirt and heavy slacks. Ann, who had been out the night before, was having breakfast with him. She was also dressed in her slacks and sweater instead of the usual morning robe. They both were clothed for the outside, and something clicked in my mind. I dashed up to the nurses' station, and called Ham at the motel.

"Get up here quick," I said. "I've got the feeling we're going to be off and running today."

"What are you talking about, Rita?"

"I'll take a bet we're going for a ride."

"You mean Mr. Kennedy?"

"Yep."

"But he's sick in bed."

"Oh, no! He's at the table eating breakfast, and he and Ann are both dressed in outdoor clothes."

Ham's automatic response was to ask no more questions. All he said was, "I'll be right there," and hung up.

The doctors had all advised that Mr. Kennedy should remain

in bed a couple of days. Essentially that was the reason for Dr. Betts' remaining at the Cape. So it was a shock to see him up. I knew something had to be done, and the only thing I could think of was to call Ham. The President had left early that morning for Washington, as planned, and Dr. Betts had gone for a prebreakfast walk along the beach.

In less than five minutes Ham was at the house. He had not stopped to finish his morning shave. One side of his face was clean, the other bore the stubble of the night's beard. He'd thrown on a fatigue jacket and a pair of slacks.

Casually, just to see for himself that Mr. Kennedy was up, he ambled into the dining room. When Ann saw him, she smiled pleasantly and asked what he was doing there so early in the morning.

Ham shrugged. "Oh, I just thought I'd look in on the boss a little early." Then, to Mr. Kennedy, he said, "How are things with you this morning, sir?"

Mr. Kennedy nodded his head warmly, for he was fond of Ham and always happy to have him around. Ann pushed back her chair and said, "Well, Uncle Joe, what do you say we go for a ride?"

Mr. Kennedy loved the idea of getting out and nodded his head emphatically yes. While she went to the closet to bring him his nylon jacket and the little black beret he wore around the Cape, I said to Ham, "What did I tell you?"

Ham's car was a tiny foreign compact which was used as a backup. "All we can do is follow her, Rita. You know that. We can't stop her."

"Then let's get ready."

He and I put Mr. Kennedy in his car, which incidentally was a powerful limousine, while Ann hunched behind the wheel impatiently gunning the motor. As Ham was closing the door, she zoomed out of the driveway.

"My car's in the lot," Ham yelled. "Let's go."

I had worn a uniform on duty that morning in respect to the doctors and had thrown a white fake fur coat around my shoulder when I went outside to help Mr. Kennedy in the car.

The coat flew off as I was running to keep up with Ham, and I naturally stopped to retrieve it; but before I was halfway to the parking lot, he had reached his car, backed it up, and skidded around the driveway, slowing down only to pick me up. I jumped in while it was still moving, and as I slammed the door, he moaned, "My God, she's already out of sight."

Ann knew that there had to be a Secret Service man with Mr. Kennedy whenever he went out, either riding with him or in the backup car, but she would often try to slip away in order to be alone with her uncle. I accepted this as a natural yearning. Privacy was a rare commodity in the Kennedy household. However, as his nurse I had a job to do, and whenever she would decide to duck out on her own, I rode in the backup car with the agent.

It was a simple procedure when we all went in one car, but on her occasional solo flights, the agent and I followed behind. On these rides, I had learned, from past experience, to keep my eyes glued to the back of Mr. Kennedy's head, for I could tell by his posture and the tilt of his shoulders if he was in any difficulty. This was not a desirable diagnostic method, but in an emergency, it worked.

I was always nervous riding backup, for the agent was compelled to keep the cars bumper to bumper. I realized that at high speed a sudden stop or quick turn could result in a pileup. That was a chance the agent had to take, for he also had a job to do, which was to stay as close to Mr. Kennedy as possible. On such drives, he also carried out his duties under severe handicaps. Even though Ham had become a good companion to Mr. Kennedy, he never forgot that he was there for the serious purpose of protecting his life. The threatening letters against him had continued to come, and we really never knew if and when a potential murder plot would become a reality. Ham, therefore, was ever on the alert.

I, too, was there on serious business as his nurse, so we never relished Ann's solo capers. The added pressure they put on us was difficult on top of everything else.

On this particular morning, Ham had responded to the situation in his usual capable way, but Ann was driving at such high speed that we bounced along the highway like a rubber ball trying to keep up with her.

A Presidential order has sobering effects, however, even if it is issued by a cousin, and she knew the President would nail her hide to the wall if she took off with Mr. Kennedy alone and something happened to him. That being the case, she observed the rules, after a fashion.

Once Ham had closed the gap and was tailgating her, she picked up more speed and never once dropped below eighty. We realized something odd was up when she took the highway that led off the Cape, and after driving for more than an hour I told Ham that I thought she was going to Boston.

He was frantic. His little car was grinding like a mixmaster trying to keep pace with the limousine, and he knew it was only a matter of time before the motor would burn up.

When we passed the Boston exit an hour or so later, we drew the only other obvious conclusion. Illogical though it seemed, she was apparently on her way to New York.

We were driving madly down a highway, miles from home, and if Mr. Kennedy happened to have an attack there would be no medicine available for him. This was my main concern, for after the previous night's seizure and the rather indefinite diagnosis, "emotional disturbances," I was quite upset and feared that any undue change in his schedule could prove severe, if not fatal. A man who, less than twelve hours prior, had had a core of top specialists hovering over him in consultation had no business taking a three-hundred-mile automobile trip.

In order to keep up with them, the little car swayed, limped, lunged, smoked, rattled, wheezed, steamed, coughed and occasionally screamed in agony. But Ham kept his foot glued to the floorboard, and with blue smoke belching from the exhaust he zoomed around trucks, passed on the wrong side, lay on the horn, spun around once, bounced off the divider regularly, and left no law intact.

We whipped through Massachusetts, then skimmed across Rhode Island, and were flying low over Connecticut when we got our first break. The most welcome sight of the day was a Connecticut state trooper hot on our trail. With shrieking siren he edged us over to the side of the road.

"Well, thank God," Ham sighed.

He jumped out of the car and left the motor running, warning, "Don't let it die, Rita. Whatever you do don't let it die."

Waving to the trooper, he shouted, "Hurry up, old buddy. We haven't got all day."

"That's a new one," the trooper snapped, taking out his book.

Ham immediately gave the trooper his identification card and began issuing orders.

"I'm following Ambassador Kennedy's car," he said. "Did you see it? Big limousine. A woman driving."

"That's a new one, too."

"Listen. This is serious."

He took his card back and began writing on it. "You call this number. This is the hot line to the Attorney General's office in Washington."

"Listen, friend," the trooper said, "why don't you take your ticket like a man and be done with it?"

Ham waved his identification under the trooper's nose. "Now, take a good look and do as I say. You call the Attorney General and speak to him! Only to him. And you tell him that Agent Ham Brown and Mrs. Dallas are after Miss Gargan. Tell him that she's got his father in the car with her, and we think she's heading for New York. Tell him my car is about to break down and ask him what he wants me to do. Got it?"

The trooper listened skeptically.

"Don't let that motor die, Rita," Ham screamed at me. "Pump it."

The little car was sputtering badly. I pressed down on the accelerator, and miraculously it chattered a bit less.

"How's he going to tell you what to do?" the trooper asked, eyeing Ham up and down. "Have you got a two-way radio in that car or somethin'?"

"That's his problem. You just get that message to him. And if you don't, ol' buddy, there'll be a lot of people in Washington wanting to know why. We're talking about the President's father, so don't just stand around. Hop to it."

"You're really going to try to get to New York in that thing?"

Ham jumped back in the car. He attempted an impressive, dramatic exit, but instead he managed to grind the gears. The little car coughed a few times and finally sputtered away belching smoke.

"Keep an eye out for them, Rita," he said. "We've got one chance in a million of catching her now. She's going to have to stop for gas pretty soon, and if we're close enough when she does, I'll have time to phone Chief McDermott in Boston. I've got to have some official opinion on this. I don't know what to do. This car's going to pieces."

I've always wondered why men coo at automobiles or at any piece of machinery, for that matter. Boats. Planes. Anything that runs, it seems. But for whatever reason they do it, it works. Ham actually talked his car into running. With the motor screaming like a wounded banshee he whispered to it, "Come on, sweetheart. You can make it. You're doing fine, baby. Just keep going."

We had to stop several times, for the hood kept flying up, but other than that, we hobbled down the highway. It was nearing noon when I saw the big car in a filling station.

"There she is, Ham," I screamed. "Pull in. There she is."

He swung into the station and stopped by an outside phone booth.

"Okay," he said. "Now you stay put. Don't get out of the car. That's an order, Rita. No matter what happens, stay put."

"But that's my patient, Ham. I should be with him."

"You stay right where you are until I make the phone call—and I mean it."

When an agent assumes his professional stance, the voice becomes dead level and the eyes harden in a most overpowering way.

"All right," I replied, meekly.

He phoned his chief in Boston, and the conversation lasted only a short minute or two. He came back and told me that the trooper had got the call through to Washington. The state police were alerted for us, and since we had reached the point of no return, meaning that we were as close to New York now as we were to the Cape, we were advised to continue on.

"What's going to happen, Ham?"

"All I know is what McDermott said. We are to follow her as best we can, but we're to have no personal contact. It's up to the Attorney General now. It's his baby."

He pulled to a pump and had his car filled. "Don't touch the motor, ol' buddy," he warned the attendant. "Just let well enough alone."

Ann, of course, saw that we were in the station but made no acknowledgment to us. She waited until Ham paid for his gas and then drove slowly onto the highway. We limped behind her. She drove only a short distance and pulled off. Ham eased in back of her. I saw her lean over and say something to Mr. Kennedy, and he nodded his head.

She walked over to the car and said, brightly, "Hi."

Ham looked straight ahead. I didn't know what to say, so I said, "Hi," too.

"Uncle Joe wanted to go to New York," she added, smiling. "So here we are . . . on our way . . . to New York."

"Well. Well," I answered, at a loss for anything more spectacular.

"What do you think, Ham?" she said. "Should we go back to the Cape?"

Ham continued to stare straight ahead.

I broke orders, something I seldom did; but Mr. Kennedy was my patient, and I owed him my attention, so I said to Ann, "Well, I imagine we're closer into New York than we are to Hyannis Port, so we might as well keep on going."

"It's whatever you say, Rita." She smiled blithely and sprinted back to the car.

"Whatever *I* say," I gasped. "Ham, I never!"

He tried hard to suppress a grin.

"You should have kept your mouth shut," he said.

"I should be up there in that car with my patient. That's where I should be."

"Okay, Rita, don't start crying."

"I'm not crying. I'm just plain damn mad."

"Now, don't get excited."

As he pulled out behind Ann, he looked over at me and grinned. Ham was a fine young man from the mountain area of West Virginia, and we had become good friends since his assignment to Mr. Kennedy. He was a great morale booster for him. All through the week, the aging man was surrounded by women, and it was to Ham he turned for male companionship. They would watch ball games together on television, or Ham would sit for hours and relate incidents of his boyhood. He was never at a loss about how to be, not only as a guard to Mr. Kennedy, but as his friend. When he grinned at me, I saw the absurdity of it all. We began to laugh, probably in hysterical relief.

"We're a sight," I said. "Do you know you've got half a beard?"

He squinted at himself in the rear mirror. "I wonder why that cop believed me."

Ann started off driving at a reasonable speed, but inch by inch she began to lengthen the distance between us. Suddenly, burning rubber, she whipped out of sight. Ham was on the alert and tried to race after her. Pounding his head with the palm of his hand, he moaned, "Where are the cops? Where's somebody?"

Suddenly steam began jutting out of the car; but Ann had slowed down again, and we were able to get close behind her. Through the steam, I could see Mr. Kennedy. He had developed a system when he was in the car of signaling when he wanted to change directions or stop by simply laying his hand on the wheel. This took the driver's attention, and Mr. Kennedy was then able to point where he wanted to go. I saw him reach across and grab the wheel.

"My God, Ham, he's trying to drive."

Before I got the words out, the car swung across the highway, plowing up grass as it bounded over the median. They barely missed an oncoming car. Sticking hot to the trail, Ham gunned the little car and when it hit the median, it shot up in the air bouncing as if it were on springs. Barely missing another car, we careened down the wrong side of the highway and landed behind them. They had run smack into the front of a greenhouse door. Luckily, only a few panes of glass were knocked out.

Ham buried his head on the steering wheel.

In the immediate distance we heard sirens, and in a second two motorcycle policemen sped by us.

"They've missed us," Ham yelled. "My God, they've missed us."

But the cyclists made a wide turn and screeched up, barely stopping. They too knocked out a few panes of glass. Two official-looking Connecticut troopers marched toward us. They came to our car, first.

One of them said to me, "Miss Ann Gargan?"

Before I could answer, he repeated, "Miss Gargan, I am to inform you that the Attorney General of the United States—"

"You've got the wrong woman," Ham interrupted. "That's Miss Gargan over there."

One trooper stayed with us, his hand resting menacingly on the holster of his gun. While he glared at us, the other officer walked authoritatively toward the limousine. I would have given anything to have heard what he said, but I took my cue from Ham and stared straight ahead.

In a few moments he stomped back to us. "The Attorney General wants these two cars to follow us to the state police barracks. From there, all of you are to speak to him. And, if you're the nurse, you're to call the doctor. Immediately."

Ann Gargan was as curious as any woman. She started to get out of the car and come over to see what was happening with us, but the trooper motioned her back.

They straddled their cycles with the order: "Follow us . . . and no funny business."

They raced their motors, popping them impressively, and

Ann, not to be outdone, roared the limousine with blasts of thunder. A few more panes of glass fell out, and poor Ham sat in his shivering machine, pumping hard to keep it going.

One officer pulled in front and motioned for Ann and Ham to follow him. The other tailgated us from the rear.

"Well," Ham said in relief, "now this makes some sense."

We drove back in the direction we had come until we reached a legal crossover. The sirens were screaming, and it was amazing to see how cars parted in obedience.

"This really makes sense," Ham repeated.

Heading again in the direction of New York, the lead cyclist turned on his sirens full blast and shot down the road "ninety miles an hour."

Ann stayed in ecstatic pursuit.

Ham beat the steering wheel and roared, "What the hell are they doing? Can't they see my car's falling apart?"

The tiny vehicle was screaming. Steam spurted from all sides, but once again, he was able to talk it into running. The motor would cough, then sputter valiantly back to life. The cyclist behind us was waving us forward with his hand and whoop whoop whooping his siren.

"Shut the hell up," Ham yelled over his shoulder.

Suddenly, I heard a terrible rattle on my side.

"Ham," I shrieked, "my door's coming off."

"Stay put, Rita. We'll make it."

"What if it flies off? What will I do?"

"Hang onto me."

He took a quick look, saw the door was waving on its hinges like a handkerchief, and winked. "Hang on, kid. We're almost there."

And so we were. We careened into the barracks' parking lot. Ham gallantly parked his car, and we sat for a moment's silence, gravely paying homage to the little machine as it shuddered its final death rattle.

Ham got out. Closed his door quietly. Walked around the car. Lifted off my door and graciously helped me out.

"Now, may I see Mr. Kennedy?" I said.

"He's all yours."

I dashed over to the limousine and was relieved to find him sitting very erect and alert. He saw me, smiled, and nodded his head, as he did every morning when he first greeted me.

"You're all right?" I asked.

He nodded, again, quite grandly.

Ham and the trooper helped him out of the car and into his chair, and then we all went into the barracks. I said to Mr. Kennedy, who was nodding to everyone pleasantly, almost gleefully, "I think you're actually enjoying this."

Ham had developed a great sense of comradeship with him, and he patted him on the shoulder and laughed, "You know, you old son of a gun, I bet you'd like to see Rita's and my head in a noose, just to see if we could wiggle out of it."

Mr. Kennedy leaned back in his chair and laughed.

The call came through from the Attorney General. Ann took her turn at the phone like a little girl caught stealing cookies. Ham spoke guardedly and did not discuss any of the details with the Attorney General in public. He spent most of the conversation "Yes sirring" and listening. I had already spoken with Dr. Betts on another line and had requested, since we were going to New York, that he have Mr. Kennedy's prescriptions delivered to the apartment.

When it was my turn to speak to Bobby, he was terribly concerned about his father.

"Are you sure he's all right, Mrs. Dallas?"

"I think he's getting a kick out of the whole thing," I said.

"He would! Let me talk to him."

Mr. Kennedy held the phone and chuckled as he listened to whatever his son was saying.

The Attorney General had told Ham that he had called Otis Air Base and that a plane was being sent down to take Mr. Kennedy on in to New York. The captain of the barracks had also spoken to the Attorney General, and he was busy giving Mr. Kennedy a big sales talk.

"Yes, sir," he said, swaying on his heels. "Your son said that nothing was too good for his dad. He's going to have the best plane at the air base come right down here and fly you people into New York. Yes, sir. Nothing's too good for his dad."

Mr. Kennedy was eating it up, nodding his head, smiling.

Fortunately, there was a state police landing field a few miles away, so we knew that with Bobby in control of the situation we would be airborne in a little while.

We knew that we had nothing to worry about. Bobby had arranged everything, and it would be the best.

One of the officers was to accompany us to the airfield, and the chauffeur from the compound would be on the plane to drive the limousine back, so after Ham made arrangements to have his car towed away, we piled in the back seat of Mr. Kennedy's car with Ann driving and once again flew off behind a police escort.

Mr. Kennedy was having the time of his life. He was in great spirits, so all of us relaxed and started laughing. Ann's remarkable sense of humor was in full swing, and when she recounted how we looked following her, Mr. Kennedy slapped his knee in a fit of laughter. Now that it was all over, Ham and I could see the funny side, and by the time we reached the airfield all of us were in high spirits.

The field offered only raw necessities, and after tipping his helmet in a smart salute to Mr. Kennedy, the officer va-voomed away.

It had turned bitter cold, and Ham was pacing outside squinting at the sky, trying to spot our plane.

"Uncle Joe," Ann said, "I'll bet you're hungry."

He nodded his head.

She lowered the window and called to Ham, "Uncle Joe's hungry. The trooper said there was a canteen in the hangar, so let's go in and get something to eat. Have you got any money with you?"

Ham dug in his pockets and came up with $2 and some change. I did not even have a purse with me and Ann never carried much more than a dollar on her. Our total treasury was $5.85.

I stayed with Mr. Kennedy while they went after lunch. He

looked great. His eyes were bright, and his coloring was better than I had seen it for weeks.

When Ann and Ham returned, they had four lobster rolls and giant milk shakes for each of us. Mr. Kennedy devoured his, and since I am allergic to lobster, I gave him mine. I was pleased to see him gulp it down. He loved milk shakes, and when he had hit bottom and his straw made the gurgling sound, I said, "Here, Mr. Kennedy, you drink mine. I'm dieting, you know."

I was not, but he was very hungry and emptied my cup in just a few swallows.

Ham, knowing that he might balk at the last minute when he realized he would not be flying on the *Caroline*, started priming him by speculating on the "fancy plane" Bobby was sending for us. Mr. Kennedy rocked back and forth, nodding.

"Bobby will do it up right, Uncle Joe," Ann said, for she also knew he was likely to dig in his heels. He loved the *Caroline*. It was his, and it would have come after us; but one of the other children was using it at that time on a junket.

Ann and Ham got out of the car to peer at the sky. I was in the back seat, but I wanted to keep an eye on Mr. Kennedy's face to notice if there were any changes, so I got out and leaned against the fender in order to see him.

A bitter wind had come up, and our breaths hung in heavy vapors. I knew Ham must be cold, for he was wearing only a jacket. Ann had the collar of her coat turned up around her ears, and I snuggled deeper into my fake fur. Despite the cold, the two of them still sipped on their milk shakes.

Suddenly I heard the hum of the electric window, and Mr. Kennedy motioned for me with a jerk of his head.

I had taught him that if he were ever out in public or sitting with his family in the living room, I would know when he had to go to the bathroom if he would casually hook his thumb in his waistband. He was an exceptionally proud man, and this was a discreet signal that we both found successful. There was never a public accident.

I leaned my head in the window and saw his thumb in his waistband. "You don't mean it?" I said.

He nodded hard and dug his thumb deeper, wiggling his fingers. We both started laughing.

"Ham. Mr. Kennedy has to go to the bathroom."

"He what?"

"Oh, Uncle Joe." Ann giggled. "Can't you wait till we get on the plane?"

"No," he roared.

I shouted to Ann and Ham, "Give me your paper cups, hurry."

They rushed over to me, and when he finished, the four of us were nearly hysterical and tears were streaming down our cheeks. Mr. Kennedy was laughing with great roars. Just then we heard the sound of the plane coming in. We looked up, and Ham said, "My God, that's not a passenger plane. It's a cargo plane."

We got busy and put Mr. Kennedy in his chair. No one paid any attention to Ham, who kept saying, "We can't ride in that damn thing."

As Ham pushed him, Ann and I tried to shield Mr. Kennedy from the wind. He was smiling up at us, his cheeks ruddy, his eyes bright.

The plane had landed, and when we reached it, we saw how huge it was. Motors began to whir, and all at once enormous double doors in the plane's belly opened up and from what seemed like forty feet in the air, a young man in fatigues looked down at us.

"How do you figure on getting him up here?" he called, cupping his hands around his mouth like a megaphone.

"Think of something, quick," Ham shouted back.

Under his breath he said to us, "This is a luxury plane?"

Ann and I began laughing again. We both had our coats open trying to make a tent around Mr. Kennedy to keep the wind off him, and she chuckled, "Leave it to Bobby. Hell or high water, he's got real class. Right, Uncle Joe?"

Mr. Kennedy chuckled, delighted by the whole adventure.

The pilot and co-pilot, standing in the door of the plane, jumped down to the ground. Why they didn't break a leg or an ankle I'll never know. They walked over to us, stared at the wheelchair thoughtfully, and finally one of them said, half-heartedly, "Don't worry, we'll think of something." The other one, evidently the co-pilot, said, "Hell, Mac, why can't we pull him up on a rope like a piece of freight?"

We held our breath, but Mr. Kennedy, without a flicker of an eyelid, sat calmly. The co-pilot swung himself back up into the plane, and Mr. Kennedy watched while a rope was tossed down. When the pilot yelled for safety belts, he nodded his head in approval. They strapped him in his chair, and then Ham and the pilot made a sling around the seat of the chair. The pilot climbed back in the plane and very slowly, with Ham guiding, they hoisted him up.

Ann and I were hauled up hand over hand.

Once inside the plane we looked around and saw that we were in a huge empty airborne warehouse. Jonah must have had the same apprehension when he found himself in the belly of the whale. There were only narrow benches on either side, and Ham stood scratching his head, saying, "How in the name of God are we going to keep Mr. Kennedy stationary when this thing takes off?"

The plane was like an icebox. I pulled my coat tighter around me, and then I noticed that Mr. Kennedy had started to shiver. He was wearing only his lightweight nylon jacket, and without thinking, I took my coat and draped it across the front of him, wrapping the sleeves around his neck. It was full-length and covered him like a cozy blanket. Ham took off his jacket and wrapped it around his feet.

Mr. Kennedy looked up at me, shaking his head no. I patted his shoulder and laughed. "Now listen, Mr. Kennedy, you're all set. You look great. I'll bet you'll be wanting to borrow my coat all the time after this."

The most wonderful expression came over his face as he looked up at me.

Ham clamped his hand down on Mr. Kennedy's shoulder, in a man-to-man gesture.

"You're okay, Boss," he said. "Everything's under control. Now all we have to do is figure how to keep you in place when this thing takes off."

Ann was huddled on a bench, staring wild-eyed at the dull interior of the plane. Ham and I both knew that she was too frightened of flying to be of any help, so he got the rope we'd used to lift up Mr. Kennedy and threaded it through the spokes of the wheelchair. He wrapped it around and did the same thing with the other end on the other wheel. Tightening it up, he said, "Now, Rita, take this end and hold it steady. I'll take this other one and pull. Let's test it."

We sat down on the floor of the plane, and Ham gave his end of the rope a hard tug. Nothing came undone.

"Okay," he said. "Now you're going to have to hold onto your rope when this plane takes off, and I mean hold onto it all the time we're in the air. Better brace your legs against the wheel of the chair and lean back as far as you can. Just keep pulling. If you let go, the chair will fly right into the wall. Can you do it, Rita?"

I looked up at Mr. Kennedy. He was watching me intently.

"Think I can do it?" I asked him.

He nodded solemnly.

"Okay, Ham, we're ready."

The plane roared off, with a former ambassador wrapped in a woman's coat, a Secret Service agent with half a beard, a niece violently ill from airsickness, and a nurse hanging on to a rope for dear life.

When we landed in New York, a limousine pulled alongside the plane and drove us to Mr. Kennedy's apartment, this time without sirens.

I immediately phoned the nursing registry and had four nurses assigned to us while we were there. Shortly after our arrival, we received a call from the compound that Captain Baird had our luggage and was flying it down with Louella Hennessey. It had been decided by the family that since it was so late in the season, we would not be returning to Hyannis Port, but would go on to Florida from New York, with a stop off at the White House.

I was mentally, physically, and emotionally exhausted by the time Louella arrived. All I wanted was a bath and some clean clothes. Stacks of luggage were brought in, and I checked through it eagerly, but I didn't see mine. I looked at Louella. "Where's mine? Where's mine?"

"Good Lord," she gasped. "I didn't think to pack it."

My uniform was covered with grime, I hadn't combed my hair since morning, and I was stranded in New York without a penny to my name. I had not stopped since we arrived at the apartment, and when I heard my luggage had been left, I went to the kitchen, flopped at the table, and buried my face in my arms. Ann came in and told me that she had talked to the office and they had rooms for Louella and me at a nearby hotel. She also said that she had called the Cape and that Dora was packing my things. Captain Baird was to return immediately to the compound and pick them up. They were to be in New York no later than tomorrow afternoon.

I was too tired to react, one way or the other, and when the night nurse came on duty, Louella and I left for our hotel. When we finally got to our rooms, we both fell across the beds, exhausted.

"Never have I spent such a day," she groaned. "You have no idea what it was like at the Cape. Bobby is furious. Phone was ringing all the time. I tell you, everybody was going crazy."

"Go to sleep."

"They were going crazy, I tell you. I had less than half an hour to pack."

"Go to sleep."

"You're sure taking a funny attitude, Rita."

"Go to sleep."

The phone rang. It was Ann. Louella answered, and when she'd hung up, she said, "You're going to take Mr. Kennedy to his office first thing in the morning."

"I'm what?" I shrieked, sitting upright.

"Ann wants him at the office first thing."

"Why can't you take him?"

"I've got to go back to the Cape, according to Ann, and help Mrs. Kennedy close it down."

The rest of the night was spent mending and washing my uniform, scrubbing my shoes, and brushing in vain my once-white fake fur coat.

Morning came all too soon, and with it I made my first of several visits to Mr. Kennedy's New York offices.

The Kennedy enterprises took up one end of a floor in the Pan Am Building in New York City, and I was always impressed by the attention and courtesy everyone extended to him whenever he arrived. The working people, in particular, seemed genuinely glad to see him. The doorman. The elevator men. The policeman on duty.

He had been very excited on the drive from the apartment, but after the wild caper he had just gone through, I could only hope for the best. When we exited the elevator on the Kennedy floor, Ham, who was handling his chair, leaned over and said, "This is all yours, Boss, so don't let anything throw you." Mr. Kennedy tilted his head up and looked at his agent. Then I saw him take a deep breath and raise his hand, slightly, signaling that he was ready for us to take him in.

Ann, at the last minute, decided she had special shopping to do and had taken the limousine, promising Mr. Kennedy that she would pick us up in time for lunch. I learned, on that visit, that she was never comfortable on the New York or White House junkets. When she was at the compound, she was on home ground, and he was her "Uncle Joe." But in the world at large, Mr. Kennedy was an important and influential figure who was treated with dignity and respect—Ann, I suppose, felt out of place in this atmosphere.

On that first visit, as we wheeled him down the long row of offices, he would put his foot out to stop us at every door to see if the men were working. He would look in, for a moment, raise his hand to them in a small greeting, and motion us on to the next. Finally, after passing through several strings of offices, we reached the executive suites, and eventually his.

It was a magnificent room, luxuriously furnished. The walls, surrounding his desk, were glass, and when we transferred him to his desk chair, he swiveled around and was able to look across the panoramic skyline. The paintings on the wall had been chosen by his daughter Jean, and though abstract, they blended perfectly with the magnificent view of the city.

Since his illness, the office had been occupied by Stephen Smith, Jean's husband, but on Mr. Kennedy's visits, all traces of Steve would be cleared out, and the room would be restored as Mr. Kennedy had had it.

Steve was always on hand during our visits in order to greet Mr. Kennedy, but he never tried to control or absorb his schedule. The understanding Steve Smith displayed was sensitive and intelligent. He would visit with his father-in-law for a few moments, then say, "Grandpa, I've got to get busy and finish the arrangements for the big party we've planned for you tonight at the Caravelle."

He'd give him a broad wink and add under his breath, "Confidentially, I've also lined up a few of the fanciest girls in town for you."

Mr. Kennedy would laugh at this, for he knew Steve was talking about his daughters. Whenever we visited New York, he belonged to them. It was "Daddy" spoiling his girls. They went on shopping sprees, and he bought them the town. He went to the theater with them and to special luncheons, and every evening they had grand parties for him that always included his old friends.

A new policy had to be established with the office staff during Mr. Kennedy's visits. On that first visit his manager called me aside and asked, "Mrs. Dallas, what are we supposed to do? Mr. Kennedy always sat in his office, and we never went in to him unless he sent for us."

I said, "He can't sit in there at his desk all alone. He is unable to call and let people know that he wants to see them."

"Well," he replied, "we just can't walk in, so what's the program?"

I had left Mr. Kennedy looking out over the city, but I knew he would become restless or ill at ease in a few moments.

"Let me go in and talk to him about it."

"You mean tell him?"

"Well, I guess I do. It's his office, and he knows what he wants. I'll ask him if he wants to see each man, and if he does, I'll come out and tell you."

Another executive spoke up and inquired, "Mrs. Dallas, he can't speak, can he?"

"No."

"So what do we do? How can we talk to him?"

"I'll keep the initial conversation going, if it lags," I said. "Then I'll step out of the room, so you can give him your reports. Even if they're not confidential, he should have executive privacy. All you have to do is form your sentences in such a way that he can reply with a yes or a no. You'll be amazed how well he communicates."

They both laughed and said that when he was well, he had a great knack of communicating. They called it "bellering." He could rattle the walls, they told me. I nodded knowingly and told them that he had not lost the knack. Interestingly enough, never once during his visits to his office did he flare up or conduct himself in any way that did not befit his position. He was always dignified and regally aloof.

No one wanted to be the first to go in and break the ice. This happened at every visit. His staff was always hesitant. One or two would go in, reluctantly, and at first I thought the interviews went quite well; but when I saw them wiping the sweat off the palms of their hands, I realized that they were in fear and awe of him. On that first visit, interviews were lagging, and I was becoming quite desperate as to who would go in to him next. I went to one executive and said, "Why can't you at least be friendly and discuss something with him?"

"Friendly?" he gasped. "Friendly with Mr. Kennedy?"

He explained that the only relationship he'd ever had with

him had been on a business level. "Things have had to change since Mr. Smith took over," he said, "and I really don't have anything to report to Mr. Kennedy now, and as for me going into his office and being friendly, as you put it, he'd throw me out on my ear."

I went into another office and asked the man in it if he would go in. He replied, "I've worked here nineteen years, and I've never been in Mr. Kennedy's office. If I started it now, neither he nor I would understand why. No, Mrs. Dallas, you'll have to find someone else."

It was difficult, but Mr. Kennedy looked forward to his New York visits. He would listen intently to his men, asking them garbled questions, and they would usually reply, logically. When he felt it was time to leave, he would shake his head no when I asked if he wanted to see anyone else. We would transfer him to his wheelchair, and he would pause a brief moment as we went through the doors, to look back. He knew he had built his empire strong enough to stand without him, but there was a deep longing in that last look he would always take. I could read in his eyes that he was remembering the fire and energy that had once been his.

Usually we would make a stop in New York twice a year. In the spring coming up from Florida and in the fall on our way back, but we never spent too much actual time at the office.

Later on, we made an annual trip to Chicago. We usually stayed only three or four days in New York, but the trips to the Midwest lasted almost a week. He adored the Merchandise Mart, and I can remember driving up to it on our first visit and thinking to myself, *Good Lord, he owns all this.* It was formidable.

Mrs. Kennedy had told me so often how, after their son Joe had been killed, Mr. Kennedy went into a low and dangerous emotional ebb. He would not work. He stayed in his room with the shades drawn. He ate only enough to keep him alive, and he became so immersed in grief that he stopped speaking. This went on for months, she said, until she had almost given up any hope of his pulling out.

It was then that he purchased the Merchandise Mart and was able to turn his mind away from his loss and become involved in something tangible. In so doing, he salvaged himself from a total breakdown.

After visits to his offices, he had no emotional reactions, at least none that were noticeable. He seemed to enjoy himself. He inquired after his interests as best he could, then left. He knew he would be forever helpless to participate, but those brief hours a year let him see the visible evidence that his world was still intact.

16

WE LEFT New York after a three-day layover and flew to Washington on the *Caroline*. Mrs. Kennedy was to leave Hyannis Port and go direct to Palm Beach to prepare the house for the winter season, and we were to remain at the White House for four days. Mrs. Kennedy never accompanied her husband on his visits to Washington, and the fact that she did not was never really questioned by the staff. We all assumed she wanted Mr. Kennedy to have his son all to himself in his Presidential surroundings. However, I often wondered if these separate visits did not deprive the President of the joy of having the two people together who had contributed the most to his career.

Mr. Kennedy was anxious during the short flight from New York to Washington, for this was to be his first visit to the White House since his son's election. I had been thoroughly briefed by the doctors before our departure, and I was instructed to have an ample supply of any possible medication Mr. Kennedy might require during the visit. I was not, except in the case of dire emergency, to have any prescriptions filled while we were at the White House. This was a Secret Service precaution against the possibility of rumors that might arise in case any prescription filled should be misinterpreted as being for the President. There were always a great deal of preliminary preparations and precautions to handle, but after our first visit, all of us fell into an easy routine. I managed to take the existing staff of nurses along to the White House, for they had already been screened and cleared by the Secret Service, and using them eliminated a great deal of work.

Arriving at the White House with Mr. Kennedy was always a remarkable experience, because of the impact of the reality of John and Jacqueline Kennedy as the President and First Lady. On the official grounds they conveyed a new and marvelous dignity. For that matter, every member of the family took on a special glow and grandeur, for protocol was impeccably observed by all.

The President and his wife would always be waiting for Mr. Kennedy when his limousine pulled up at the portico. They would stand quietly until he had been removed from the car; then the President would step forward. He would be the first to bend down to kiss his father.

"Welcome, Dad," he would always say, in a soft personal whisper.

The First Lady would then come to him, put her arms around his neck and say, "Grandpa, Grandpa, how good it is to have you here with us."

After the welcoming, we would then be escorted through the public area of the White House and into the Presidential private elevator, which would take us up to the family quarters on the second floor. Mr. Kennedy was always given the Lincoln Room, and I stayed nearby in the John Quincy Adams Room.

There are a hundred and thirty-two rooms in the White House, but the family living quarters, during the Kennedy administration, consisted of a living room, five bedrooms, a dining area, and a kitchen.

On our first visit, both the President and the First Lady were quite concerned over Mr. Kennedy's condition. Nothing elaborate was planned for him on our first night at the White House so he would be able to rest after his trip. He dined with the President and his wife, visited a little with them after dinner, then retired early. He was excited at being there, and he had some periods of aphasia reaction, suddenly laughing or crying for no particular reason. Both the President and his wife were deeply concerned over these reactions.

About ten thirty that same night, the President's personal valet came to my room with word that the President would like to see me. I had been with the family long enough to know that a call late at night meant business, so I dressed hurriedly and followed him down the long dimly lit hall. We walked through the silent living room and stopped before a closed door. The valet knocked politely, opened it discreetly, and said, "Mrs. Dallas is here, Mr. President."

"Oh, fine," I heard him say. "Come in, Mrs. Dallas, come in, please."

The valet opened the door and stepped aside to allow me to pass. I walked head on into a bathroom and John Fitzgerald Kennedy.

He was stretched out full length in the tub, his hands locked behind his head, soaking placidly.

"Nice of you to come, Mrs. Dallas," he said.

What else could I answer except "Nice of you to have asked me"?

He went on in his most polished Harvard manner, telling me that he and his wife were terribly anxious about his father.

"After all," he said, "you're the one who's with him constantly, and you should know better than anyone else how he's doing. How he's really doing, I mean. I get reports from the doctors, and Ann keeps me posted; but I want your personal opinion, Mrs. Dallas."

I was listening to him, of course, but all I could really think of was what in heaven's name does one say to a naked President.

But with the Kennedys, you could not survive with a middle-of-the-road attitude, so I took a washcloth off the rack, tossed it in the tub, and said, "For heaven's sakes, cover up."

He splashed the water with his hands like a gleeful boy, then with an appealing look of mock contrition, made a fair attempt to cover up by ceremoniously draping the cloth over himself. He grinned and motioned for me to sit down—on the toilet.

I could not bring myself to do it.

"Thank you," I said, "but I'd rather stand."

As the President of the United States lay stretched out in a bathtub, clutching at a floating rag, I gave, in my most professional tone, my opinion of his father's health.

We talked back and forth for about ten minutes, and then he started to get out of the tub. I asked quickly, "Is that all, Mr. President?"

He sat back down, fished for the washcloth and said, with great dignity, "Why, yes, Mrs. Dallas . . . and thank you for coming."

Grappling for protocol, I muttered something like, "Thank you for asking me, Mr. President."

I recall passing the valet and frowning at the twinkle in his eye.

The next morning, when Mr. Kennedy finished his breakfast, we went out into the hall where the President, Caroline, and Bobby were waiting for us. The First Lady came out when she heard us and hugged and kissed Mr. Kennedy, then took Caroline and left him alone with his sons.

The boys were standing around talking aimlessly with their father when, all of a sudden, he started shouting and shaking his fist at them. They looked at each other, then back at their father.

"Dad, what's wrong? What's the matter? Are you sick? What is it?"

The President turned to Ann, who was standing alongside Mr. Kennedy, and said sharply, "What's the matter with him?"

By that time Mr. Kennedy was yelling at the top of his lungs.

"I don't know," she said. "I have no idea."

She bent over him and asked, "What's wrong, Uncle Joe?"

He shook his fist at her and bellowed all the louder.

I was standing behind his wheelchair, and during the pandemonium my mind was racing because I knew that soon the President was going to say to me, "What's wrong with him, Mrs. Dallas?" and I would have to come up with some sort of satisfactory answer.

An idea suddenly flashed across my mind, and since I was

standing behind Mr. Kennedy, he did not see me motion for the Attorney General. I told Bobby that while I was learning Mr. Kennedy's past habits, the New York office had informed me that he never believed in personal visits during working hours. I whispered to him, "I don't know whether this could relate to you boys or not, but perhaps he's trying to say, 'Get to work.'"

Bobby looked at me and grinned. "You hit it, Mrs. Dallas—and thanks."

He walked back and stood beside the President. He said, "Well, Dad, I think we've fooled around long enough."

The President immediately grasped his brother's thought and said, "Yes, Dad, we can't stand around entertaining you all day. I think it's time for me to get to my office and start running the country."

To his brother he grinned. "And as for you, Mr. Attorney General, you'd better get over to the Justice Department and take care of all the law and order."

With that, Mr. Kennedy broke into a wide smile and put out his hand to his sons. As Bobby Kennedy bent over to kiss his father's forehead, he looked across at me and winked.

They both went their separate ways, and Mr. Kennedy was satisfied.

During our White House visits, all of Mr. Kennedy's children were around in full force. The First Lady and Ethel, in particular, made it a point, during the day, to keep very close tabs on him but with his sons at work, he was once more encircled in a woman's world.

The Secret Service was not permitted on the second floor or in the family quarters. This was the private area, unencumbered by the evidences of official guards, but this privacy also left Mr. Kennedy without the masculine companionship he had come to rely upon from Ham.

He was delighted when his daughters-in-law came for their "drop ins"; but the White House can become a lonely place, and he brooded when we were alone. He became so melancholy that I took it upon myself to phone Ham Brown and ask him to come and stay with Mr. Kennedy.

"I can't, Rita," he explained. "None of us are allowed up there."

That evening, when I took Mr. Kennedy to dinner with the President, I told him, privately, that I thought his father was falling into fits of depression. "I think he misses Ham," I said. "With you and the Attorney General gone all day, he becomes very restless."

"Well, why isn't the agent with him?"

"It's against orders," I said.

He laughed. "You get right on the phone and tell the chief that the President said that he wants his father's agent up with him. Now. It's an order. A new order."

I did as he instructed, and when Mr. Kennedy saw Ham waiting as we came out from dinner, he smiled from ear to ear and waved his hand. After that, Mr. Kennedy was pleasant and responsive during his visits. He and Ham spent the long hours watching television and discussing ball games. When I say "discussing," I mean that Ham had adjusted to Mr. Kennedy's garbled tongue and responded to him in conversation almost as though he understood verbatim.

The first time Mr. Kennedy visited the famous Oval Room was a very special and moving experience for him. The First Lady had been visiting with him and after about an hour she surprised him by saying, "Grandpa, Jack wants us to come to his office this morning. He's going to call up just as soon as he's free."

This was something Mr. Kennedy had been looking forward to, the chance to see his son in the office where he carried out his business as President. He was very excited and full of anticipation for the rest of the morning, but it wasn't until after lunch that the President could send for us. The First Lady had not been able to wait, for she was working with a photographer on a special White House album. However, before she left for the appointment, she made certain we would have an escort to the President's office.

Shortly after one o'clock he called for his father. We hurried down, and he was waiting for us at the door to his office. I wheeled Mr. Kennedy into the Oval Room, and he was very solemn as he motioned his son to sit behind the long, wide desk.

The President sat very straight and dignified and began to point out different mementos on his desk. Suddenly he and I were both aware that silent tears were streaming down Mr. Kennedy's face. There was no sound, simply tears of pride. The President kept talking as though he were not aware that his father was weeping, and Mr. Kennedy was able to get himself under control with dignity.

The President got up from his desk and walked over to his father. He took the wheelchair himself, something he seldom did, and moved him to another area of the room, near the windows.

"This is my rocker, Dad," he said, and sat down opposite his father. "It looks as though we both need special chairs, doesn't it?"

Mr. Kennedy smiled but he pointed to his son's chair and shook his head no.

A moment's silence passed between the two men. Then the President called in his father's agent, and the three of them chatted for a moment.

As Mr. Kennedy was being wheeled from the room, the President held me back.

"Mrs. Dallas," he said, "I want you to try out my rocking chair. It seems that it's becoming quite famous, so you sit in it and who knows, it might be something for you to tell your grandchildren someday."

He stood over me smiling and kept urging me to "keep rocking." I knew his father was waiting, so I thanked him and left. As I expected, Mr. Kennedy was in the hall, extremely fretful and curious about why I had been detained. I laughed him out of his approaching bad disposition by saying, "I've been rocking in your son's chair, Mr. Kennedy. I just couldn't resist it."

With that he was all smiles and we spent the rest of the day pleasantly.

When I checked on Mr. Kennedy at various hours, often late at night, the upstairs lights would be turned low. It gave the whole area a solemn tone. At one end of the hall the Presidential living room would be softly and dramatically lighted. There would be muted music mingling with the shadows.

The First Lady would be sitting on the couch, outlined by a gentle halo of light, and then the President would step from the elevator that opened onto the living room. He would stand very still, waiting, while his wife rose from the couch to come to him. He would rest his hand on her cheek and then take her in his arms for a quiet embrace.

How often I thought, if the world had ever seen those moments there would be no doubt that Camelot existed.

At such times I found it indeed sad that Mr. Kennedy could never have been welcomed openly to the White House, as I knew the President and his wife would have wanted. Even after his stroke, he was kept so under wraps that very few outsiders ever realized he could not speak. In order to prevent any major outbreak of rumors, our visits were often cut short if we happened to be at the White House and an important guest of state came unexpectedly. We had to pack up and be gone within an hour.

Ann was always the one who was given the unpleasant task of telling her uncle that he had to leave.

I remember when news came that Andrei Gromyko, the Soviet Foreign Minister, was arriving. Ann came to us and said, "Get packed. Here we go again."

It was an awkward situation for everyone concerned, but the President, in protecting his position, could not afford to have his father there for fear that a hostile press would report that the Ambassador was present and directing his son's affairs.

When we left the White House after that first visit, Mr. Kennedy was invited to fly to Florida by the First Lady as her special guest. He was delighted at her invitation, but I was concerned because they were flying in her government plane, which was a Jetstar. The doctors felt that there would be no medical problems, but Mr. Kennedy was accustomed to his own plane, the *Caroline*, and although he seemed to accept the idea of a different plane, I was worried about his disposition.

All the way to the airport the First Lady was marvelous with him. She sat up front in the limousine with her arm around him telling him all about her Jetstar and saying how pleased she was to be able to have him as her guest. He was floating on air when we arrived at the airport; the First Lady stayed right by him, keeping him at ease during the complicated procedure of strapping him into the special chair that is always used to transport handicapped persons onto an airplane. Just before he was carried up the steps, she took out her rosary and blessed him. Very quietly, she whispered a special prayer for a safe flight. Then Mr. Kennedy was carried up the steps by Agent Brown, the pilot, and the First Lady's Secret Service agent, Clint Hill.

Everything had gone smoothly, but once on the plane, he reacted violently because of its unfamiliarity. The seats looked too narrow, and he didn't want to be strapped in. He got very upset and started shouting. Throughout all of it the First Lady was beautifully calm and gentle with him, and he never directed his outbursts at her. He would stomp his foot at us and then turn to her, pat her cheek and smile. He didn't want to get off the plane, and he didn't want to sit in the narrow seat, so finally Ham, Clint, and I decided to hold his chair in position while the plane took off. The First Lady watched in amazement as we struggled over Mr. Kennedy's chair.

As the plane shot in the air, I could see Ham and Clint bracing against each other with all their strength. I had to fight to keep from toppling over Mr. Kennedy, but since he was well strapped in, he rode the almost vertical incline in complete comfort.

"Shame on you," I grunted. "Shame, shame on you."

His lips twitched mischievously, and he cocked his eyebrow as if to say, "Next time better make sure it's the *Caroline*."

"Is it always like this?" the First Lady said in amazement.

"Not always," Ham replied between clenched teeth. "Not always."

As the plane leveled, Mr. Kennedy raised his hand, motioning us away, and with a regal gesture indicated that he would now sit in the seat. In midair, Ham and I transferred him into the one facing the First Lady.

When he was settled, Clint and Ham took seats in the back of the plane, and I started to sit alongside Mr. Kennedy; but the First Lady said, "Sit by me, Mrs. Dallas." She knew that in facing him, I would be in a better position to observe his reactions. I sat down as she reached across and held his hand. With her other one she began saying the rosary.

Suddenly he started laughing at the top of his voice. His face was flushed, and he had a wild, confused look in his eye. I immediately took his pulse and found that it was dropping, rapidly. Ham came running up the aisle.

"What's wrong, Rita?"

"I think he's having a reaction to the altitude," I said. "See if the pilot can drop down."

It was as I thought. He was having an anoxic reaction, and it was causing him to behave as though he were roaring drunk.

The First Lady never asked a question about her father-in-law in his presence as though he were not aware or capable of understanding. She never said, "What's wrong with him?" or "How is he?" She related to him always in the first person, and even though she was startled by his behavior, she said calmly, "Grandpa, I'm so glad you're really enjoying yourself."

She had no idea what was happening to him, so she gave me a quick, questioning look, and I nodded, reassuringly.

The pilot told Ham that he could come down to two thousand feet, but no more, and that he could not fly at that altitude for any length of time.

Mr. Kennedy's pulse had dropped to thirty-eight, but as the plane came down, it picked up, slowly but surely. For the rest of the flight, we went up and Mr. Kennedy became giddy, we went down and he leveled off.

An anoxic reaction has almost the same effect as laughing

gas, so hilarity reigned between Washington and Palm Beach. The First Lady, through it all, was marvelous with Mr. Kennedy, but by the time we finally landed at Palm Beach she seemed a bit frayed. Mr. Kennedy had settled back to normal once we were on the ground, and kissing him, she chuckled. "Well, Grandpa, I must say that traveling with you is certainly a different experience."

He nodded his head and grinned.

On the drive to his Palm Beach estate he made an unusually moving gesture. Once again the First Lady rode in the front seat between him and the chauffeur, and as she had on the drive in Washington, she started to wrap her arm around his shoulder. He raised his hand to stop her. Turning slightly in the seat (an effort for him), he stretched his left arm across the back of the seat and wrapped it around her shoulder, holding her close.

"Grandpa," she said solemnly, "thank you again for flying down with me. It was a difficult trip for you, and I know you'd have been more comfortable on the *Caroline*; but it was grand of you to go through what you did, just to be with me."

Her eyes were moist, and she leaned her head on his shoulder. "If I'd only known, Grandpa, I wouldn't have put you through it for the world."

Mr. Kennedy hugged her with his good arm and patted her cheek. We rode the rest of the way home in silence.

More and more I saw evidence of this remarkable relationship, and I often regretted that my knowledge of their devotion came only after his illness. Many people catered to Mr. Kennedy and his power, but between him and the First Lady there was a beautiful and equal devotion.

She was a loner who stood her own ground and refused to compromise her identity or mesh it even with her husband's. Mr. Kennedy knew this and obviously respected her for it. She had the strength to stand up against the whole family if necessary. Jacqueline Kennedy had a special place in his life, as I saw time and time again. I believe he actually considered her as much of a Kennedy as he did any of his blood relatives.

17

Ann had become a public figure by the end of that first year. Apparently the Kennedy public relations staff had been alerted to introduce her to the press, for suddenly, she seemed to burst on the horizon, appearing regularly in columns and national magazines as "Ambassador Kennedy's niece and devoted companion." This was done with such professional timing that it was not surprising that the American public assumed she was his nurse. Without ever saying so, the stories left this impression, and knowing the thoroughness of the Kennedys, this did not happen by accident.

Once the decision had been made at Horizon House, Ann became Mr. Kennedy's ever-present link, not only with the public, but with his family as well. To my recollection, there was never a photograph printed after Horizon House that did not show the two of them together, nor was there an article relating to Mr. Kennedy that did not include Ann. Family unity was confirmed, and the endearing impression it made on the general public was pure genius.

Ann became obsessed in her devotion, and she often would not leave Mr. Kennedy's side. She was so firmly ensconced in her authority that by the end of the first year it was affecting the open relationship that his family had with him. They had put their father's care into the hands of a nonprofessional, and as the years went on, she acquired the authority to overrule them all.

Mrs. Kennedy would say, "Ask Ann. Ask Ann," until it became a habit. All in all, when the family relinquished their decision-making power over him, they became as vulnerable as he.

Part of the difficulties with Ann stemmed from the fact that they were openly demonstrative and affectionate toward one another, but this attitude never included outsiders. Even Mr. or Mrs. Kennedy's sisters and brothers were not involved in the inner circle, and Ann, being an outsider, was placed in a provocative and difficult position. They were all polite to her and very much aware of her needs, but there always remained a wide gulf between them. She was not a Kennedy, and they, above all others, knew it. It was the same with her brother, Joe Gargan. Mr. Kennedy had selected him to be Teddy's playmate when he was a child, and Joe was always in the background until after the Chappaquiddick incident.

He would stand outside a room until he was invited to come in, and even then he would never sit down unless he was asked to do so. Teddy was fond of him, but he was not a Kennedy.

In a year's time, however, Ann had achieved complete domination over Mr. Kennedy, and if the family ignored her or provoked her in any way, she was able to cut them out of the picture. It took very little to set off a chain reaction. If one of them would tease her dog or be a little brusque questioning her about their father's condition, she used the only means she had available to retaliate, and that was to deprive them of visiting their father.

When Ann was miffed, she would tell them that he was not feeling well enough to visit. They would seldom challenge her decision. I would listen to her describe his condition to the family with such intelligence that not only did she convince them, but there were times when she nearly convinced me. I would be tempted to check back through the record book just to reassure myself that we were on the same case. The other nurses were aware of this situation, and they would come to me and say, "Who's right around here? How can we take care of a patient with this kind of snafu going on?"

"Don't worry about the snafu," I replied. "It's our job to pick up the pieces and go from there."

And we did. When one door closed on Mr. Kennedy, I would try to open another.

Eunice, in particular, had been pleased when she learned that Pat Moran and I were continuing with our efforts to rehabilitate him. She was especially delighted when I told her that he was learning how to write with his left hand.

"Good for him," she said, as she went in to congratulate him on his accomplishment. She stood over him while he painfully showed her a sample of his writing, and he was doing quite well until he was told by someone that he should not learn how to write his name.

"You can never tell what might be put in front of you to sign and without knowing it, you might give away everything you have."

A frozen look immediately swept over his face, and I knew that it was the end of writing for him. He tried often during the next two or three weeks, but his incentive was blocked by fear. He would take his pencil in his left hand, and there were times when he would become so tense that he would snap it in two.

Eunice, however, never gave up. She would say, "Dad, what's wrong? If you'd only write, we'd know what you wanted. It would be so much easier for you. Just learn a word at a time. When you want a Coke, just try writing it out, and as time goes on, soon you'll be writing more and more. It's worth a try, Dad."

He would take the pencil again, but would freeze physically and mentally. I'm sure Eunice realized what had happened, for one day she said, "Quit trying to write your name, Dad. Don't bother with it. Just try to write the things you want."

The frustration made his therapy ineffective, and later the same deterrent occurred with his speech.

Eunice frequently came in to work with him using flash cards. We both believed he could learn to speak, and we were supported in this by the evaluation of a prominent therapist from Chicago who had come to observe him. His letter to the President confirmed that he was capable of speech rehabilitation and urged that he be allowed to continue dictating to his secretary and conversing as often as he wanted. He kept at it until one afternoon he was told curtly that no one could understand him. "Don't you realize you jabber? Don't you realize it's embarrassing to have to listen to you mumble and pretend we all know what you're saying?"

His body trembled; then he clamped his mouth shut, and I never heard him try to say another word except no or yes. Eventually even this stopped.

I have seldom wept tears of hot anger, but when I heard one of the young men who had been hired by Ann to act as a physical aide to lift and move Mr. Kennedy refer to him as "mumbles," I became violent.

"Don't you ever say a thing like that again," I shouted. "Ever."

I so frightened the poor boy that he left the job, and at the time nothing could have pleased me more. In retrospect I feel that he was innocent of intentional mockery. He had no doubt heard similar disrespect from outsiders, but as a member of the nursing staff it was something I could not tolerate.

There were many frustrations working on the Kennedy case. I had to request that a sensitive intercom system be installed between his room and the nurses' station. Ann did not want to permit a nurse in her uncle's room even to administer his general treatment and medication, so the only means the other nurses had of communicating with the patient was by listening to him over an intercom. If he called out, struggled, or gave any peculiar sound, they could thus be alerted.

When I took the Kennedy case, there were no sickroom aids available, such as oxygen. It seemed to me that Mr. Kennedy was quite susceptible to cardiac arrest or other similar attacks because he had a modest history of coronary arteriosclerosis, and so I requested an oxygen tank, in order to be on the safe side. When my requisition was not filled, I purchased a small emergency tank of oxygen at the drugstore for my own peace of mind.

He had his first cardiac arrest at Hyannis Port during the

second summer, and I was able to revive him with closed cardiac massage. He came to quite rapidly and had no evident side effects. But after this first arrest it was apparent that he was highly susceptible and would require careful attention. The sickroom supplies I had requested were immediately made available.

A cardiac arrest can be a frightening thing to witness for an untrained person and also very dangerous for the patient because even if he recovers, there is the possibility of brain damage.

It can happen at any time and completely without warning. With a faint gasp or moan the victim passes out. His heart has actually stopped, and there is no pulse. The flesh often will turn a dusty gray, and if the eyes were open at the time of the attack, they will usually remain open and rolled back in the head.

People who have had cardiac arrests say that they had a feeling of impending death just before it happened. Another interesting thing is that when they recover, they usually regain consciousness calmly. It's as though they have been asleep, and when they come to, they may feel a little groggy, but usually the premonition and fear are gone.

Short of an operation for heart massage, the basic treatment for a cardiac arrest outside a hospital is for a trained person to pound the chest rapidly and hard directly above the heart. This is called closed cardiac compression. It is complicated because the rhythm must be perfect, and once the heart begins beating again the chest must be pounded in a counterrhythm until the patient revives. Brain damage can occur owing to a lack of oxygen if the heart is not revived soon enough (usually within five minutes).

As a nurse I was deeply concerned after the first cardiac arrest because I felt I needed a backup nurse in the event of another emergency. It wasn't until after his second attack that I was able to get one. It happened on a warm evening that same summer. All his children were with him, and they all had spent a pleasant cocktail hour together. In Mr. Kennedy's house only

Dubonnet wine was served, and it was the custom for his children to show up about six and gather around Mr. and Mrs. Kennedy for what Teddy referred to as "fun time." Gradually, so as not to tire him, they would drift away, and he would later dine alone with his wife.

He had particularly enjoyed his children that evening, but after they left, I noticed he appeared to fall into a blue mood. I attributed it to despondency or loneliness. Suddenly, he gave a faint gasp. Instinctively I knew what was happening to him, and I went to work immediately. I yelled for Ann over the intercom. She dashed into the room and saw me hammering her uncle on the chest.

"Get the family," I called over my shoulder.

She was stunned.

Still beating on him, I shouted, "Don't stand there, get the family. Call the doctor."

In a matter of seconds, it seemed, his children were filling the room, watching me hammering on his chest with all my strength. They stared at their father, transfixed. Mr. Kennedy was still unconscious.

Bobby pushed his way through and cried, "Mrs. Dallas, that's too hard for you. Let me do it."

By that time I was in rhythm, and the heart had started, so, without stopping, I snapped, curtly, "Get back. Let me do my work."

With that, Bobby stayed by the bed, his face glued to his father. I glanced up and saw his lips moving, silently. He was praying. The rest of the room was as quiet as a tomb except for the almost inaudible whispers of silent prayer.

Mr. Kennedy revived calmly, and although it was not critically necessary that he be given oxygen, I administered it to him to make him more comfortable.

Not until I was certain he was out of danger did I look around the room. The President and the First Lady, Bobby and Ethel, Eunice and her husband, Pat and Jean and their husbands, Teddy and Joan—all of them were there, and when I saw Teddy kneeling at the foot of his father's bed staring at him, I realized that he was basically a very young man. The shock of being so close to death deeply frightened him.

"He's fine," I said, knowing that they all needed reassurance. "He's asleep now."

Ann had put in an emergency call to the local doctor, and after he arrived, there was a big conference on whether or not Mr. Kennedy should be rushed to the hospital. The doctor kept insisting that he should be where he could be observed.

While the discussion was going on, I kept my eye on my patient, and I thought I saw a slight twitch in his eyelid, so when Bobby drew me aside to say, "What do you think, Mrs. Dallas? Should we send him to the hospital?" I decided to play it by ear.

"Well," I said, "knowing your father as I do, I don't think he'd be very happy waking up in a hospital."

Just then Teddy gave out a loud war whoop. "Dad," he shouted, "you're an old faker! I saw your eyelids! You're awake! You've been lying there listening to us!"

Mr. Kennedy opened his eyes and grinned.

His children poured over him laughing and teasing. The doctor shook his head and left, saying, "What a family."

I stepped out of the room, for I was exhausted. Bobby followed me. The President was right on his heels. They each took my hand, and the President said, "Is 'thank you' enough, Mrs. Dallas?"

"He made it," I replied. "That's the important thing, and thank God he came out of it soon enough."

I explained the danger of brain damage, and both boys groaned in relief.

Later that night, as I was leaving, I stopped in the kitchen to tell Matilda that Mr. Kennedy was fine. She and I were having a cup of coffee when Joan came into the room.

"I'm glad I found you, Mrs. Dallas," she said. "The Senator has been wanting to speak to you, but he's still with his father. He wants to tell you how glad he is that you saved his dad's life tonight."

I expected no thanks. It was my job, but it was rewarding

when all the Kennedy children, one by one, made a special effort to express their gratitude.

The next morning it rained very hard, and Bobby was the only one to visit his father before lunch. I suggested to him that it might be a good idea if an alarm system could be set up, and within hours workmen were at the compound wiring in an elaborate system.

An alarm button was installed at the head of Mr. Kennedy's bed which activated an amplified alert that could be heard all over the compound. Throughout the years this alarm was to sound many times.

At that same discussion with Bobby I stressed that there should always be a backup nurse on the case. Ann simply was not qualified to assist me, and after seeing an arrest, Bobby realized this. In the event of seizures or attacks, his father was in the throes of a life-and-death emergency, and it was more than one nurse could handle.

"It might never happen again," I explained. "Or another arrest could occur within hours. Caring for your father is complicated, and I feel we should cover any potential emergency that could arise. I know it will be an added expense but—"

"Wait a minute, Mrs. Dallas," he interrupted. "It's Dad's money we're talking about and whatever it takes—if it takes all of it to make him comfortable—then, well, it just takes it."

That was one of the few times I ever saw him drop his eyes in embarrassment. I'm sure he was aware of the tensions and complications that were resulting from having Ann placed in charge of his father, but Bobby was as committed as all the other Kennedys to maintaining the image of the whole. Individual needs came in second, and the choice had been made regarding Ann, never to be altered and, as far as I could see, never reconsidered.

The Kennedys were dazzled by the brilliance of their own destiny, and there was little time to slow down or look back or reconsider. During President Kennedy's short-lived hour in history, the whole family emerged on the national scene with extraordinary intensity. They were a whole, a unity, and they often seemed driven by a sense that they had to maintain their identity as a family in order to keep from being shattered by the hurtling forces of their own momentum.

Their blood loyalty surpassed any tie I've ever known. It bordered on a fetish. They were loyal to the extreme, and it seemed as if they clung to each other not to survive as individuals, but to survive as Kennedys. Theirs was not the ordinary love of brother and sister—it went far deeper than that.

The strength of this family blood bond seemed to be a guarantee that the comet would never fall or burn out. And the Kennedys were not alone in this belief in themselves. It seemed to be universally shared. Even those who had voted against the President felt that a political dynasty had been established that could reign eternal. It appeared that the Kennedy era was indestructible. The goal had been won, and the laurel of victory rested comfortably on the brow of JFK.

To them belonged the spoils.

Celebrities swarmed after them. The public fought for a cherished glimpse. Multimillionaires sought favors and the international jet set claimed them as their own. Royalty besieged them. Artists clamored for commissions, and impersonators became rich through mimicry.

Life was a hurdy-gurdy, grinding out a new and exciting melody, and in looking back on the final year of this high, wide, and handsome era, I recall the whole Kennedy clan as a family voluntarily caught up in a wild frenzy. It went beyond political adulation, and it was more than any of them had anticipated. There was joy, overwhelming joy to savor and the promise of an unlimited horizon. Only occasionally in unguarded quiet moments did the puzzling question appear: "What happened?" But the tempo of the New Frontier swept on, hardly pausing for such moments of questioning.

Plans were already formed for the next election. Campaign committees were activated, and press agents worked overtime to perpetrate the image. Speech writers churned out reams of political philosophy. Professional comedy writers provided glib and witty one-liners that were memorized and held in reserve for press conferences, national interviews, campaign speeches, and world tours.

Everything about them was news, and it had its effect and took its toll.

The Kennedy comet had roared across the heavens at such a breakneck speed that someone had to be cast in the role of the villain. So, as long as his older brother was alive, it was Bobby who tolerated the reputation of being ruthless. It was Bobby who took the brunt. While the President brought art and intellect to the White House and received public accolades for doing it, Bobby was in the grubby back rooms of the political world, making enemies for himself, instead of for his brother. The load carried on the slight shoulders of Bobby Kennedy was a burden that would have staggered most other men.

But although he was scorned for his supposed ruthlessness, Bobby seemed to hold a firm grip on himself and kept to the job at hand. If there was ever a man who owned his own mind and whose public generosity was based on a deep inner personal integrity, it was Bobby Kennedy.

The other members of the family played their roles in different ways. Strong-minded Eunice caught the golden ring, took it in stride, and placed her influence and personal devotion at the service of the mentally retarded. Pat was somewhat disenchanted, but she accepted the role of sister to the President with high-spirited finesse. Teddy and Joan Kennedy's heads were young enough to be turned by the fame and flattery, but there was genuine joy and exuberance in their heady participation. Jean, quiet and elegant, rode the crest of prominence, and Ethel Kennedy, bearing child after child, added to the reputation for enchanting frivolity by having her house and the light bulbs in it sprayed every day with Arpège perfume.

They were told they were "the beautiful people," and they behaved as such.

Mrs. Joseph Kennedy took on the role of matriarch and with each passing day became more and more stereotyped.

The President himself was a man of great style and sophistication. He radiated such a personal confidence in himself and in his abilities that, had they come from a lesser man, the egoism would have been unbearable.

But John Kennedy was not an egoist. He was an image, and there were times when I realized that a part of him had been manufactured by a slick advertising campaign. According to the image, to which he adhered, the smile was flawless. Every physical motion was carried through with the studied precision of a dancer. The voice was used with studied inflections to evoke just the right response. The mind was constantly stimulated and prompted by a brilliant think tank. The clothes were so immaculate and expertly tailored that every muscle was advantageously set off. The walk was brilliant, and the stance of British royalty was often emulated.

It was, indeed, an image that was the personification of the romantic novelist's man of destiny.

But the image never forgot that it was the culmination of skilled plans and maneuvering or that it had unlimited financial support to keep it alive.

There was, however, more to John Kennedy than the apparent potpourri of commercial perfection. He was also friendly, perceptive, inquisitive, tender, and powerful. The most pertinent thing he was, however, was Joseph Kennedy's son, and he never forgot it.

It overwhelms me to think back on that last year before the President's death, for I cannot see it as it was actually lived. It is clouded with the memory of tragedy and sorrow, and yet John Kennedy is as eternal in my mind as is the flame that burns over his grave.

He was a President, yes. But I also knew him as a father, a brother, a husband, and a son.

Caroline idolized him and no matter where he was, if he would clap his hands, you could hear her high happy voice call, "Daddy, Daddy, I'm coming."

His young son, John, was a scamp of a child. He adored airplanes and did everything he could to "bum a ride" on anything that flew. The President would let him go along as often as he could, but when he could not take him, he would give him a tiny toy plane as a substitute, very much like those that can be found in a crackerjack box.

"You can't go with me this time, John," he'd say, "but here's a play plane for you till I get back."

He must have bought them by the gross, for they were everywhere. This usually pacified young John, but if it failed, the President would bend down and whisper in his ear, "You fly this one, son, and as soon as you grow up, Daddy's going to buy you a real one."

The little boy would look at him solemnly with his great round eyes and say, "Promise, Daddy, when I grow up. Promise?"

The President would hold him tight and, with his face buried in his hair, say, "I promise. Someday I'll get you a real plane." Little John would run off telling everyone the news. He'd tug at us, wave his toy plane, and say, "My daddy's going to get me a real one when I grow up."

Caroline had a great tolerance for her smaller brother, but not so much that she'd step aside and not vie for her father's attention.

If she would balk at doing something, as any child will, all that one would have to say would be, "Don't you want to make your daddy happy, Caroline?" and she would do anything you'd ask her if she thought it would please him.

I remember the first time she was to water ski. She was such a fragile-looking little girl, and she appeared even more so as she sat huddled on the upper deck of the *Marlin*. She was terribly frightened and had been whimpering a little.

When it came time for her to get in the motorboat, she began to tremble. Her mother was already waiting for her and called, "Come on, Caroline. Come on."

Caroline buried her face in the crook of her arm and cried. The First Lady climbed back on the *Marlin* and raced to her. Taking her daughter in her arms, she soothed, "Darling, darling, don't be afraid. You don't want others to think you're not brave, do you?"

Caroline, her face buried in her mother's lap, mumbled, "No."

The First Lady turned up her chin and kissed her.

"Now dry your eyes, there's nothing to fear, so come on and let's do it. It will make Daddy so proud of you when he comes home this weekend."

Caroline followed her mother with some hesitance and climbed in the motorboat. Her first lesson was a fantastic thing to watch. She took two or three spills but got right back up. Her mother would jump in the water and swim to her with each tumble, and in less than a half hour, the little girl was handling the skis like an expert.

She and her mother made a pact with the rest of the family not to tell the President about it, and when he came that weekend, everyone went out on the *Marlin* as usual. When his wife and daughter took off in the motorboat without any fanfare, he hardly noticed, but when they raced by with Caroline on skis, he began to wave and clap his hands. A great cheer went up from the rest of the family, and Mr. Kennedy clapped by slapping his leg. When Caroline made a turn and came back again, the President squatted down by his father and yelled over the cheers, "Look at her, Dad, just look at her."

When she came back on board with her mother, the President greeted her in true Kennedy manner. He stood at attention and applauded.

Caroline looked up at her mother, her face aglow, and the First Lady very gently brushed a strand of wet hair off her face and whispered, "Now, go to Daddy."

John Kennedy was a member of a large Catholic family, and as such he had a great longing for children. He and his wife had had tragic difficulties in having a family, and therefore, the two they had were indeed precious to them.

Where all children were concerned, he was the unquestioned hero of the hour, and it was always a special treat when he would load the golf cart to overflowing with nieces and nephews and ride them around the estate. Caroline always took the special place on her father's lap and would go on every ride. He would make sure that each child had a turn, and even though some of them were too young to realize that he was the President, they loved him just the same and never wanted to miss out on "Uncle Jack's ride."

The President and Eunice were very close and had a great competitive relationship. They loved visiting their father together, and he got a great kick out of hearing them challenge each other. The President always went through his speeches with Eunice, seeking her opinion. They would huddle together in the library and then stop back at Mr. Kennedy's room, so Eunice could say, "He's pretty good, Daddy . . . but I could do it better."

"Maybe so"—her brother would laugh—"but I'm the President, and that counts for something."

Eunice was the one who always took charge whenever there was a crisis or an emergency, and she had a tough, don't-give-an-inch attitude when there was trouble. The President always admired her for this.

Once, in Florida, they were all swimming off the *Marlin* when someone suddenly spotted a school of sharks. Everyone scampered back onto the boat except Eunice. She continued her swim, undisturbed. The sharks flirted around her for quite a while, then turned and swam away.

The President had been watching with intense concern, but once he saw that his sister was out of danger, he yelled out to her, "See, Eunie, even the sharks are afraid of you."

He had a great sense of humor, and I remember one time during the winter season at Palm Beach when he and I met head on. Literally!

Always in Palm Beach, we were notified of his arrival, and everybody prepared for the visit. The kitchen was alerted to make his favorite dishes, and the house was given a general cleaning.

Somehow, on this one visit, I did not learn that he was coming for the weekend, and I decided to go into town on an errand. On my way out to the parking lot I waved to the cook and got in my car to run my errands.

Pulling out of the driveway onto the street was always hazardous. It was a very bad, sharp corner set on an incline. In order to see what was coming from the left, mirrors had been installed to provide a view of oncoming traffic around the corner.

I was always frightened, pulling out onto the street, for I am not the best of drivers, and that day I was concentrating on squinting into the mirror to see if it was clear. I did not look to the right. I simply forgot. I pulled out, and as I did, I heard screaming brakes. I turned and gasped, for there was the President and Caroline, in his car, with a backup car of Secret Service men behind him. Caroline stood up in the seat of the convertible and yelled, happily, "Hi, Mrs. Dallas, how's Grandpa? We're coming to see him."

I froze. All I could see was the President sitting behind the wheel, laughing at me.

I couldn't back my car up, and I couldn't go forward. I just sat there.

"What's wrong, Mrs. Dallas?" Caroline giggled. "Are you sick?"

I saw one of the agents wave his hand, motioning for me to back up. It's probably a good thing I did not move, for I would, no doubt, have shot the car in reverse and plowed through the kitchen, or else I would have flubbed and driven straight into the President.

I raised both my hands, helplessly, and the President doubled up.

There we sat inches apart, neither car making a move. One of the agents started toward me, but the President called, "Leave her alone. She's just a typical female driver." Then he teased me: "You're nearly as bad as my mother."

He called to the agent in the backup car, "Move out, fellows, and let a lady pass."

They backed down the street, and then the President backed up his car so I could get out of the driveway.

Caroline was still sitting up on the back of the seat, calling out directions. When I was out of the drive, I waved to the

President as I drove off, touched by the man's courtesy, humor, and consideration.

He always seemed especially to enjoy his father's birthday parties. Every member of the family would attend, children and grandchildren alike.

There would be ice cream and cake in the dining room, with party favors at each place. Dora would work all day long putting up festoons and paper streamers from the ceiling.

The daughters would elaborately decorate one of his extra wheelchairs with ribbons and balloons, and when they came for him to take him to the party, he would be gruffly embarrassed. It was all an act, however, for he rode in it like a king on a throne.

As soon as he entered the dining room, the grandchildren rushed to him to give him his birthday kisses, all twenty-three of them.

Mrs. Kennedy would sit next to him at the table, and they would pose while their children took pictures of them together.

During the ice cream and cake, the room shook with the celebration. After everyone had finished eating, his sons would wheel him into the living room, and they would all settle down while the grandchildren entertained. Ethel Kennedy usually wrote the skits, and it was the most touching part of the festivities. They would all participate, even down to the youngest child taking roles. All parts were perfectly memorized, and how Ethel found the time not only to write the plays but to rehearse them is remarkable. All in all, it was a professional presentation, for no one ever blundered or forgot a line.

When the skit was finished, the "actors" were rewarded with resounding applause and bravos. They would then all line up in front of Mr. Kennedy in family groups—grandchildren in the front and the parents standing behind. Every voice would be lifted in a rendition of Happy Birthday.

Joan Kennedy would play classical favorites on the piano, and then Mrs. Kennedy would be coaxed into playing. She would always protest, "But I'm so rusty, let's hear more from Joan." They would all beg and applaud until she gave in, and then she would go to the piano to play all the old nostalgic songs of Ireland that Mr. Kennedy loved. They would push him close to the piano, and the children would gather around to sing along.

Teddy sang "When Irish Eyes Are Smiling" so loud that the veins in his neck stood out. Unfortunately, he usually sang off-key, but this only added to the fun, for Mrs. Kennedy often hit wrong notes. Mr. Kennedy would keep time with his foot, and if a particular jig struck his fancy, he would also tap out a rhythm with his hand.

These celebrations were strictly a family affair, and I always sat just outside the room in the hall. It was necessary that I keep an eye on Mr. Kennedy, but I wanted him to be completely surrounded by his family during these special occasions. The President, however, never stopped urging me to join in. He would drag a chair alongside mine and sit by me to watch the proceedings.

"Did you get your cake and ice cream?" he'd want to know. Or, "How about some more?" Or, "Let me get you a Coke." Or, "Are you sure you won't have a drink?"

He would be missed shortly from the group and someone would call out, "Come on, Jack, sing harmony on this one."

Later he would come back and sit down for a moment. I could tell by the way he would ease himself into the chair when his back was causing him pain, and rather than let the family know, he would slip away for a moment's ease.

It was always a late evening for Mr. Kennedy, and when it was over, his children escorted him to his room. One by one, they would kiss him, say, "Happy birthday," and leave. The President was always the last to wish him well.

"Happy birthday, Dad," he'd say, after the others had gone. "And may you have many, many more."

The President was a romantic, and when Ham Brown married Jan Tyrell, the hostess of the *Caroline*, he and the First Lady saw to it that the plane was put at their disposal. Everyone in the family was especially delighted at the marriage, and Mr. Kennedy, in particular, was ecstatic in his approval.

The President was always joshing me about my "love life," as he put it.

"When do you go out, Mrs. Dallas?" he'd ask. "Every time I see you, you're here with Dad. You should cut loose once in a while, you know, and have some fun."

"Mr. President"—I laughed—"if you can find me a staff of nurses, I promise you I'll 'cut loose.' Just find me the staff."

"I see what you mean," he'd say, "but please try to take some time off." I rarely got the chance to, but I was always touched by his concern.

John Kennedy was very special to his father, and I remember one particular incident that occurred at the Cape shortly before he left for Dallas.

All the Kennedys liked cider, and the President and his father were particularly crazy about it. There was a special orchard nearby that had a prize apple crop and bottled exceptionally good cider. When it was in season, it was Teddy's responsibility to see that his father was well supplied.

Mr. Kennedy's physical condition made us encourage him to take as much liquid as possible, which was sometimes difficult, but when his "vintage cider" was available, he would drink as much of it as we would give him.

Teddy kept close eye on his father's stock, and when it was down to the last gallon, he would see to it that another jug was put in the refrigerator.

After dinner one evening, the President and his mother came alone to visit Mr. Kennedy. They were all in a good humor, and the President was especially elated over the baby he and the First Lady were expecting within the week. It had been decided that it would be a boy, and his name would be Patrick. Mrs. Kennedy and the President filled Mr. Kennedy in on all the plans that were being made. The baby would be delivered at Otis Air Base Hospital, and in that way they could all visit, including Mr. Kennedy. He was very alert and jovial as he listened.

Knowing how much the President liked cider, I said, "Mr.

Kennedy, would you like me to serve you and the President a tall cold glass of your special drink?"

"Yaaaaa." He beamed and smacked his lips.

I hurried to the kitchen, but there was not a sign of a jug in the refrigerator. I could not understand it, for early in the afternoon there had been more than half a gallon. I made a quick check on his chart before I went back to the room, just to make sure that he had not had that much liquid intake. I shook my head in bewilderment, for I knew no one would dare touch Mr. Kennedy's cider.

When I went back to the room, I said, "I'm sorry, Mr. Kennedy, but the whole jug is missing."

He gave me a black look and grumbled. Mrs. Kennedy was also perplexed.

"Teddy knows he's to keep his father's supply up," she said. "I'll speak to him about it in the morning, Joe."

The President was in the big lounge chair, his long legs stretched out in front of him, and he burst out laughing.

"Mrs. Dallas," he said, "I'll bet you're the only woman in history to catch a President stealing."

He unwound himself from the chair and went over to his father. "Dad, I'm caught, so I'll confess. I stole your jug. It's at my house."

Mr. Kennedy rocked with glee.

"Oh, Jack"—Mrs. Kennedy chuckled—"you don't have to steal, you know."

"Well"—he grinned—"it's like watermelon. It tastes better that way, huh, Dad?"

Mr. Kennedy nodded and wiped the tears from his eyes.

"I'll tell you what, Mrs. Dallas," the President said, "you run over to my house and bring back the jug. Now that I'm caught I might as well give up the loot."

"Don't go out without a coat," Mrs. Kennedy warned. "It's bitter cold."

With that the President took his jacket off the back of the chair and dropped it across my shoulders. It was a heavy winter

Air Force jacket with the Presidential seal on it, and it was so large on me that it served as a wraparound coat.

I dashed over to his house, picked up the cider, and returned. I filled two large glasses and a pitcher of cider and took them to the President and Mr. Kennedy. They were still chuckling over his antics, especially when the President said, "If Bobby had been home, I could have blamed it on him, like we did when we were kids." He and his parents spent the rest of the evening talking about the days when the President was young, and they relived many warm, humorous moments of family history. It had been a rare evening for Mr. Kennedy, and he went to sleep that night with a full heart.

The cider incident was one of the few relaxed moments in those last weeks before November 22. The President was under a lot of pressure and often looked very worn. It was a tremendous blow to him and the First Lady when they lost their baby son, Patrick. They both took it very hard, and the President seemed to become haggard and drawn. The First Lady decided to go away for a while to take her mind off her sorrow, and when the President was at the compound during her absence, he was listless and moody.

The weather was bleak, even for November, and the last weekend he was ever home, he commented that the one bright thing on the horizon was: "Jackie's coming back."

He was to meet her in Washington. They were going to Florida for a few days to be alone together, and then to Texas.

Less than a week later John Kennedy was murdered.

When President Kennedy was shot, not only did the United States lose a President, but Caroline and John lost a loving father, the other grandchildren lost a fun-loving "Uncle Jack," Eunice lost an energetic and admiring companion, Jean and Pat a strong brother, Teddy and Bobby lost their closest friend, Mr. and Mrs. Kennedy lost a son who had filled their dreams and quiet moments, and the First Lady lost her husband.

I thought of them all that long night while I stayed with Mr. Kennedy, and I remembered President Kennedy's last words over and over. "Take care of Dad until I get back."

18

THE MORNING AFTER the assassination was full of the dull pain of an unbearable loss. We were all emotionally drained after the shocking intrusion of death, and the realization was beginning to seep into us that a vital, loving man was suddenly no more. But somehow our work went on, and my full attention was on Mr. Kennedy.

He had been told the night before that his son was dead, and he had not slept well. He was awake very early, and I wondered how he was going to face this day. It was always his custom to have a glass of juice and read the morning paper before breakfast, and I knew I had no right to break his routine, but when I brought the paper in with the dreadful news, I did not want to offer it to him. I laid it on the dresser, hoping that he would not ask for it. The headlines were horrifyingly vivid, and the reporters were having a field day speculating on the assassination and the family's reaction to it.

He drank his juice, then, much to my despair, motioned for the paper. He looked at the headlines, read for several minutes, then slowly laid his head back on the pillow and listlessly brushed the paper off his bed and onto the floor.

There had been no conversation between us. When I brought his juice, I had said good morning, but nothing more. I did not move around the room but sat quietly in a chair near his bed and waited.

I looked at the front page of the paper which had fallen faceup on the floor. Edged in black was a large picture of the President, and I stared at it, almost transfixed, for it seemed impossible that he was dead. Utterly impossible.

I looked back at Mr. Kennedy and saw that he had gripped the sheet in a tight knot. His eyes were closed, and two tears ran down his cheeks. I turned off the intercom and said, "Mr. Kennedy, I'll be outside the door if you should need me."

He did not open his eyes or make a sound. He gave a small nod of his head, as I put the rosary in his hand and left him alone.

There are moments of grief that cannot be shared and by the nature of their intensity must be suffered alone. Mr. Kennedy needed time to grieve alone. It was his right as a man and as a father.

I waited outside his door until Dora brought up his breakfast. I took it in to him, but he turned his face away.

All morning long his eyes stared straight ahead into nothingness. He took his medication in a listless way and became more withdrawn as the morning passed. He seemed emotionally frozen.

Father Cavanaugh had come to be with him; but apparently the grief and shock had been too severe for him, and he had gone to bed under doctor's orders. Ann, too, had collapsed and was under sedation. Mrs. Kennedy, on her way to and from mass, had looked in on her husband but did not disturb him.

Teddy and Eunice had not come in, but Mrs. Kennedy said they would see him after lunch.

"There's so much to do," she said, "and they're taking care of it for me. So many friends are calling, and I simply can't talk to them, so they're doing it."

I brought in his lunch, and he paid no attention to it. He simply stared straight ahead. I returned the tray to the desk in the nurses' station and sat down for a moment, trying to decide what I could do. He was a helpless man who had lost a son, but even more, he was a man yet to be comforted by his family, yet to be told anything except that his son had been murdered. Old friends were being talked to, but the father of the slain man had lain for hours with hardly a word of condolence.

I knew he could not be allowed to withdraw further into

himself, so I made a decision. I went back to his room and stood at the foot of the bed. "Mr. Kennedy," I said.

He gave no indication that he heard me.

"Mr. Kennedy, I must talk to you, and I know you can hear me."

His eyes never moved from their fixed stare.

"People all over the world are wondering what this will do to the President's father," I said. " 'Will he have a heart attack?' they're saying. 'Will he give up? Will it be too much for him?'

"Now, Mr. Kennedy, you and I both know that you're a tough Irishman who knows how to fight back, so fight, Mr. Kennedy. Fight hard.

"Come downstairs and be with the rest of your family. They need you. Bobby and the girls are in Washington with the First Lady, and Teddy and Eunice are here to stay with you and Mrs. Kennedy, so think how hard this is on them—and if you give up, so will they.

"Mrs. Kennedy needs you. Teddy and Eunice need you. So, if you have any strength left, give it now. Don't let them down, Mr. Kennedy. For their sake and yours, don't let them down.

"Mr. Kennedy?"

Slowly he raised his left hand and motioned for me. I walked around his bed and stood beside him. He reached for my hand and clamped it in a viselike grip. He raised it to his cheek and gave a long, agonizing cry.

"I'm going to wait outside, Mr. Kennedy. I'm going to turn the intercom back on so I'll be able to hear if you decide you want to go downstairs."

I took my hand away, and as I left the room, I said, "It's up to you, Mr. Kennedy. It's all up to you."

It was nearly ten minutes before he called, and it was a long wait for me. When I finally heard him, I wanted to dash back into the room, but instead, I went in normally and said, "What is it, Mr. Kennedy?"

He motioned to his wheelchair.

"Do you want to go downstairs?"

He nodded yes. He pointed to his robe and slippers and helped while I put them on him. In his paralyzed condition, dressing could be quite difficult if he decided not to cooperate, but that morning, he assisted me in every way he could.

I did not call for help to get him into his wheelchair but said, "Let's see if we can do it on our own, Mr. Kennedy."

He nodded his head firmly and made every effort he could to get himself from the bed to the chair. In just a few minutes he was ready, and when I followed the usual custom of handing him a mirror in order for him to see himself, he brushed it aside.

We went downstairs, and Teddy was in the sun room. We found him sitting on the arm of a chair, staring moodily through the window at the flag flying at half-mast. He was startled when he heard us, but he put on a wide smile and said, "Why, Dad, I didn't realize you'd be coming down today."

Mr. Kennedy gave no answer but pointed outside.

"What do you want, Dad?"

Mr. Kennedy pointed outside again and jabbed his finger for emphasis.

"Do you want to go out?" Teddy asked. "Is that it?"

Mr. Kennedy nodded his head yes and made a rambling diagram in the air with his finger, which we all knew meant that he wanted to take a ride.

"Get him ready, Mrs. Dallas," Teddy said, "and I'll go warm up the car."

I did not want to put him through the ordeal of dressing, so I merely wrapped a heavy blanket around him and put on his little beret. We waited inside the front door until Teddy drove up. He jumped out of the car and took his father's wheelchair. Without help, he bundled him in the front seat, then opened the back door for me. The car was warm, and Mr. Kennedy settled down as his son put the chair in the trunk. When Teddy got behind the wheel, he reached over and laid his hand on his father's shoulder.

"Okay, Dad, which way do you want to go?"

Mr. Kennedy first pointed us to the Hyannis Airport, and we knew that he wanted to check on the *Caroline*. When we arrived, Teddy explained why the plane was not there.

"Captain Baird will be back this afternoon, Dad, and he'll be on standby the rest of the time. I thought maybe I'd go down to Washington late tonight, if it's okay, and come right back."

His father nodded his approval and was very explicit in his directions after we left the airport. We drove to Bass River, taking all the back roads, and during the whole ride there was no talk of the assassination, nor did Teddy ever force conversation.

He spoke about the weather and of spending Christmas in Florida. He told his father about some of the boat races he'd won during the summer and mentioned that he wanted to buy the house next door to Bobby's in order to be able to live on the compound.

"The man won't sell it, Dad, and I'm sure disappointed."

They talked of other things, and we drove for more than three hours that day, going up and down the back lanes until Teddy finally slowed down the car and said, "Dad, I'm lost, you'll have to help me find my way home."

Mr. Kennedy smiled for the first time, faintly, and pointed out the directions. Through all the twists and turns he never lost us, once.

I have no way of knowing whether Teddy was lost or whether he felt merely that his father needed the reassurance that he was still the one they depended on. But Teddy did have a notoriously bad sense of direction, and helping his son find his way home helped prevent a dangerous withdrawal by Mr. Kennedy. Life would go on, and he was given a sense of his importance to his family by this simple act.

I'm sure Mr. Kennedy kept us out on such a long ride in order to tire himself, for by the time we returned to the compound he was worn out. Teddy helped me get him to his room, and he was very passive when we put him to bed. He was soon fast asleep.

While he was napping, Mrs. Kennedy sent for me. Teddy had told her about taking his father for a ride, and she said, "I know it's been hard on you, Mrs. Dallas, for none of us have been any help, but thank you for taking care of my husband.

We mustn't let him get in the shape he was in when we lost Joe. My husband is a strong man, but when something hurts him, he withdraws. He never wants to show a weakness, but this kind of pride can destroy him, as ill as he is. Getting him out today was a miracle, and I thank you for it."

While she was talking, I noticed two black mourning veils laid on her bed. One was full and quite heavy. The other rather delicate and somewhat ornate.

"I wanted to ask your opinion," she said. "You're a widow, so you might know which veil I should take to the funeral."

She gave a dry laugh and continued, "I'm wearing the same dress I've had in the closet in case Mr. Kennedy died. How ironic it is that I'll be wearing it to Jack's funeral. We never know, do we, Mrs. Dallas?"

"No," I said, "life gives us no assurances."

She fingered the sheer veil, then looked at the heavy one. "My husband and children always want me to look right, so which one do you think will be best, Mrs. Dallas?"

"Mrs. Kennedy," I said, "you're going to be very much in the public eye during all this, and if you want to shed a few tears behind the veil, then I believe if I were you, I'd wear the heavy one."

She touched first one, then the other. She looked up at me with deep pain in her eyes and sighed. "Perhaps I should take them both."

When I saw the pictures taken at the funeral, she was wearing the heavy veil, and I grieved for her in her terrible loss.

Word started coming in regarding the funeral, and an important decision had to be made. Would Mr. Kennedy attend? Eunice and Teddy were the only two of the children who had been staying at the compound, and they left only for brief flights to their brother's bier. Otherwise, they remained with their parents. The rest of the children were in Washington assisting the First Lady with the unimaginable details that confronted her. Either Eunice or Teddy went to mass with their mother, and almost hourly family prayer sessions were conducted in the home.

As the hours passed, more information regarding the funeral came in, and when we learned of the long walk involved, everyone felt that it would be impossible for Mr. Kennedy to make it. The doctors made the final decision and explained it to the family. Eunice listened, her face intent and set firm. Teddy stood by, wetting his lips and occasionally running his fingers through his hair.

We knew that with his last ounce of strength, Mr. Kennedy would make the effort to attend the funeral, if it was up to him. I believe the man would have laid down his life, willingly, in order to pay a last homage to his son, but apparently the doctors felt the risks were too great.

There was also Mrs. Kennedy to consider. She was standing strong; but her strength had a breaking point, and the added tensions and concern that she would naturally feel regarding her husband's well-being might prove too much. No one ever told Mr. Kennedy of the decision. He sensed it and accepted it.

During those terrible days, squadrons of guards were assigned to the compound, and security was increased, for no one knew whether or not a conspiracy existed. Fear mounted in us all. Was it a plot against the family, and if so, who would be next? And why?

Then like a shock wave came the horrifying news that the accused assassin, Lee Harvey Oswald, had been murdered—shot down before the eyes of the nation. When Mrs. Kennedy was told, she let out a weird, high cry of, "My God, my God."

From that time on the house existed in an eerie silence. The staff went about their chores with muted sorrow. No one cried. No one talked. Father Cavanaugh was still in bed. Eunice was a mainstay to her mother. She handled every detail. Teddy's presence was a great comfort, for he was a visible assurance that there were other sons strong enough to pick up the torch and carry it for their dead brother. Bobby was in Washington but would phone several times a day, and Pat and Jean remained at the Capitol, assuming obligations that would otherwise have fallen on their mother's shoulders.

The evening before the funeral the family left Hyannis Port for Washington. Mrs. Kennedy, Teddy, and Eunice came to tell Mr. Kennedy good-bye, and there were no displays of emotion. They informed him of the time of the funeral, in case he wanted to watch it on television, and he nodded solemnly to each one as they stooped to kiss him. I fought hard to hold back tears.

When they left, he covered his eyes with the back of his hand and remained in that frozen position until he heard the motors of the *Caroline* signal as it flew over the compound. Captain Baird always used this means to let Mr. Kennedy know that all was well.

He looked at me after the sound of the plane had disappeared into the night and motioned for me to turn down the lights. I knew then that regardless of the personal cost, he should have been going with his family, and had he been consulted as to his wishes, I know what his decision would have been.

He had not watched television since he had heard the news from Teddy and Eunice and had only briefly glanced at the paper that first morning. I suppose there was nothing more for him to know. His son was gone, and the morbid details did not concern him.

The room was blanketed in the soft shadows of twilight, and we sat together in silence.

The next morning he refused his breakfast and would not get out of bed.

We sat together, watching the clock in silence.

The hands limped the minutes away, and finally the hour came.

I took his rosary from the nightstand and laid it in his hand. I pulled my chair near his bed. His eyes were closed, and his face was granite in its composure.

"Shall I say the rosary, Mr. Kennedy?"

He nodded faintly.

So it was, while a nation watched their President laid to rest with fitting pomp and ceremony, his father prayed alone, in a still and near-deserted house.

Tragedy, like a black and evil bird of prey, hovered over the compound. Its giant wings cast a long, ominous shadow that was never again to be lifted.

Mr. Kennedy remained alone for two days after the funeral. At that time, Mrs. Kennedy returned to the compound. The next afternoon Teddy, Pat, Eunice, and Jean came home with their families for Thanksgiving, but Bobby and Ethel were not with them. Bobby had been so exhausted that he needed to get away from everything, so he went to Hobe Sound, Florida, with his family.

It was a most peculiar homecoming. One could not tell from outer appearances that a son and brother had just been buried. Life picked up where it had left off, or so it seemed. But underneath the collective calm lay evidence of shattered hope and desperate sorrow.

Teddy laughed louder than usual. Eunice was stiff and a bit more brittle in her attitude. Jean, always quiet, wore a stoic expression. Pat, who was always high-strung, became more on edge than ever. Mrs. Kennedy's shoulders seemed to sag, and the lines in her face appeared deeper.

Unexpectedly, on Thanksgiving Eve, word came that the First Lady had landed at Hyannis Airport and would be arriving shortly. Everyone, even the family, was tense, awaiting her arrival. All of us wondered what we would say or do.

Mr. Kennedy was not told, for they felt he would want to see her immediately, and everyone thought she would go straight to her own home and not join the family until Thanksgiving dinner, if then.

I was sitting with him in his room when I heard her voice coming from downstairs.

From the tone of it, she sounded aggravated and determined. I could not hear what was being said back to her, but her voice was louder than I had ever heard it.

"I'm here to see Grandpa," she almost shouted. "No, I'm not upset. I'll rest after I see Grandpa. Please, please, leave me alone. I'm fine. I just want to see Grandpa."

Mr. Kennedy heard her, of course, and he motioned for me to find out what was going on. The First Lady sounded almost panicky, as if she were trying to pull away from someone.

"She'll be here," I said, "she can handle it."

He let out a deep, quivering sigh and shook his head woefully.

I did not want to leave the room and get involved in a family situation. Obviously someone was trying to convince her that she needed rest or that she could see Mr. Kennedy tomorrow. This, I'm sure, was being done with best intentions and was in consideration for the tragedy she had just passed through, but Jacqueline Kennedy was a woman of strong conviction, and regardless of her own exhausted spirit, she was determined to see her father-in-law. She had given of herself willingly to the world during her tragedy and had fulfilled every obligation of state. Now she was home, and her first personal thought was of him.

The scene downstairs got so loud that Mr. Kennedy again motioned for me to find out what was actually happening. Reluctantly I went out into the hall and stood there, for a moment, trying to decide what I should do. Just then the First Lady came running up the stairs, alone.

The last time I had seen her was just before she had been taken to Otis Hospital for the delivery of her son Patrick. I do not know what I expected. I suppose I felt she would carry a horrible and visible mark of her tragedy—but there were no changes in her, at first glance.

When she saw me, she ran down the length of the hall.

"Mrs. Dallas," she cried. "Oh, Mrs. Dallas, I want to see Grandpa."

"He's waiting," I replied.

Her eyes seemed to be frozen, and her shoulders, usually so straight, slumped a bit—but she was still the same Jacqueline

Kennedy, and I realized that the wounds were too new for the scars to show.

In her arms she had a furled flag, and as she stood before me, her voice dropped to its familiar gentle whisper.

"May I see him?"

"Of course. I think he's been waiting for you all along."

She stopped outside his door and stood for a moment in deep thought. She cradled the flag, then embraced it. Holding it close, she said, "Mrs. Dallas, this is Grandpa's."

She handed it to me, and her hand lingeringly gave it a final caress.

"It was Jack's."

I nodded.

"I want you to keep it, and when I leave, please will you give it to him? I can't, Mrs. Dallas, but I want him to have it. It's his. Will you give it to him for me? After I'm gone."

I nodded again, for I was too choked to speak.

"And please," she said, "one more thing. Come in with me while I talk to him. We both want you."

I followed her and laid the flag on the dresser behind a stack of papers. Mr. Kennedy did not notice, for he was welcoming her with his outstretched arm. She leaned her head on his shoulder, and they embraced.

"Oh, Grandpa," she whispered. "I'm so glad that at last I'm here with you. I've been so worried. Are you all right?"

He nodded yes.

She pulled up a low footstool and sat down beside his bed. They were at eye level. She took his hand in hers and studied it, thoughtfully.

"Grandpa," she said solemnly, "Jack's gone, and nothing will ever be the same again for us. He's gone, and I want to tell you about it."

Her voice never wavered, and I shall always marvel at how so young a woman could cope with reliving and retelling—in total detail—the most harrowing experience of her life.

She began with the day they had left Washington for Texas and told him everything through to the final service and burial.

His eyes never left her face, and she never faltered. She would caress his hand or hold it tightly from time to time, and when she finished, she stood up, straightened the covers over him and kissed him good-night.

"I'm going home now, Grandpa. I'm very tired, but I'll be over tomorrow to have Thanksgiving dinner with you."

She bent over him again and closed both eyelids with kisses.

"Sleep well, dear Grandpa," she said. "Sleep well."

I had been standing near the door, almost in the same spot where I had waited while Teddy and Eunice told him his son had been killed, and as she slipped quietly past me, she took my arm and said, "Walk to the head of the stairs with me."

As she started to leave, she said, "Thank you, Mrs. Dallas. Being with us made it easier."

Then her tired eyes looked into mine, and she spoke softly, "Is Grandpa all right?"

"He's doing well."

"Did he see it on television?"

"No. He didn't want it that way."

"Did he read the papers?"

"He glanced at the front page that first morning, but that was the only time."

"Then perhaps you were right. Perhaps he was waiting to hear it from me. Oh, thank God, thank God, I came."

She brushed her hand across her forehead. "I'm so tired, so very tired," she said. "I need rest; but I'll be over in the morning, and if you will, please let me know when you've given him the flag."

"I will tonight, if he's still awake. Otherwise, in the morning. But I'll call you."

"Thank you." She smiled wanly.

I watched her as she slowly descended the stairs, her hand dragging on the banister, and I have never seen a woman who looked so alone.

I went back to Mr. Kennedy and found him awake, staring thoughtfully at the ceiling.

I brought the flag to him.

"The First Lady wants you to have your son's flag," I said. I laid it beside him, and he ran his fingers over the tightly folded triangle, in deep meditation. In a moment he motioned for me to put it on his desk. I felt his eyes following me as I laid it down gently and reverently. He leaned his head back on his pillow and closed his eyes. I sat down in a chair I always kept near the foot of his bed and waited until I knew he had fallen into a deep sleep. The night nurse took her vigil, and after one last look at Mr. Kennedy, I left for my home. Like him, I was also soon asleep.

At two in the morning my phone rang. It was the night nurse telling me to "come quick." All I got from her was that Mr. Kennedy was in a state of panic, and when I rushed to his room, I was horrified at the wild, terrified expression on his face.

I was given the following story from the nurse. According to her, Mr. Kennedy had slept soundly. Ann had gone into his room quite late saying that she was going to "tuck him in" which she often did. After a while she came back out and went to her room. The night nurse settled down at the desk in the nurses' station and kept her ear close to the intercom because we were all quite concerned about Mr. Kennedy during this period of deep grief.

A few minutes before two o'clock she was startled when she heard Mr. Kennedy screaming. She rushed in and found him lying in bed, stiff with terror, his eyes wide with fear. Draped over his bed like a blanket was the flag that had lain on his son's casket. Apparently Ann had covered him with it when she had gone in before. Later, when he awakened and in the dim glow of the night-light realized what was over him, he went to pieces.

He was so distraught that I spent most of the night attempting to calm him down.

The next morning Ann was bewildered by the distress her gesture had caused him when we told her what had happened. No one else knew about the incident and the flag hung in the living room for a while until Mrs. Kennedy had to take it down because it bothered her so much. It was put away, and several years later when it was requested for the Kennedy Museum, it seemed to be lost, and it took all of us days of searching before it was found.

Thanksgiving Day came bright and crisp and as had always been the custom, the family celebrated it together. It was dismal enough facing the loss of the President, but to have Bobby spending the holidays away from the family made it even more desolate. Apparently the death of the President and the difficult responsibilities of carrying out his office as the Attorney General had proved too much for him. It was reported there was an incident at the birthday party the First Lady gave for young John at the White House, the day after the funeral, that finally broke him down.

They were gathered around, arms draped across each other's shoulders, and someone started to sing "Heart of my Heart," one of the Kennedy favorites. Bobby fled from the room, completely shattered, and it was decided, for his own good, that he needed a few days away to himself.

Many people, even those closely associated with the family, found it impossible to rationalize their apparent lack of sorrow at the President's death. There was a great deal of criticism by the staff when they all gathered on the front lawn and played a boisterous game of touch football after Thanksgiving dinner. Mrs. Kennedy took her usual walk, and it was almost as if nothing had happened.

The next morning I met the governess of Teddy's children as she was driving off the compound. I waved at her, for she was always a pleasant, friendly woman who seemed extremely proficient in her position. She stopped her car, and in contrast with her usual calm exterior, her face was tense.

"This is good-bye, Mrs. Dallas. I'm leaving."

"What?"

"I've quit the Senator."

"I don't believe it. Why?"

Her voice livid with anger she said, "Enough is enough. The President was just buried, Mrs. Dallas, and the Senator had the gall to have a gang of so-called friends in last night. I never saw anything like it. They stayed up all night, laughing and drinking. They actually made a game of seeing who could tell the most outlandish stories about the President and the family. It was the most disgusting spectacle I've ever witnessed, and I'll not work another day for that heartless man."

"Oh, please," I said, hoping to soothe her, "the Senator wasn't being heartless. He was having his own wake for his brother. Haven't you ever heard of an Irish wake?"

"I don't care what you call it. I've resigned, and I never intend to work another day for such people. I let him know that I thought he was thoroughly disgusting."

She drove off incensed. I am Irish and was able to understand what Teddy was doing. However, I admit I understood the feelings of the governess because I had also been taken aback a bit when I watched them throw themselves into the game of touch football with such vigor and good humor as if nothing had happened.

There is no doubt that we Irish are a mysterious and peculiar people. Perhaps the only way to endure an unbearable loss is to find some kind of mirth.

Such was the case on Thanksgiving weekend when Cardinal Cushing called and said he would be up for a visit with his old friend, Joe. When he arrived at the house, Ann and Mrs. Kennedy were in Mr. Kennedy's room, and we could hear the cardinal's booming voice carrying all the way up from the living room.

"I've come," he roared, "to repeat the eulogy for Joe. I'm redoing it in its entirety."

"Oh, Lord, no," Mrs. Kennedy shrieked as she scampered from the room. "Tell him I'm not doing well. Tell him I'm in my room. Tell him anything."

Ann, laughing, was hot on her aunt's heels. "Rita, it's all yours."

I looked at Mr. Kennedy, and he was shaking the bed, laughing.

"We're hooked," I said. "Lord help us, we're hooked."

Just then the cardinal burst into the room. "Joe," he shouted with arms outstretched, "Joe! Joe! Joe! I've come."

Mr. Kennedy raised his hand in a warm wave, trying hard to keep his lips from twitching.

"Joe, the eulogy was magnificent. Absolutely magnificent."

Everyone in the family idolized the cardinal, for he was a dear man with a charming grace and humor, but he had a voice that would defy description, and once heard, it could never be forgotten.

Without any preliminary, he took out a sheaf of papers, cleared his throat like a clap of thunder, and with all the majesty and volume that he had conjured at the services in Washington, he roared out the eulogy word for word.

I was grateful that Mr. Kennedy kept his eyes pasted to the ceiling through the oratory, for had he looked at me, I know I would have shamed my Catholic heritage forever by spouting laughter all over the good cardinal's eulogy.

Mr. Kennedy kept his mouth pressed in a tight, serious line, but I could see the edges twitching as he fought to control himself.

Finally, the cardinal finished. He folded up his papers elegantly and boomed, "Well, Joe, didn't I tell you it was magnificent?"

Mr. Kennedy could no longer control himself and burst out laughing.

Fortunately the cardinal took it as "one of Joe's situations," and was not hurt or upset.

I, however, ducked out of the room as the cardinal was shouting, "Laughter is good for the soul, dear Joe. Indeed, yes."

I saw Mrs. Kennedy peeking around her bedroom door, and she crooked her finger, motioning for me.

"He's finished?" she whispered.

I had held back my laughter so long that my eyes were watering.

"Yes," I sputtered.

"Well, then," she said, grandly opening the door, "I must take this opportunity to welcome the cardinal."

She started to her husband's room, then stopped and looked over her shoulder. "You're really sure he's finished, Mrs. Dallas?"

I nodded just as Ann tiptoed down the hall.

"Is it over?"

We both took a fit of laughing. "Poor Uncle Joe," she said, wiping her eyes.

"Poor Uncle Joe, my eye. Poor Uncle Joe and Rita Dallas. You two really left us flat."

The cardinal was one of Mr. Kennedy's dearest friends, so I felt my laughter was venial. It was, however, days before I could get the picture of Ann and Mrs. Kennedy scampering out of the room and the dear cardinal, oblivious to everything and everyone, leaning over Mr. Kennedy, reenacting the entire eulogy at the top of his voice.

His visit was good medicine for Mr. Kennedy, and the fact that he was able to respond to humor gave me assurance that he would be able to cope with his great loss. The cardinal was correct when he had said, "Laughter is good for the soul."

A few days later Mr. Kennedy was able to make the flight to Palm Beach for the winter season without incident, and it was not until Ham Brown came to say good-bye that he fell back into a blue and desolate mood.

With the President's death, the government could no longer provide an agent as his bodyguard, so Ham was being reassigned. We all got the full impact after he left. The direct phone line to the White House was removed, and the White House trailer was hauled away. The Presidential flag was taken down, and the *Honey Fitz* sailed out of the blue Florida waters. As each day passed, we became more acutely aware that the Kennedys were no longer the First Family.

At that time Jacqueline Kennedy made a permanent decision about her children, and that was to guard their right to privacy with a fierce and determined fervor. Had she not done this, I doubt if Caroline could have coped with life as well as she has.

The widow did not attempt to compensate her daughter's loss in any superficial way, and she never grew lax in her training and discipline. She succeeded in providing her daughter and her son with a life they could accept without interference, and today when I read that she is still vigilant and constant in her determination to keep them from the limelight, I know that only a woman with her inner strength could have waged such a formidable battle.

Caroline was shattered by her father's murder, and she became a pitiful little girl in her grief. She seemed to age before our eyes. She stayed to herself, lost in thought, and her eyes, once so pert and dancing, were listless and stared into a bleak nothingness.

Children seldom clench their fists, but her tiny hands were always knotted. She toyed with her food, and the special desserts that had always tempted her were pushed away.

This child was at a crucial age, for she was old enough to realize what had happened to her father. But like the rest of us, she could not rationalize why anyone would have wanted to destroy him.

19

FOR THE NEXT TWO and a half years Robert Kennedy became the central focus of strength and hope for the family. Bobby gave of himself with extraordinary intensity and generosity. Despite his own grief and loneliness, he radiated an inner strength that I have never seen before in any other man. Bobby Kennedy has always been controversial, but I saw him as a man of enormous personal integrity and honesty.

Much has been said about his unique devotion to Jacqueline Kennedy, but none of us who were close to the family at this time ever felt his actions were exaggerated or strained. Whatever he did, he did as a natural instinct. He was there when she needed him, but he never pushed his protectiveness on her. The fact that she turned to him was enough, and to my knowledge he never let her down.

Shortly after the assassination, a television program was scheduled to be carried via worldwide satellite. I believe this was the premiere telecast via satellite, and the First Lady was offered this opportunity to acknowledge her gratitude to people around the globe for the worldwide response of deep concern at the death of her husband.

She made a specific request for Bobby to appear with her, which, of course, was accepted by the producer. Charles Collingwood was selected as the narrator, and although the appearance was to be brief, a great deal of planning went into the project. The First Lady chose not to broadcast from her own home, but from Mr. and Mrs. Kennedy's living room, instead.

The TV crew arrived three or four days in advance, and the night before the program, Mrs. Kennedy's secretary and I had dinner with Charles Collingwood and the producer. They peppered me with questions about Mr. Kennedy, some of which I felt I could not answer. Apparently they had been warned of his unstable behavior patterns, and they suggested that I might be able to keep him away from the living room during the setup and the telecast.

There was no possible way for me to agree to such a request, and I reminded them that they were using his home and also that if the First Lady was "willing" to chance his being unruly, then no one else had any reason to worry about it.

The next afternoon workmen and equipment began to arrive at the house by the van loads. Technicians swarmed over the estate, running in and out, shouting orders, stretching special lines. Remote trailers sat bumper to bumper in the drive and parking lot, and the house was so noisy that even Mr. Kennedy, who was upstairs in his private quarters, could not help hearing the commotion. He could see strange men running up and down the hall, carrying rolls of electrical wiring over their shoulders, and he knew something out of the ordinary was going on in his house. As I expected, he decided to find out what it was. He threw his leg over the side of the bed and pointed emphatically to the elevator. I could tell by the fire in his eyes that he was boiling mad, so I took it upon myself, since no one else had, to explain to him what was happening. He listened with a deep frown covering his face until I said, "I'll take you downstairs anytime you want to go, Mr. Kennedy, but please don't get angry. Remember, the First Lady and Bobby want it done this way, so don't spoil it for them."

He pulled his mouth down and scratched his chin thoughtfully, and I held my breath until he looked up and nodded his head briskly. He was all business, and I knew, regardless of the invasion that was going on in his house, he would remain calm and agreeable. It was for his son's widow, and that made the difference.

When we got off the elevator, we had to pick our way

through the hall, dodging workmen and equipment. No one paid any attention to us. When I spotted Mr. Collingwood and the producer in the sun room, I said, "Those are the men in charge, Mr. Kennedy. The man with Mr. Collingwood is the producer of the show. Would you like to meet them?"

He nodded, but his eyes were busy taking in the hordes of people practically falling all over each other in their activity. I crossed to the sun room and told the producer that Mr. Kennedy wanted to meet him. He was aghast.

"Now, don't get upset," I said, "he's fine. If you'll just explain to him what's going on, he won't cause any trouble."

"You're sure? He could blow this thing wide open, you know."

"He'll be all right just so long as you explain everything to him."

"If you say so, Mrs. Dallas," he agreed, with reservation.

"I'll try to understand what he wants to know. If he asks a question, just make sure you explain everything, and remember, this is his house and he is Joseph P. Kennedy."

When I introduced the producer and Mr. Collingwood, they were charming. They greeted him with great dignity, calling him Ambassador Kennedy. As they explained the show, I wheeled him all over the downstairs, bumping his chair across the thick cables that were strung everywhere, but he didn't seem to mind. He wanted to go into the living room, and the producer showed him where the First Lady and Bobby would sit during the telecast. The producer had the massive television cameras maneuvered around for his examination, he pointed out the wattage of all the lights, and then told him that this program would be picked up by satellite and beamed around the world. He won Mr. Kennedy over completely when he said, "Your son's devotion to the space program has made this kind of televising possible, Ambassador."

With that, Mr. Kennedy waved his hand in great dignity and signaled that I could return him upstairs.

That night, a short time before the show, Bobby sent word that he would like me to be downstairs during the program.

Everyone in the family was very keyed up, and they were afraid Jackie would faint. I left Mr. Kennedy with the backup nurse, for he was in good spirits and smiling broadly as I left. I decided I would not go into the living room, so I picked a spot on the main stairway and sat there. I was in a position to hear the nurse if Mr. Kennedy happened to need me, and I could also see the First Lady and Bobby on the couch. If she fainted, as everyone was afraid she would, I could get to her.

Bobby and the family were waiting for her in the hall when she came in. She looked around at the mass of equipment and technicians, and her eyes got very large. Bobby did not make a dash; he simply smiled and walked easily toward her. She clung to his hand while he guided her past the rest of the family, pointing out the cables on the floor carefully, and eased her into the living room.

She nodded silently to the producer and Mr. Collingwood. Still clinging to Bobby's hand, she followed him to the couch, and they took their last-minute cues from the producer.

With her first words, her voice trembled, ever so slightly. The cameras were on her face, and Bobby quickly moved in closer and rested his hand on hers.

She spoke about the assassination and expressed her gratitude to everyone who had extended her their sympathy and prayers.

When it was over, she stood up, thanked the producer and Mr. Collingwood, and made a special point of acknowledging every workman and technician.

She came out to the hall and saw me sitting on the stairway. "Mrs. Dallas"—she smiled—"thank you for being around. Only I'm so glad I didn't need you."

She was a beautiful young woman, held in high esteem by the world. Everyone adored her in her grief. She epitomized the sorrow of every American and everyone around the world who had loved and admired her husband. I watched her go to each member of the family to thank them for their support. Finally, she grasped Bobby's hands and kissed his cheek, and my eyes filled with tears of admiration. But somehow I could not help wondering what would happen when this extraordinary woman would finally lay aside her widow's weeds and seek another life for herself.

"What then?" I wondered. "What then?" When the answer finally came and the public that had worshiped her turned against her, I wept.

Since the family were all together for that occasion, a special mass was held at home the next evening. Eunice's son Bobby Shriver was only a young boy at the time, but he was selected to assist Teddy as altar boy.

The altar was set up on the piano, and I was kneeling where I could look in the living room and keep a watch on Mr. Kennedy.

It was a sorrowful gathering. The First Lady was there with her sister, Lee Radziwill, and everyone was very tense.

As the mass began, I noticed that young Bobby was getting quite pale. He was serving beautifully with his uncle, but he suddenly began to tremble. I slipped over to the edge of the living room and motioned for him to come to me. Teddy saw what was happening and nodded to the boy that it was all right to leave. He managed to tiptoe out of the room, but once in the hall, he slumped against the wall, and I knew he was on the verge of fainting.

"What's wrong, Bobby?"

"I feel dizzy. I think I'm going to be sick."

I put my arm around his shoulder and whispered, "Come on upstairs with me and lie down for a moment."

His eyes were glassy, but he mumbled, "Will it be okay for me to leave, Mrs. Dallas?"

"Of course," I whispered in his ear and held him close. We tiptoed up the stairs, and I took him to one of the small bedrooms where he stretched out on the bed. I wiped his face with a cool cloth and then covered his eyes with it. My son had been an altar boy, and I remembered his first experience in serving mass. He had suffered a similar reaction, so I felt I knew what was troubling Eunice's boy. I waited until he seemed calmer and then I asked, "Were you nervous, Bobby?"

"Oh, I don't know," he said weakly.

I took his hand in mine. "Well, it's understandable if you were, what with the priest at the altar and everyone watching you . Did you forget what you were supposed to do?"

He looked out from under the cloth at me. "Oh, no, Mrs. Dallas, it wasn't that. It was just that while I was serving, I realized that I was so close to God. That's what frightened me. It's a scary feeling, Mrs. Dallas."

I sat quietly for a moment, unable to speak.

Then he talked for a few more minutes about his feelings, and finally I said, "We're not supposed to be afraid of God, Bobby. Why don't you show Him your love by getting up and going back downstairs and finish serving?"

At first he was a little reluctant.

"Do I have to, Mrs. Dallas?"

"No, you don't have to, but don't you think you should?"

He let out a long sigh, stood up, and said hesitantly, "Well, okay, but you've got to go with me."

"I'll go as far as I can, but the rest is up to you."

The two of us walked back down the stairs, and as he started into the living room, he held out his hand. "Thank you, Mrs. Dallas," he said, shaking mine. As I watched him slip away and take his place beside his uncle, I felt a great wave of admiration for the young boy.

A day or so after this incident, Mr. Kennedy's man from the New York office came to the house with some papers for Mrs. Kennedy to sign. Late in the afternoon she called me to her room and said "I'd like you to witness my will."

Her voice was very tight and unnatural.

"I've named Bobby now as my executor," she said flatly. "It was Jack, until he died."

I quickly signed the papers, and as she gathered them up, she said, "So many details. So many cold, impersonal details."

Later I thought of all the responsibility Bobby had to face.

It seemed too much for one man, and yet there was a calmness about him that made one wonder from what rare fiber he was made. Teddy was a great emotional solace to his parents, but Bobby was the one who welded the pieces back together.

It was a slow process, and even after the wound began to close, there were the scars. Mrs. Kennedy and the First Lady were very much alike in the way they maintained their control and dignity despite the extraordinary pain of their loss as mother and wife. Both had suffered their grief under a ruthless, public limelight, and they had kept their dignity intact; but it had taken a severe personal toll.

I recall the day the First Lady returned from the Norfolk Shipyards after her daughter, Caroline, had christened the *John Fitzgerald Kennedy*. Once again she visited Mr. Kennedy to give him a lengthy and personal account of the ceremony, and it was evident, especially to him, that she was under a heavy strain. When the visit was over, I walked out with her, and she said, "Mrs. Dallas, I've reached the point where I cannot go through any more public functions . . . and it's the last time I will ever subject my children to them. Today was heartbreaking for both of us, and I can't keep it up."

"Why don't you try and get away by yourself for a while?" I said. "Shake off some of these memories. Be alone."

"Oh, how I wish I could, Mrs. Dallas." She sighed. "But life is too complicated for that now. Everything is so exaggerated. I wonder if I'll ever again know the security of privacy."

I watched from the upstairs window as she walked slowly to her home. It was a clear, bright day, but I understood the shadows she had to endure, for a few paces behind her the Secret Service man matched her steps.

She turned and gave a weary nod to him as she went inside and he took up his solitary post at her door.

I saw them both as impersonal prisoners, bound together by invisible chains, for a bodyguard is an ever-present reminder that danger, even death, is a constant companion.

20

AFTER THE ASSASSINATION we became acutely attuned to potential dangers, and I quickly developed the nervous habit of taking secret but sweeping glances around me out of the corner of my eye.

Early one afternoon (shortly after the arrival at Palm Beach), I needed to phone the pharmacist in order to go over Mr. Kennedy's supply of medicine. As was their custom after lunch, Mr. Kennedy was napping, and his wife had gone to her bedroom to rest. The domestic staff had settled down for their habitual afternoon break, so not wanting to disturb anyone, I decided to do my telephoning from the kitchen.

I took a shortcut and used the back stairs or "the maids' stairway," as Mrs. Kennedy called it. This stairway stopped at a small landing by the kitchen, and from it there were four or five steps that led in another direction that opened onto the patio. The patio was attached to the long arbored walk that led to the front door.

I was being very quiet, hoping not to disturb anyone's afternoon siesta, and was just dialing the phone when a cold sense of "something's wrong" swept over me. A moment later out of the corner of my eye, I saw a man dash across the patio.

I was frozen in my tracks. He opened the door, and I watched as he actually seemed to slink up the few steps of the landing. I was terrified, and call it woman's intuition if you will, but I sensed danger.

He spotted me in the kitchen, and we both stared at each

other for a moment. Then he made a dash through the house. I ran after him, shouting, "Who are you? What do you want?"

He stopped abruptly, turned to face me, and said in a completely calm voice, "Oh, I'm the TV repairman. I've been called to pick up a set."

I knew that the televisions were always serviced ahead of our arrival, both at Palm Beach and Hyannis Port, for Mr. Kennedy would not tolerate a malfunctioning set. He was a fanatic about it, for his family was constantly in the news, and he never wanted to miss a report about them.

The man was lying. I knew that every set was working perfectly. There was another reason I knew he was lying. Whenever a service call had to be made, the staff was notified, for nothing was ever removed from the house. The broken appliance was taken to a spare room and repaired on the premises. This had been enforced for security reasons when the President was alive, for with him constantly in and out of the house, every precaution was taken. There was always the danger that a bomb could be planted.

I also knew all the repairmen the family used, and this man was not one of them. And even more important, I saw that he had no service case and no uniform. He was wearing a white shirt without any trade insignia and a pair of black sport slacks. He offered no identification and to my knowledge had not rung the bell to gain admission to the house.

I knew he was an intruder, and even though I was terrified as we stood facing each other, perhaps my years of nurses' training had taught me to remain calm in an emergency. Still and all, I had no idea what to do. I had felt very insecure since the Secret Service men had left. Our new security force was made up of local men from the police force who were doing the job on the side. I knew they were good men, but I had no idea how they would react to a crisis. With my mind flashing all these thoughts, I knew I had to do something.

I decided to act nonchalant with him. "Stay here," I said, hoping he did not notice the tremor in my voice. "I'll check and see what set needs repairing."

He shrugged, and I dashed from the kitchen, ran through the hall, and threw open the front door. I looked in all directions for a guard. One had been assigned to cover the front part of the grounds but was nowhere in sight, so I ran the length of the house and finally found him in the parking lot sitting in his car, eating a sandwich. Mrs. Kennedy did not want the men to eat in the maids' dining room, so they either had to bring their lunch or leave the premises and eat at the drugstore. If they left, that meant the house and grounds would not be covered.

I rushed over to his car and told him what had happened. Together we headed back to the house.

The kitchen was empty.

"He's gone!" I said in panic. "Oh, good heavens!"

I pointed the guard in one direction and started in the other. We covered the downstairs quickly and met back in the kitchen. He followed me as I dashed up the back stairs. Halfway up I stopped and thought, *What am I doing? He's the one who should be going first.* I stood aside and motioned for him to go ahead of me. When we reached the second floor, I was frantic. Again, call it intuition, but I felt he was nearby.

We turned into the main hall and saw him at the fuse box with the door of it opened. The policeman drew his gun and shouted, "Freeze," which he did.

Ann heard the commotion and came tearing out of her room. She saw the guard holding the man at gunpoint and ran back, slamming the door. I heard her calling me from behind it. Through it I told her what had happened, and she said, "I'll call Bobby."

The guard had the man handcuffed and was shoving him down the stairs, but the intruder was in no way ruffled.

Bobby's reaction to Ann's call had immediate results, and within minutes police cars surrounded the property. They arrived without sirens, so as not to alarm either the household or the neighbors. They took the intruder outside and stood him in the middle of the parking lot. His ankles were then manacled, and a ring of policemen encircled him.

The district director of the Secret Service sent a division of agents, and when they arrived, they took over and went into action.

I was told to identify the man, and as they walked me across the lot, the circle of guards parted, and we stood face to face again. He was completely calm.

"Is this the man you saw entering the house?" the agent asked.

"This is the man I saw *in* the house," I corrected.

"Was he carrying a bag or suitcase or package of any kind?"

"No."

"Were his hands in his pockets?"

"No, they were swinging free. When I first saw him, he was moving fast and he was swinging both arms freely."

"That's all, Mrs. Dallas, and thank you."

I was escorted back to the house, and the ring of guards immediately swallowed up the intruder. I was told to remain indoors until I received further instructions.

"Stay close to Mr. Kennedy," the agent ordered. "Under no circumstances are you to leave him."

I returned to my patient and watched from the bedroom window which offered me a good view of the parking area.

The intruder stood motionless, as if he were planted to the cement. I was perplexed by his remote attitude. He had accepted the arrest without any kind of reaction. He merely dropped his hands from the fuse box and voluntarily lifted them above his head.

I knew that if he had been there on bona fide business, his whole attitude would have been different. Any normal citizen would first of all be upset at being arrested. He was not. He should have protested or identified himself. He should have said, "Call my boss." Or, "I live at such and such a street." Or, "My name is so-and-so." Anything. But to my knowledge he said absolutely nothing to the arresting officer. When I identified him, there was no reaction in his eyes. He was the calmest man I have ever seen, and I knew this was not right.

Mr. and Mrs. Kennedy napped through all the excitement, but when Mrs. Kennedy was awake, she was informed of the incident. Again she reverted to habit and went ahead with her routine of golf. The chauffeur drove her through the squad cars, and she sat in the back seat with her eyes straight ahead. From the upstairs window, I noticed an unmarked car trailing close behind hers.

A few moments later an agent came to Mr. Kennedy's room, and I was told to prepare to take him for a ride.

"The bomb squad from Miami will be here any minute," he said, "and a thorough search of the house and grounds will be made. The Ambassador's wife thinks it best that he not be told about all this, so we'll take him for a ride until it's all clear."

Mr. Kennedy was awake and quite agreeable to a jaunt. Ann wanted to see the "goings-on," so an agent drove Mr. Kennedy's car.

"How will we know when to bring him back?" I whispered.

"I'll know," he said. "Don't worry about it."

They had removed the intruder, and as we drove through the gate, I could not see any police cars; but the street was packed with what I knew were unmarked Secret Service vehicles.

I tried not to show any undue tension to Mr. Kennedy, and I was relieved when I looked through the back window and saw a car tailgating ours. I knew it would be equipped with a two-way radio and that some prearranged signal had been set up with our driver to let him know when the all-clear was issued.

Mr. Kennedy loved to ride, but we were out so long that he became restless. He kept laying his hand on the steering wheel, indicating that he wanted to return home. The agent was an expert at maneuvering. Mr. Kennedy would point right, and he would turn left, with an immediate, "I'm sorry, sir."

Mr. Kennedy was losing patience, and I dreaded the impending scene, but not a moment too soon the agent was apparently given an all-clear from the backup car, for he suddenly picked up speed and followed Mr. Kennedy's directions perfectly all the way back to the house.

Mr. Kennedy was quite aggravated and glared at the agent as he was helped from the car. I looked around and there was no evidence to indicate that things were not normal, but that evening, as I was leaving for my own home, I asked one of the high-ranking guards about the intruder. I received a brief answer. "He has connections in Dallas."

My stomach turned to lead. Strangely enough, not in fear of my own safety, but for the aging parents who had already suffered through so much.

"How do you know?" I asked.

"I've already said too much," he replied, "but you were involved, so I'll stick my neck out and tell you that he let something slip."

I was not tempted to pursue with further questions, but instead of going home, I went back to the house. I was heartsick. I had left Mr. Kennedy in the library, and when I went in, he was sitting in his lounge chair, his good leg stretched out in front of him, hunched forward absorbed in a television news program.

I sat on the couch and studied his face. Overnight, almost, faint lines had become deep creases, and there was a veiled look in his eyes. They had lost their sparkle. He drummed on the arm of the chair with his good fingers, beating out a nervous, staccato rhythm.

Mrs. Kennedy came by and, without interrupting her husband's viewing, sat down and watched through to the end of the program. When it was over, he motioned for me to turn off the set. Mrs. Kennedy chatted with him about her golf score and mentioned a few of the people she had met at the club. She asked how he was feeling, and he nodded at her and smiled.

She turned to me and said, "Nurse, I think it would be nice if we had a glass of iced tea. Won't you see to it for us?"

It was odd hearing her call me "nurse," but from the time she had returned from the funeral, she had never addressed me by my name. It was as though she could not bring herself to speak the word, and several months passed before I again became "Mrs. Dallas."

Later that same week I asked one of the local guards if he knew what had happened to the intruder. The incident had not been reported by the press, nor had any correspondents tried to contact the staff. He answered me in a strange way.

"I don't know, Mrs. Dallas. One day they've got him in jail. The next day he's gone, just like that. Nobody's talking."

That was the last I heard about the man. Someone had clamped on a lid and no one would ever be able to pry it off.

I, like most every other American, still have deep questions about the assassination, and I have no information to challenge the final assumption issued by the Warren Commission, except that I have never rested easy within my soul.

The events that surrounded the assassination will always plague the minds of everyone, but even those of us close to the Kennedy household never witnessed a discussion regarding it. There was no open speculation either among the domestic staff, the professional personnel, or any members of the family. There was, however, an apparent dread in everyone, a jumpy nervousness. A feeling of apprehension and unrest.

Life, of course, went on. People came and went, but we lived in a different world.

A few days after the intruder, Mrs. Kennedy called me to her room and said, "Nurse, I want to ask a favor of you."

"Of course, Mrs. Kennedy."

"Well"—she hesitated—"I don't want you to think I'm afraid or even worried about anything. It's nothing like that. But I'm wondering if you will stand at the window and watch me when I go for my swims. I don't want to change my habits, and I do enjoy the ocean. But if I should disappear, I would want my children to know what happened to me."

She continued with a weak, embarrassed laugh and raised her shoulders in a helpless gesture. "If I disappeared, they'd wonder, you know, so if you'd just watch when I'm out, I'll feel safer . . . for their sakes. Now mind you, I'm not worried. It's just . . . well. . . ."

I wanted to help her, but I knew I could not give her the feeling of assurance that she was apparently seeking.

"Mrs. Kennedy," I said, "I don't think I'm the best one for

the job, for if your husband should need me, I would have to take care of him."

Her shoulders drooped. "You're right, of course," she said.

I noticed, from then on, that either her secretary or her chauffeur stood discreetly at the seawall and watched while she swam.

It seemed she sensed that a chain of tragedy had begun and she was helpless against it. I believe she sincerely felt that fate would strike out against her, and that if it did, she wanted no mystery for her children to unravel.

She never complained or allowed herself to be drawn into an open circle of grief, but all of us knew how deep her suffering was. Night after night, she could be heard pacing back and forth in her room, deep into the wee hours of the morning.

Often she would spend the night in the attic, and we could hear her overhead, moving things around. When morning came, she would always say, "If I disturbed anyone last night, I was just in the attic looking for some of the money my husband is supposed to have."

We knew better, of course, for the attic was stacked with precious memories of her children's infancy and youth. When sleep would not come, she would seek the tokens of the past to cling to for stability.

Pat spent a great deal of time at the Palm Beach house that season and she grew critically haggard. She suffered from insomnia, and her long sleepless nights left her drained with exhaustion.

Christmas arrived solemnly, and a private mass was offered at the house on Christmas Eve, with Teddy serving as altar boy.

Everyone came with the children, and the tree was an extravaganza that touched the ceiling.

It was a sad-happy celebration with packages being opened and ribbons strewn through the house, but during the mass, every thought turned to the man who was so critically missing.

Bright and early the next morning, Christmas Day, Mrs. Kennedy issued orders to get the tree down.

"Do it now," she said. "I don't want to see it when I get back from mass."

It was a huge thing, and it would have taken hours to untrim it, so there was only one thing to do. The staff carried it outside, still trimmed, and hid it on the laundry patio. The lights and ornaments were later taken down, but when Mrs. Kennedy returned that morning, the living room was back to normal.

We saw very little of Bobby during the first part of December, but when he did come around, I was shattered by his appearance. If ever a man suffered, it was he. Not only was he burdened by his brother's murder, but he was laboring under a hostile change of administrators.

There was no love between himself and the new President, and it became apparent to everyone that President Johnson did not want a Kennedy, especially one named Robert, to remain as a member of his Cabinet.

President Johnson did, however, make a personal visit to Mr. Kennedy in order to express his sympathy, and the day he came proved difficult for everyone.

Mr. Kennedy was always fastidious about his appearance and never received a guest unless he was groomed to the hilt. That day, not only would he not get dressed, but he would not get out of bed or change from the pajamas he had slept in. Neither would he allow us to do so much as comb his hair.

President Johnson arrived and was escorted in by Mrs. Kennedy. He was very sympathetic and polite, but Mr. Kennedy would not so much as look at him.

Mrs. Kennedy was thoroughly embarrassed, not only by her husband's behavior, but by his obvious snub. She tried in vain to make conversation, but it was obvious to everyone that Mr. Kennedy would have no part of it.

In just a few minutes, President Johnson departed, and no sooner was he out of the house than Mr. Kennedy was ready to get up. He was quite a man, this patriarch, and even though he was lying flat on his back, his old "to hell with you" attitude was still intact. He had been like a Roman emperor that day.

It was thumbs up or thumbs down. Even though he could not speak a word, he left no doubt as to how he felt.

He was aware of the open rift between President Johnson and his son, and he would not feign friendliness when he was filled with such deep resentment.

Before Christmas, Bobby had made a public decision that rocked his entire family. He picked the remote and unscaled mountain in the middle of the Canadian Yukon Territory named after his brother and announced that he intended to climb it in order to establish it as a living monument. Bobby had never done any mountain climbing before, but he took on the challenge of this high, rugged, ice-covered tower with a violent ferocity and a wild-eyed, hell-bent determination.

Mr. Kennedy would watch the running reports of his son's climb on television and shout, "Naaaaa, naaaaa, naaaaa," at the top of his voice. He would shake his fist at the set and scream, or if he found a picture in the paper of Bobby in his mountain gear, he would angrily grind it into a ball and throw it across the room.

He was uncontrollable, and when word came that Bobby had finally reached the top of the mountain, he screamed all the louder. Nothing anyone would say would comfort or console him.

Finally, Bobby came home, and his eyes, usually so blue and brilliant, were pale in their weariness. He was an exhausted but proud man. He knew his father was angry with him, but I doubt if he was prepared for the onslaught he received.

Mr. Kennedy was actually violent when he saw his son. He threw anything near him and screamed until he was hoarse, but the saddest thing of all was that he would not look at his son.

Bobby had brought back a framed picture taken from the top of the mountain and had also had a piece of the rock from it embedded in lucite for his father, but Mr. Kennedy would not accept it. He shouted his son out of the room.

Bobby was visibly shaken. We stood outside in the hall, and he took both my hands in his.

"Mrs. Dallas," he said, "why can't Dad understand? I had to do it. I had to."

"I know," I replied. "And he'll understand in time. I think he's still petrified with the thought that something might have happened to you, and he probably feels you were risking your life for nothing."

He went away with his head tucked deep in his shoulders, saying, almost to himself, "I had to climb it. I had to."

Mr. Kennedy would not give in. Over and over Bobby tried to talk to him, but he'd turn his face away and roar until his son left the room. I saw it was destroying Bobby. Every day he looked more haggard.

After he had had a terribly disturbing visit with his father, he said, "Mrs. Dallas, it's useless. I might as well go home."

"Wait," I urged, "give him a chance. Don't go yet."

Bobby slumped down in a chair and buried his face in his hands, and I knew something had to give. I also knew that it had to be Mr. Kennedy. I went back to his room, clicked off the intercom, and said, "I want to have a private talk with you, Mr. Kennedy."

I think he knew what was coming, for he propped himself up on his elbow and glared at me.

"Mr. Kennedy," I began, "I don't know why you're treating Bobby as you are, and I am very disappointed by what you're doing. I've never known you to be unfair before, but you are now."

He flopped back on the bed and grumbled.

"I don't care what you say. Bobby doesn't deserve this kind of treatment from you, of all people. Don't you realize what he was doing when he climbed the mountain? What he was saying?"

He looked at me with a curious frown.

"He chose the tallest peak he could find, one that was rugged and steep, that had never been conquered, and he conquered it, Mr. Kennedy. He climbed it because it was named after his brother. Kennedy Mountain towers above all the others, and what do you think his thoughts were when he got to the top?

He scaled cliffs that were covered with ice, that went straight up, Mr. Kennedy, and he did it to touch the clouds. Don't you realize how close he was to his brother at that moment? He was as close to heaven as his human body could get him.

"Can't you see him standing there, slashed by the wind, covered with cuts and bruises? Can't you hear him when he said, 'This is my brother's mountain'? And when he planted the black mourning flag, can't you read the thoughts he must have had? Can't you hear him thinking, 'I did it, Jack, and it's all yours'?

"Other people are going to build monuments to your son. They'll name schools after him and libraries and highways, but Bobby was the first to give him a monument, and no one can ever match what he did.

"He gave of himself.

"He couldn't wait for committees to be formed, and blueprints to be drawn up, or masons to lay stone. He let the greatest architect of all build his brother's monument, and none other can ever compare to it. It was God-given.

"And all you can do is scream at him and turn your face away."

I clicked on the intercom and left the room.

In a few minutes I heard him and went back in. Bobby's rock and picture had been put in a desk drawer, and Mr. Kennedy pointed to it. Without saying a word, I took them out.

"Where do you want them, Mr. Kennedy?"

He pointed to the top of his television, and after I had set them there to suit him, he motioned for me to come to him. He took my hand and, in a gesture that conveyed everything, pressed it to his cheek.

I knew I was about to cry, so I cuffed him lightly and said, "Oh, come now, here we are acting like a couple of sentimental Irishmen."

He grinned and waved me out of the room. I found Bobby sitting glumly in the library.

"Why don't you try one more time to talk to your father? One more time."

He pulled himself out of the chair and gave a long sigh. "It's just about to get me down, Mrs. Dallas, but if you think I should, all right."

"Give it another try."

He raised his shoulders and let them drop heavily. "Okay, Mrs. Dallas."

I was at the nurses' station when he came bouncing out of his father's room. His face was aglow.

"He's got my picture and rock on the television, Mrs. Dallas. My God, he understands. All of a sudden, he understands."

He stopped and stared at me intently. He had the same piercing eyes as his father. They could bore right through you.

"Did he tell you to put them on the television?"

"Yes."

"Do you know what made him change his mind about me?"

"I suppose he thought it over and realized why you had to do it."

"Mrs. Dallas. . . ."

"Let's not talk about it. Everyone has a mountain he has to climb. Each one in his own way. Your father's climbed them all his life, and I think he realized what you had to do. He'll be proud of you for it, too."

"Mrs. Dallas. . . ."

"Be off with you now," I said, pretending gruffness, "and go find another mountain to climb."

Bobby Kennedy never mentioned the incident to me again, but after his death, I received a picture of him from his wife taken when he reached the top of Mount Kennedy.

Bobby Kennedy was unforgettable. He had the rare ability to stand in another man's shadow and be able to do so without bitterness. Although he stood only five feet ten and was the smallest of the three brothers, I never knew a man who could equal his stature. He had unique courage and loyalty. I never saw him fail to recognize and accept the responsibilities of his destiny. Not only was he there for his family, but he continued to perform for his country right through a time of intense personal tragedy. And there seemed to be no letup.

In mid-June of the same year, a little more than six months after the assassination, Teddy, who was already campaigning for his second term in the Senate, was critically injured in a plane crash. This accident not only cost the life of the pilot but also plunged the family into new anxieties and fears.

I remember the night of the crash vividly. It happened on June 19, 1964. Teddy was scheduled to make a political speech in Northampton, Massachusetts, and he had attempted to commandeer the *Caroline* to fly him to it, but Captain Baird refused to take the plane up, for severe fog and weather warnings had been issued for that area.

Teddy was upset and angry about the rejection, but Captain Baird remained adamant in his refusal to fly. Refusing to respect the experience of his father's pilot, Teddy chartered a plane on his own and started out. In his party was Birch Bayh, the Senator from Indiana.

Earlier that afternoon Captain Baird had flown Bobby into Hyannis Port, and I remember, when he came to the house to visit his father, he told everyone that Teddy was chartering a plane because Captain Baird would not risk flying him in the weather. No one seemed particularly disturbed about it, but that night I was to have dinner with the crew of the *Caroline* and met them at the Candlelight Motel. Captain Baird was quite upset over the fact that Teddy was determined to fly.

"It's bad weather," he said. "This fog is really rolling in."

Just then Isabel Stearns, the owner of the Candlelight, came running to our table. "Mrs. Dallas, quick. They're calling you from the big house. Ted Kennedy's been in a plane crash, and they need you."

At that moment another call came through. It was Bobby for Captain Baird. He wanted to be flown to Boston immediately. He held the line while the captain checked with Flight Control at Hyannis Airport to see if the weather was clear enough to make it to Boston. He received emergency clearance but advised Bobby that he would have to go by car from Boston to Northampton, for the airport there was still closed in by fog. Bobby accepted this plan and told the captain to pick him up at the house. He said that if I had not already left, I should come with Captain Baird. "We want her with Dad when he finds out," he said.

At that point no one knew the full extent of the crash, so before Captain Baird left the motel, he phoned his wife, for he wanted her to know that it was not the *Caroline*. News reports would be coming through, and he wanted to assure her that he was safe.

Bobby was pacing up and down the driveway when we drove up. He gave me a quick nod as I got out, jumped in the front seat and said, "Gun it." The car took off at top speed.

Inside, the house was bedlam. Every phone was ringing. All the family were there, and the girls were doing their best to man the lines. I ran up to Mr. Kennedy and was relieved to find him still asleep. Mary Sullivan, an RN who lived in the neighborhood and often volunteered to help out in emergencies, was sitting by his bed.

Eunice asked me if I would take the phone in the butler's pantry, and since Mary would remain with Mr. Kennedy, I was happy to pitch in.

The first call I received came from Defense Secretary Robert McNamara. He wanted me to assure the family that he was assigning a top crew of medical corpsmen to the Senator and that they would remain with him until he recovered—however long it might be.

Such calls went on most of the night, until word finally came from Bobby that Teddy would be all right. Senator Bayh had pulled him out of the wreckage. His back was injured, but he would live.

Not much comment was made around the house about the pilot's being killed, and very little attention was given to his death in the papers. I suppose no blame was cast since he was willing to fly the Senator despite the weather warning; but another man was dead, and the endless cycle of tragedy seemed to have picked up momentum.

As soon as the family learned that Teddy had been rushed to

the hospital in Northampton, they all began to make arrangements to go to him.

When Mr. Kennedy was told of the accident and assured that Teddy was basically safe, he did not show any signs of panic and seemed to take the news with a kind of calm resignation.

Between Mrs. Kennedy and the girls, a constant vigil was kept at the hospital in Northampton. The doctors decided not to allow Mr. Kennedy to visit Teddy because they did not think it would be good for him to see his son while he was in a critical condition. Mrs. Kennedy, however, would come in as soon as she arrived back from her daily visit to the hospital and reassure her husband that Teddy was doing well. The girls were also thorough in their reports and never failed to give him their personal accountings of their brother's condition.

They were all reassuring, but there was an unspoken fear in their manner. It was too soon after the President's death for them to face another tragedy, another loss.

Mrs. Kennedy, always meticulous in her religious habits, made daily masses, not only for the souls of her dead sons and daughter, but for Teddy as well.

There were constant prayers and private masses being said at the house by his family, and finally the news was brought to Mr. Kennedy that his son was well enough to be transferred to the New England Baptist Hospital. It was a joyous day for everyone, especially Mr. Kennedy, for with the transfer he was told that he could visit his son.

However, Mr. Kennedy's upcoming visit presented another problem. He had previously not been told the serious extent of the injuries that Teddy had suffered because the doctors did not want to risk a setback for Mr. Kennedy due to worry over his son.

Now they were concerned because Teddy was lying in an orthopedic frame, and if Mr. Kennedy were not told this ahead of time, the shock of seeing Teddy this way could be severe. But they knew Mr. Kennedy would become worried and suspicious if he were kept from visiting his son after the transfer to Boston, so the decision was made to inform him fully of Teddy's condition. They knew that Mr. Kennedy would be more relieved from worry when he actually saw his son despite the shock of seeing him in the frame. When they told him, he took the news fairly well and was anxious to go to see him.

Mrs. Kennedy was not in favor of her husband's making the trip until Teddy was completely out of danger, and agreed only after she was assured by her husband's personal doctor, Dr. Boles, that he would accompany us on the visit. This pacified her to some extent.

"But he still looks so bad," she said sadly, "and I don't think it's good for my husband to see him like he is."

The doctors told her it would be months before Teddy was fully recovered, and in their opinion, it would be detrimental to Mr. Kennedy to keep him away any longer than necessary.

Dr. Boles met us at the hospital, and as we wheeled Mr. Kennedy down the hall to Teddy's room, I was startled at the noise and commotion that was going on. Mr. Kennedy looked at Dr. Boles questioningly, then bristled with pride when Dr. Boles told him that despite Teddy's serious condition, he had brought his office staff from Washington and had them set up in a series of rooms across the hall from his hospital suite.

"Business as usual." Dr. Boles chuckled.

Part of the wing on Teddy's floor had been turned into a wheeling-dealing campaign office. It was sheer bedlam, and Mr. Kennedy loved it.

We wheeled him past the temporary offices into his son's suite to find that it, too, was packed with people.

Teddy's personal doctors were there with an orthopedic surgeon, a neurologist, an internist, and two nurses. His wife, his secretary, Dr. Boles, Ann, an aide, and I made up the rest of the entourage.

As soon as Mr. Kennedy arrived and had exchanged a warm round of greetings with Teddy and Joan, the doctors began discussing the operation that they felt should be performed on Teddy's back.

Teddy was listening to them intently and would glance over at his father and then look back at the doctors during the discussion. Mr. Kennedy also listened very carefully to every word that was said. He was almost perched on the edge of his chair. Suddenly he began shaking his head fiercely, bellowing, "Naaaaa, naaaaa, naaaaa."

The outburst startled everyone, and the doctors dropped their consultation with Teddy and began hovering over Mr. Kennedy, trying to understand what had caused him to have such a sudden and violent reaction. But there was no way for them to get near him. He was like an oncoming Sherman tank when he let fly with his good foot and fist.

"Naaaaa, naaaaa, naaaaa," he roared.

Teddy, ashen and shaken, kept saying, "What's wrong, Dad? Can you tell me? Dad, please, what is it? Tell me."

Ann was behind his wheelchair, leaning over his shoulder, crying, "Uncle Joe, Uncle Joe, what's wrong? Are you sick?"

"Naaaaa, naaaaa."

I stepped out in the hall, for I thought it would be best to clear the room for a minute. Having cared for him so long, I knew something had upset him. I sensed that he desperately wanted to communicate something important. This was not just an aphasia reaction.

The shouting became louder from inside the room, and I thought to myself, *This is not good,* so I went back in and stood by Mr. Kennedy's side in order to observe him for a moment.

He kept pointing to the doctors, then to Teddy, then back again to the doctors, and would shake his head rapidly and roar, "Naaaa, naaaa."

"Do you want to discuss your son's operation, Mr. Kennedy?" I managed to get in. "Is that it?"

He fell back in his chair, waved his hand and said, "Yaaaaa."

Teddy took it from there, and with very few questions we were all able to understand that he did not approve of his son's undergoing surgery.

Teddy watched him, thoughtfully, then said, without hesitation, "Dad, you've never been wrong yet. So I'll do it your way."

And he did.

When Mrs. Kennedy learned of the incident, she said, "I understand my husband's fear. When Jack had to undergo his serious back operation, Mr. Kennedy never left his side. The last rites were said for him three different times, and my husband never left him for a moment. I think he feels that unless it's a matter of life and death, he doesn't want Teddy to go through what Jack did."

After Teddy had turned down the doctors' recommendation that he be operated on, he concentrated, with typical vigor, on his convalescence and rehabilitation.

It was not surprising when, on most of our future visits, we found him on the balcony of his room taking his sunbath, for he was an outdoor man and the restrictive walls of his room were depressing to him.

He would lie on an exercise table, facedown, and talk about the book he was writing or about the fact that he had taken up painting. When the therapist would come in to turn him faceup, he would grin at his father. He would discuss his campaign and laughingly say, "Joansie is taking my place and winning more votes than I ever could."

Mr. Kennedy loved this son so much that he was constantly reaching out his hand for an affectionate touch.

One day Teddy called the house from the hospital and specifically requested that his father be brought to visit him the next afternoon. He wanted to give him a surprise.

He was waiting for us when we arrived, and as his father was wheeled in, he waved his hand.

Then he stood up and walked for the first time since the accident. Mr. Kennedy took a deep, startled breath, then grinned from ear to ear. Bursting with pride, he struggled to his feet and stood beside his son.

The scene was magnificent, and Teddy had a reporter and photographer in from *Life* magazine to record it.

Teddy was overjoyed that day, and it was heartwarming to

see the gratitude in Mr. Kennedy's eyes when he saw for himself that his son would walk again.

"I've got a long way to go, Dad," Teddy said, wrapping his arm around his father's shoulder, "but with your help, I can't miss."

21

BOBBY KENNEDY HAD BEEN carrying the heaviest responsibilities after the death of his brother. He had continued on as Attorney General without a break right through the funeral, and he also had to hold the family together when Teddy's accident happened. Finally, when President Johnson eliminated the possibility of his seeking the Vice Presidential nomination by disqualifying all Cabinet members, Bobby came to a decision and resigned his post on August 25, 1964. It was exactly ten months after his brother's funeral and only two months after Teddy's plane crash.

However, life went on, and the Kennedy drive to take their place in history could not be stopped no matter what the cost.

With Bobby's resignation, speculation began that he might try to unseat Johnson, and when reporters pressed him for a comment, he grinned and said, "I have no Presidential ambitions, and neither does my wife, Ethel-Bird."

When he announced that he would run for the United States Senate from New York, he breathed new life into the family. Bobby's decision to run for public office rekindled a flame that had all but died. Although Teddy was continuing with his campaign from the hospital, it was Bobby who lifted them up to a new and exciting crest.

He was, without question, a political genius, keenly conscious of timing. Three days after he announced that he would run, he appeared on television at the Democratic National Convention in Atlantic City, and the country was swept up once again by a Kennedy. He introduced a filmed tribute to his brother, and upon its completion, he stood with his head bowed during a wild and frenzied sixteen-minute ovation.

He had brought the Kennedys back to life, and once more they flashed before the public with all their color and magnetism.

A scintillating energy took over the family. Not one of them doubted Bobby's victory. Deep thought, of course, had gone into his decision, and they knew it would be difficult to unseat the formidable incumbent, Kenneth Keating, but the determination to win wiped away all thoughts of defeat. The horizon was clear.

His campaign took place in New York, and Mr. Kennedy made several trips to the city in order to get a firsthand account of his son's progress. Mrs. Kennedy was also deeply involved and excited by his election. She was alive again with a fresh burst of energy and began making public appearances and giving speeches in her son's behalf.

Mr. Kennedy always watched carefully when she appeared on television. He would want the volume turned to full strength so as not to miss a word. Sometimes he would shake his head and frown, but most often he was pleased with the results and would wave at her image on the screen and say, "Yaaaaa. Yaaaaa."

It was apparent that Mr. Kennedy sanctioned and approved of Bobby's decision to run. He still yelled at him and shook his fist under his nose, but it was in a different way, for he knew that in this son rested the hope and future of the Kennedy image.

When we were in New York, Bobby would always arrive at the apartment very early in the morning to have breakfast with his father, and even though Mr. Kennedy was not able to make himself understood, he was still actively giving instructions and advice.

Bobby never let on that his father's speech was garbled. He would prop his elbows on the table and peer intently in his eyes. He absorbed every sound. Mr. Kennedy's voice would rise in excitement and then fall into a low, confidential whisper, while Bobby listened carefully.

I had often watched the President concentrate on the inflection of his father's voice. He would lean back in his chair, cocking his ear as if to pick up a clear word or rest his elbow on one knee and cup his chin in his hand thoughtfully. The President was an imposing figure, mature and magnificently handsome, but Bobby was never imposing. His hair, as unruly as a boy's, grew in stubborn profusion, and his great hooked nose overpowered his face. Lines cut deep ridges across his forehead, and the steel blue of his eyes flashed like the blade of a sword. He did not have the flair and sophistication of his older brother, but he bristled with energy and excitement.

He was always tousled, and whenever I saw him "dressed up," he still looked to me like a small boy wearing his first long trousers.

Bobby never relaxed when his father spoke. He hunched and strained to hear every garbled word, almost as if he expected clarity to burst forth. There were times when I felt he was actually trying to pull words from his father's mouth.

He visited his father as often as he could. He would be red-eyed from lack of sleep and hoarse from hours of speechmaking, but he never failed to report to his father when we were in New York.

I can see him sitting with his hand in a pan of warm salt water trying to relieve the swelling that was caused from hours of shaking hands.

While he explained to Mr. Kennedy a new strategy he was planning, I would keep the water warm and massage his fingers.

Robert Kennedy was sincerely devoted to the underprivileged and deprived and would give vivid and often harrowing descriptions of living conditions that existed in the tenement districts. His voice would lift and explode. "I'll make changes, Dad," he'd say. "You know I'll make changes. Millions of people need help. My God, they need help."

Mr. Kennedy would nod his head solemnly, then reach out

his hand to his son—but whenever Bobby said something that did not sit well with his father, he still roared and shook his fist.

One afternoon, during one of our visits, Stephen Smith, Jean's husband, came to the apartment and urged Mr. Kennedy to go with him to Bobby's campaign headquarters.

"Grandpa," he said, "you're really the one who started all this, and it would be a great boost to the workers if you'd show up."

Mr. Kennedy smiled but waved a gracious no, and despite his son-in-law's sincere invitation, he still refused. As with the President, he stood firm in the decision to remain in the background.

Both sons won their elections. We were in New York with Bobby, and two gala parties had been planned as victory celebrations.

On election afternoon I received a call from Mrs. Kennedy's secretary, telling me that Mrs. Kennedy wanted to make sure that I would come to the victory party. Later I received a call from Bobby's secretary, extending a personal invitation from him to attend.

One party was to be held at his headquarters and was open to all the workers who had contributed their time and efforts to his victory. The other was a private gathering at Delmonico's.

I told Mr. Kennedy about the invitations, and he seemed quite pleased and nodded that I should go. However, he decided to stay up that night and watch the returns on television, so it was quite late before he retired.

I was able to get a call through to Bobby's secretary and told her that since it was so late, I'd better spend the rest of the night on standby for Mr. Kennedy. She insisted that "the Senator" was anxious for me to be at the party. "You'll never see anything like this again, Rita," she said. "It's like a resurrection, so get someone to take over and please come. He's expecting you."

I did not want to be away too long from Mr. Kennedy, for he

had been very excited when he had gone to bed, so I told the night nurse where I would be, in case Mr. Kennedy needed me, and took a cab to Bobby's headquarters.

The street was jammed with shouting, cheering people, and it took me more than half an hour to push my way up to the door of the building. I squeezed into the lobby only to find it blocked by a long row of desks. Behind them scores of men were doing what they could to stop gatecrashers. I did not have a written invitation, nor did I see a familiar face in the crowd to identify me, so I was refused admittance. I couldn't get in, and I couldn't get out. Suddenly, above the yells and cheers, I heard a voice ringing, "There's the Ambassador's nurse, let her in."

The most amazing thing of my life happened. People were so packed that it was impossible to move, but I suddenly felt myself being lifted off the floor. The two men on either side of me got me around the waist, and I was bodily handed over the heads of the crowd. I started screaming, "Put me down, put me down," but my voice was lost in the loud, happy hooting of the mob.

It was the wildest thing I've ever experienced. I found myself stretched prone in the air, actually being tossed from one hand to another until, amid catcalls and whistles, I landed almost headfirst behind the row of desks.

I struggled to my feet, but there was no way for me to be angry with the crowd, for they were delightful. I have never seen so many radiantly happy faces.

Headquarters was made up of five or six large rooms. In them people were sitting on desks, floors, filing cabinets, window ledges, laps, and anything else flat and available, including upturned wastebaskets.

I was a little relieved when Bobby's secretary pushed her way toward me and said it was time for us to leave for Delmonico's. When we arrived there, we stood in line with a glittering crowd of people—glamorous men and women—all friends and supporters of the new Senator from New York.

Once again I did not have a written invitation, but when I

gave my name to the extremely posh maître d', he bowed deeply and said, "Ah, yes, madame, we have your table." The secretary and I were seated together, next to Senator Kennedy's table.

An impressive list of big-name entertainers were scheduled to appear that evening with Tony Bennett headlining, but there was no way for anyone to hold the crowd's attention. The excitement of waiting for Bobby had them in an uproar. Tony Bennett tried but laughingly shrugged his shoulders and gave up.

It was pandemonium!

Suddenly the cry went up: "Here he is, here he is! He's here! He's here!"

The applause was so deafening that it completely drowned out the orchestra playing his victory song.

The crowd enveloped him. Women were kissing him, wildly pulling his hair, tugging at his clothes. Men gripped his hands, and all I could see was an occasional glimpse of the top of his head.

His secretary had pushed her way through the crowd to greet him, but I could not bring myself to plunge in and try to get to him. I did what everyone else did who was not in the crushing mob. I stood up on my table and applauded. How he spotted me among the sea of faces, I'll never know, but suddenly I realized that he was pushing his way toward me. He came to my table and helped me down. His eyes were misty when he kissed my cheek and said, "Thank you for coming, Mrs. Dallas. I know you must be tired having been with Dad all day, and it was a lot to ask that you come here tonight and wait for me, so I do thank you." He kissed me again and said, "How is Dad?"

"Happy"—I laughed—"and, I hope, sound asleep."

"Will you tell him about this for me?" he said, giving a sweeping gesture to the room.

"I would not dare show up in the morning without being prepared to give him a step-by-step account. He knows where I am, and he'll want every detail. I went by your headquarters and, now, to see this celebration—well, Senator Robert, I'll be able to keep him busy for days just telling him about everything I've seen."

He clasped my hand so tightly that my ring cut into my finger. "Thank you," he whispered again and was quickly swallowed up by the crowd.

I was emotionally shaken by the depth of his sincerity, and as I watched his body being churned and twisted by well-wishers, I felt a deep and piercing sorrow. Even though he laughed and waved at everyone, he seemed very alone. He had wanted me there, I think, because he knew I would carry the experience to his father. I was simply a fortunate messenger, chosen to relay the good tidings of victory to the absent source of power.

I left shortly afterward, and the next morning, when I went in to Mr. Kennedy, I brought the newspapers with me. The banner headlines screamed, BOBBY WINS. I held a paper up in front of him, and when he saw the headline, he reached out his hand and grasped mine with the same intense grip that his son had the night before.

I sat down by his bed and he settled back with his left hand cradled behind his head, a position he usually took when he was extremely comfortable. I went over every detail, and when I told him how I had been carried over the heads of the crowd, he roared. Knowing how concerned and interested he was with minute details, I spent the rest of the day trying to recount and remember everything that had happened. I described what the ladies were wearing. I told him about the thrill of seeing the mass of workers celebrating at campaign headquarters. I told him about Tony Bennett being drowned out by the cheers for his son, and he was ecstatic.

Late in the afternoon Bobby called and told his father that he wanted to take him out to dinner that night. We were planning to leave for the Cape the next morning; but the Senator wanted to share an evening with his father, and our departure was gladly delayed.

Mr. Kennedy dressed with meticulous care, scrutinizing every detail of his dinner suit. He fussed and fumed until I had his black tie exactly right. He brushed his hair until it glistened, and when Bobby came for us, Mr. Kennedy received him with all the respect due a United States Senator. Sitting erect and proud in his wheelchair, he bowed his head low and offered his hand in congratulations.

Bobby had won, and as he bent and embraced his father, I heard him whisper, in a husky voice, "We made it, Dad! We made it!"

22

BOBBY THREW HIMSELF into his role as United States Senator with fierce concentration. There was never any speculation or discussion around the house that Bobby might give up this work to run for the Presidency in 1968. There were always rumors from the press about it, but nothing was ever brought up in the family or staff. Then, midafternoon one day, while Mr. and Mrs. Kennedy were having lunch together in the dining room, Bobby came home unexpectedly.

He sat down with them and, over a soft drink, said, "I came here first because I wanted both of you to know my plans."

Mr. Kennedy's eyes shot up, and he peered at his son intently.

"I'm holding a press conference in the morning," he said, "to announce that I will run for the Presidency. The field is wide open, with Johnson out of the way, and I'm going for it."

Neither parent spoke. His mother looked at him blankly, and Mr. Kennedy put his head down and stared at his food. There was an eternity of silence. Then Mrs. Kennedy got up from the table and walked around it to kiss him. She began peppering him with questions, trying to be gay and light, but both of them kept their eyes on Mr. Kennedy, who had not moved.

He would not touch his lunch. Instead, he motioned to me that he wanted to be taken to his room.

Bobby waited until he knew his father would be retiring for his nap, then he came up and kissed him good-bye.

"Try to understand, Dad. I think I'm doing it the right way," was all he said.

On looking back to that day, I realize that no one said to Bobby that it was a wonderful decision he had made. No one congratulated him. There seemed to be a pall over all of us, and when we would see pictures of him dashing here and there on his campaign, it sent a cold wave through everyone.

Bobby spoke to the nation the next day on television and in a few brief words set the pace for his campaign.

"I do not run for the Presidency," he said, "merely to oppose any man, but to propose new policies. I run because I am convinced that this country is on a perilous course, and because I have such strong feelings about what must be done, I am obliged to do all I can. I run to seek new policies—policies to close the gaps between black and white, rich and poor, young and old, in this country and around the world. . . ."

After listening to the speech, Mr. Kennedy accepted his decision to run and gave him the *Caroline* to use on his campaign tour, as he had the President.

The crew of the *Caroline* idolized Bobby, and they were quickly caught up in the excitement his appearances generated. Maggie Cooney, the stewardess, urged me to take a few days off and travel with them.

"You've got to see Bobby in action," she said. "I've heard of human dynamos, but he's the first I've ever seen. People are going crazy. You'd think he was a messiah the way they try to get to him, just to touch his hand. I never saw a man like him. He fears nothing. The agents are losing their minds. Bobby sees a crowd and rushes right to the middle of it."

He became the only topic of conversation at the compound. It was Bobby! Bobby! Bobby! Every television was left on, and even his parents were caught up in the new aura.

They would watch the news together, whenever possible, and when the coverage was especially full, they would look at each other softly and smile.

He preached against the Vietnam War with a severe intensity, and when Mr. Kennedy would hear him lift his voice against it, he would nod his head in complete agreement.

When the broadcasts were over, Mrs. Kennedy would leave after kissing her husband.

"We have good reason to be proud of him, Joe," she'd often say, and Mr. Kennedy would smile warmly.

When Martin Luther King was assassinated, Bobby was speaking in Indianapolis and was scheduled to appear that night at an open rally in the heart of the ghetto. Everyone urged him to cancel the engagement, but he never backed down. He refused the additional squads of bodyguards assigned to him and stood up before a hostile and potentially riotous throng of blacks.

He threw away his prepared speech, grabbed the mike in his hand, and poured out his soul to the people.

He came home for a day after attending Mr. King's funeral, and he was showered with attention by his family and intimate campaign advisers. He looked on the brink of collapse.

As he had done during his campaign in New York, he constantly reported his progress to his father. He could schedule only one-day visits as the heat of the campaign picked up, but I remember one evening, after he had spent several hours with his father, he came to the nurses' station and slumped wearily on the edge of my desk.

He sat there for a long time studying the toes of his shoes. Finally he lifted his head and said, "Mrs. Dallas, I want to ask you something, and I want you to give me a straight answer. Don't pull any punches."

"All right, if that's the way you want it."

"It won't go any further than between us, but I have to know something. Dad's bad off. He's fought hard, but he's failing. I guess he doesn't have much of a life the way things are, but I want to know, Mrs. Dallas, do you think my dad could have walked?"

I met him eye to eye, and answered, "Yes, Senator, yes I do. In fact, I know your father could have walked with a brace and a cane. He had everything going for him in the beginning.

He had that special kind of drive. But he's given it up—as far as walking is concerned. That's past. But there's plenty left in him, or he wouldn't be alive at this moment."

He looked up at me, and his eyes glistened.

"My God, my God!" he said. Then he just ran out.

When I saw him a little later that evening, he seemed far away and disconnected from the family.

But it turned into an electrifying night for everyone. Even the First Lady had come over from her home to fete Bobby, and she was more excited than I had seen her for years. When Bobby called out the favorable statistics of the latest polls, she did not applaud politely, as she usually did—she led them all.

When he finished his reports, he grinned, while the family cheered, and said, "Looks like we're going to make it."

The First Lady called from across the room, "Won't it be wonderful when we get back in the White House?"

Ethel Kennedy had a very sharp and often brittle wit. "What do you mean 'we'?" she said.

Jacqueline Kennedy looked as if she'd been struck. She flinched as though a blow had actually stung her cheek. The room was crisp in its silence.

Ethel gave a careless shrug and walked away.

The First Lady looked helplessly around the room, gave a shy embarrassed smile, kissed Bobby fleetingly on the cheek, and went to her home alone.

No one offered to stop her.

For the rest of the night I could not forget that look of startled pain that had clouded her eyes. Often I wondered what would have happened if Mr. Kennedy had witnessed the scene. I don't believe he would have allowed her to walk away like that, for there was a deep and irrevocable love between them. Although love cannot repair shattered dreams, it can at least add dignity to the memories.

During her years as the President's wife Jacqueline Kennedy had been openly generous and gracious in sharing the honor of the Presidency. The White House had overflowed with Kennedys. All during her married years she was devoted to the whole Kennedy family. Even after her husband's death she had borne the tragedy of assassination with a dignity that brought honor to the Kennedy name. She had the mind and heart of a poet, and I will never forget the poignant words she wrote for *Look* magazine and the "JFK memorial book."

"I should have known that it was asking too much to dream that I might have grown old with him."

When the family let her walk away alone that night, I think she realized that although she still carried the name, her place in the Kennedy montage had to come to an end. Her husband had been gone for almost five years, and although she loved the family deeply, she had come face to face with a decision about her own future.

The next morning she stopped in to see Mr. Kennedy. Her hair was tied back with a silk scarf, and she was wearing black slacks and a black long-sleeved sweater. She looked somber and very tired. She stayed only a few minutes and said she'd be back later. She kissed him on the cheek and whispered softly, "I have some thinking to do today, Grandpa."

On her way out, she sat down in the chair by my desk and said, "Grandpa looks tired, but his eyes were very bright. Bobby's campaign seems to be doing him some good—at least I hope so."

"He's right on top of every detail," I said, "and seems to love every minute of it."

"He's a magnificent man. Magnificent."

She fiddled with a paper clip and then said shyly, "Mrs. Dallas, you've been a widow a long time, haven't you?"

"Twenty years," I answered.

"It's hard, isn't it—being alone, I mean."

"Mrs. Kennedy," I said, "don't make the mistake I've made. Find a life for yourself. It won't be the same, I know, for nothing ever is, but don't destroy your future. You can find a new happiness. You can find another kind of security. You have two children to raise and trying to do it without help is hard, as you say. I know. I've raised my boy alone, and it's been difficult. I don't mean financially difficult, I mean, the spiritual and emotional difficulties that come with trying to raise children without the wisdom and strength of a man to help guide them."

She stood up thoughtfully.

"I'll think about what you've said, Mrs. Dallas. I'll think about it."

That evening her Secret Service man, Clint Hill, came by the house exhausted. She had spent the entire day walking. She had walked to all the familiar places that were dear to her and the President. The tiny coves along the beach, Squaw Island, the long stretches of fields that lay behind the compound, the private picnic areas, the horse barns, and it was well into evening before she returned home.

Mr. Kennedy had been anxiously awaiting her, and when she finally came in, she said, "I'm sorry I'm late, Grandpa, but I'm very tired. I won't stay long. I've had a lot of thinking to do today."

He raised his brows as if to ask, "And what have you decided?"

She laid her cheek on his hand and whispered, "You'll always know I love you, won't you, Grandpa?"

Quickly she kissed him good-night and was gone. In a few days she left for her apartment in New York.

Jacqueline Kennedy had come to a decision to free herself from the past for the sake of her own future and the future of her children.

Bobby's campaign rushed on, building momentum and excitement both in the family and all over the country. His energy and dedication electrified the whole nation, and the atmosphere around the compound was charged with the anticipation of victory. The Kennedy comet was flashing on the horizon again, and nothing seemed to be able to prevent the inevitable reemergence of the Kennedy phenomenon on the national scene.

Everything was building to the climax in California, but before he left for the Coast Bobby telephoned from Philadelphia that he was coming to visit his father.

When Mr. Kennedy learned that his son was arriving, nothing would do except that we meet the plane. He was thrilled and excited that Bobby would take time out to come to him at such a crucial point in his campaign.

California was the big one, and the whole family was committed to helping him in it. Since his father could not actively participate, Bobby was doing the next best thing—he was coming to give his father a last-minute report, first hand.

Ann had one of the medical aides drive us, and when we reached Hyannis Airport we waited for more than half an hour. Mr. Kennedy kept looking up at the sky for a sign of the *Caroline* and was growing nervous and restless.

Finally, Ann sent the aide into the airport for information. He came back in a few minutes with news that something had gone wrong with the plane, and that Senator Robert would not be able to take off.

Mr. Kennedy was crestfallen. When we got home, he had us wheel him into the sun room and sat there alone, blue and dejected.

The phone rang, and it was one of Bobby's men with a message for Mr. Kennedy.

"Your son is hitchhiking home," he said. "He bummed a ride on another plane and will be at the airport any minute."

I believe if we had not stopped him, Mr. Kennedy would have tried to run to the car. We drove at breakneck speed, with him urging us on, and we had just pulled up at the runway when a plane landed. Sure enough, we saw Bobby. Behind him was his adviser Dick Goodwin, and I have never seen two men so completely exhausted.

Even from a distance I could see the lines that were deeply etched in Bobby's face, and it seemed to me that he was dragging himself off the plane. But when he spotted the car, he broke into a run.

Mr. Kennedy's face lit up and he waved his hand excitedly

as his son ran toward him. Bobby skidded up to the car window, stuck his head in, and kissed his father.

Bobby still had his head stuck in the window in deep conversation when Mr. Goodwin finally arrived at the car. He had walked wearily from the plane, and when he got to the car, he leaned against it in exhaustion and began talking with us. I asked if he and Bobby had had any difficulty chartering a plane at the last minute.

He laughed and said, "We didn't charter one. When the Senator found out the *Caroline* would be down for a few hours for repairs, he went right back into the airport and checked around until he found a plane that was going to New York. He asked if we could hitchhike a ride, and if they would be willing to take a slight detour and come by here to drop him off so he could see his dad."

He shook his head in a puzzled way, and mused, "You know, nothing was going to prevent him from seeing his father today. He was going to make this trip or else. He said, 'If I can't hop a plane, I'll thumb a ride, but I've got to go home.'"

Bobby pulled his head out of the window and said, "I'm going to drive Dad. You folks ride backup."

We drove close behind, and I could see him in the car, turning his head toward his father, laughing, talking, and being elaborately emphatic with his gestures. Mr. Kennedy never took his eyes off his son. He was completely absorbed by every move, every word, every gesture.

Bobby helped get him out of the car when we arrived home and wheeled him into the house. Mr. Kennedy wanted to go back to the sun room, and once Bobby saw that he was settled, he said, "I'll go find Mother, and then I'll be right back."

It wasn't long before he returned and said to his father, "Just the three of us are having dinner tonight, Dad. Alone. Just us."

Ann flinched and walked away. In a few minutes I saw a sight that had become so familiar to me. She was out in the driveway with her dogs. She started running with them across the lawn and down to the pier, all by herself. So many times when the family was gathered around having "fun time," as Teddy always called it, I would see this slender young woman go out with her dogs to run and play with them. She would bend down and hug them tightly, and as hard as she made it for all the nurses, I realized she was still a frightened, lonely girl at the charity of a family who had given her a job to do and a role to play, but who had never taken her into the warmth of their lives.

There was much laughter and gaiety that day between Bobby and his parents. He kept saying over and over, "Dad, I'm doing it just the way you would want me to—and I'm going to win."

He hugged Mrs. Kennedy and said, "How will you feel being the mother of two Presidents? That makes you quite a girl, doesn't it?"

For a brief moment her face froze in fear and tension, but she quickly pushed her memories aside and smiled at Bobby warmly, kissing his cheek. Nothing was going to let her spoil his day.

Dinner was very festive, and Mr. Kennedy was bubbling with excitement. When the meal was finished, Bobby wheeled him to his room and kept right on talking while we put him to bed. When Mr. Kennedy was settled, Bobby said, "Dad, I'm leaving for California in a few days, and I'm going to fight hard."

He bent over to kiss his father good-bye and added, "I'm going to win this one for you."

He stood up straighter than I had ever seen him. Usually his shoulders were hunched over with his head tucked between them, but as he stood before his father, he pulled himself to his full height. Mr. Kennedy held out his hand and they said good-bye with a tight, lingering grip.

I went out to the nurses' station, for I felt they should have a last moment together. When Bobby came out, he gave me his famous victory sign. He was halfway down the hall to his mother's room when he abruptly stopped, turned around, and came back.

He stood directly in front of me. Placing both hands on the

desk between us, he leaned over and looked directly at me. His eyes were the purest blue I had ever seen them.

He stared at me intently, then said evenly, "Mrs. Dallas, take care of Dad till I get back."

I can still see him walking down that long hall with his shoulders bowed. He knocked at his mother's door, and as he started in, he looked back at me, flashed a wide grin and held up two fingers.

His sign of victory.

I never saw him again.

Despite his unexpected defeat in Oregon, no one doubted that Bobby would ultimately be victorious, and plans were formulated for his campaign celebration.

A day or two after he left droves of workmen converged on Bobby and Ethel's home to carry out a crash program of redecorating and remodeling.

It was to be Ethel's surprise gift to her husband.

Shrubbery was dug up, and majestic greens were replanted. All around the house breathtaking flowers were set in, and the rooms inside the house were brilliant with their bright, happy colors.

The home became a picture postcard, and none of us could wait to see Bobby's expression when he saw it. It was evident that Ethel had worked in diligent secrecy in order to coordinate this major undertaking so it would be finished, almost overnight. Everything turned out perfect.

We were all glued to the television during the California primary, and every day Mr. Kennedy would get an up-to-the-minute report by telephone on how things were going.

On voting day, long before the polls closed, word came that it was apparent that Bobby had won. Mr. Kennedy gave a great sigh of relief and signaled that he was ready for bed.

The big house also settled down, for it seemed to know that the battle was over. Half the war was won. He had to capture the nomination at the Chicago convention, but riding on the crest as he was, no one doubted that victory was his.

Mr. Kennedy was soon asleep, and Bea Tripp came on for the night shift. After we chatted a few minutes, I slipped across to my house and sat on my porch for a while to unwind.

It was a beautiful summer night at the Cape. The stars were hanging low over the ocean, and a gentle breeze stirred the air.

I rested for a moment, but knowing the excitement that would strike the compound the next day when the word was official, I decided to go to bed. In a few moments, I too was comfortably asleep.

The harsh sound of the telephone jarred me awake, and I knew something was wrong. It was Mrs. Tripp.

"Bobby's been shot," was all she said.

"Is he all right?"

"No, Rita."

"He's dead?"

"No."

"Oh, thank God."

"Rita, he won't make it."

"What about Mr. Kennedy?"

"He's still asleep."

"Mrs. Kennedy?"

"She knows."

I hung up, staring at the phone.

My mind was racing, full of confused thoughts, but somehow I managed to dress quickly. I rushed over to the big house and slipped in the side entrance. I went immediately to find Mrs. Tripp, and she told me how she had heard the news. She said she had gone to awaken Mrs. Kennedy for mass as usual and just as she arrived at the door, she heard Mrs. Kennedy's television come on. She realized Mrs. Kennedy wanted to see the news reports confirming Bobby's victory in California.

Suddenly the door flew open, and Mrs. Kennedy stood staring at her, crying.

"It's Bobby! It's Bobby!"

She slammed her door shut, and behind it Mrs. Tripp could hear her cries over the television.

Just then Ann had come into the hall, ashen.

"Aunt Rose—she knows?"

She then told Mrs. Tripp that one of the children had telephoned during the night with the news that Bobby had been shot. Ann had been told not to awaken either parent. She had suffered through the terror in solitude. Mrs. Tripp said she stood in the hall, weaving on her feet, trembling and sobbing, "I can't help anyone. Somebody, do something. Oh, God, what are we going to do?"

Mrs. Tripp had guided her to her room, where she had fallen across her bed gasping.

Then she had gone to call me.

She told me that Mr. Kennedy was still asleep. We decided Mrs. Tripp would stay at the nurses' station to listen for Mr. Kennedy and I would wait in the hall for Mrs. Kennedy to come out. We knew that as soon as she had composed herself she would tell us what she wanted to do about telling her husband. Her first thought would be to call her children, and then a decision about him would be made.

While I was waiting in the hall, the chauffeur came upstairs and said, "She's going to mass."

"By herself?" I asked.

"That's what she says."

"She'll be destroyed by the reporters."

"Well, all I know is she called up, pretty calmlike and said, 'I'm going to mass, as usual.' "

In about five minutes she came out of her room and she was unlike I had ever seen her. Her face seemed to have collapsed. She had on her black coat and had wrapped a heavy black scarf around her head, looping it under her chin. She almost seemed like an ancient peasant woman who had been creased and worn by toil. As she followed the chauffeur down the hall, her quick, aggressive walk had disappeared. She no longer had her ramrod-straight composure. As I watched her, her shoulders were rounded, almost hunched, and she seemed to hobble as she walked. She had spoken to none of us, only nodded, with her eyes hidden.

When she returned from mass, she was terribly upset. The photographers and reporters had swarmed into Hyannis Port during the night and were merciless in their pursuit of her. She was crying and unconsciously twisting a handkerchief in her hands.

She looked at me and said, hardly above a whisper, "I'm going to my room for a few moments before I go in to my husband."

About ten minutes later she opened her door and was perfectly calm.

For the first time since I had come on the Kennedy case, she went into her husband's room alone and closed the door after her.

I went over to the nurses' station and turned off the intercom.

She was not with him too long, and when she came out, she glanced at me and began weeping.

"Stay with him, Mrs. Dallas, please."

I went into the room. Mr. Kennedy was lying on his back, his hand covering his eyes. Two tears moved slowly down his cheeks, and for a moment, I was so overcome that I did not even notice the television was on, cruelly blaring out the news.

There were no hidden tears when Bobby was shot. No stoic emotions. No curbed grief.

Mrs. Kennedy paced her room restlessly. Ann wept. The maids cried. The aides. The secretary. The gardener. The chauffeur. The cook. Everyone was in tears.

Throughout the house, televisions were blaring at full volume. The set in Mr. Kennedy's room was kept on at his insistence, and he stared at it without blinking.

No one could stay with him for very long. Ann would come in and try to say something but would flee, sobbing. Mrs. Kennedy would slip quietly in, but at the sight of her husband lying so stiff in his bed staring at the television, she would cover her face and run back to her room.

Robert Kennedy died twenty-five hours after he was shot, and all that time everyone in the house hung on a thread of hope, staring at the television while he fought to live. Six of his children had been flown to California to join him in his victory celebration. They were watching television when they saw him shot, and they too hung on with hope.

His wife had been at his side when the bullets hit, and Jacqueline Kennedy, who had been in New York, had flown immediately to Los Angeles. When Ethel's grief overwhelmed her and she was put under sedation, it was Jacqueline who remained at Bobby's side during the agonizing hours he fought to live. This woman, who had moved the world with her incredible dignity in grief when the President died, stood by Bobby and wept unashamed.

And after twenty-five hours it was over.

He was gone.

Sometime later Mrs. Kennedy called me to her room. "I'm going to New York to be with my children. I must be there when Bobby comes."

Her face was set in a frozen expression.

"He will be at St. Patrick's, and I'm going there to wait for him. I'll stay at the cathedral until he comes."

Her eyes were lowered, and in a trembling voice she asked, "Can you take care of Mr. Kennedy?"

"Yes."

"You'll be on your own, Mrs. Dallas. Ann is under a doctor's care, and you'll have to watch over her, too. Can you do it?"

"Yes."

"Can you be strong and not break down in front of him?"

"Yes."

"Will he be all right, do you think?"

"Oh, Mrs. Kennedy, I don't know. What assurance do we have of anything? He's stable now, but how can I answer you?"

"I know you'll do your best, and I have to leave him in your care. I must be with Bobby. I must."

Later in the afternoon she came in to tell her husband good-bye. She stood by him for a long, silent moment and then left very quietly, all by herself.

That night, on television, I saw her sitting alone in an empty cathedral, dressed in black, her head bowed in prayer . . . waiting for Bobby . . . waiting for her son.

Television coverage exposed every detail, and Mr. Kennedy's set was never turned off. I tried to get people to come in and sit with him—the household staff, anyone—but as soon as they saw him watching the grievous coverage of his son's murder, they would start to cry and have to leave the room.

His children called regularly; but there seemed to be nothing to say, and Mr. Kennedy would hand the phone back to me listlessly.

I kept waiting for him to want the television off, and finally, when I saw him take a long, shuddering sigh and put his head back on the pillow, I said, "Mr. Kennedy, I don't know about you, but I can't take much more of this."

He nodded his head and closed his eyes. For the first time in uncounted hours, his room was silent.

A local doctor came to check on him and found his condition stable. He did not stay long, and as he left, he said, "Mrs. Dallas, most of my time will be taken up with Ann. If you need me for the Ambassador, call me."

Although Ann was in almost constant hysterics, she had somehow managed to arrange a mass for the dead to be offered for Bobby at St. Francis Church in Hyannis Port. It was for the staff at the compound and also for friends on the Cape who had not been requested to join the family at the funeral.

When I learned that the doctor would not be attending Mr. Kennedy at the time of the funeral because he planned to accompany Ann to the mass, I called him. Mr. Kennedy was his patient, and I felt that he was in far greater danger than Ann. It was his son they were burying—his third son.

"What about Mr. Kennedy?" I asked him.

"I will be available for him if he needs me, but I feel Ann must have the security of a doctor close to her, and I'm going to the mass. She has invited me, and I think I should be there. If anything comes up, you can call my wife at home, and she'll get in touch with me at the church."

My mind flashed back to the President and the time when he was so furious that Admiral Burkley had left his father even for a moment, so I did as I thought the family would want me to do—I called the priest at St. Francis and asked if he would post someone at the phone in case Mr. Kennedy needed the doctor. He assured me he would.

I wondered, to myself, *How much more can he take?*

When the doctor called to say the priest had been in touch with him and added, "Mrs. Dallas, it's just that I'm worried about Ann. I'm afraid she will collapse," I was at the end of my patience.

Knowing her strength as I did, I assured him that she would not.

I hung up the phone and went to Mr. Kennedy's room. The television was on again and would remain on during the desperate hours that followed.

We watched numbly as it presented its tragic details.

Robert Francis Kennedy had died on June 6, 1968, at 1:45 A.M., Pacific Coast Time, at the Los Angeles Good Samaritan Hospital. He had been forty-three years old.

We watched as his casket was placed aboard a Presidential jet plane that would fly him to New York.

His widow, his two eldest children, his remaining brother and his sisters stood on the lift, and as the coffin was raised, they joined hands to make a circle around him.

Jacqueline Kennedy mounted the steps to the plane alone, her head bowed.

At LaGuardia Airport, his widow and brother rode in the hearse, past the thousands of people who lined the way to St. Patrick's.

Inside the cathedral, his mother was waiting.

The steps of the pallbearers echoed in the emptiness as the

coffin was carried to its place on the catafalque. Archbishop Terence Cooke blessed it, and prayers were offered. Then, one by one, his family left their pews and came forward to kneel at the casket and kiss it. Slowly they left, and only Teddy remained. All through the long night he knelt beside the velvet-draped coffin that held his brother's remains and prayed.

At dawn, the doors of the cathedral were opened, and the people came by tens of thousands. An honor guard stood at solemn attention over the coffin, which had now been draped with an American flag.

The cathedral was closed at five in the morning of the next day, and it was then that his wife returned to pray alone in the vast silence.

At nine the doors opened again to admit the people who had filled Robert Kennedy's past. Lyndon B. Johnson and his wife. The Vice President. Cabinet members. Senators from across the land. Governors. Celebrities. Workers of all kinds. Two thousand people filled the hall.

His brother stood to eulogize him, in a voice unsteady and broken.

Mr. and Mrs. Joseph Kennedy had borne nine children. Only five were left, and as her last son's voice filled the cathedral, Mrs. Kennedy wept behind a heavy veil.

In Hyannis Port, Mr. Kennedy, silent and alone, listened with his eyes closed as his last-remaining son spoke:

"My brother need not be idealized or enlarged in death beyond what he was in life. He should be remembered simply as a good and decent man who saw wrong and tried to right it, saw suffering and tried to heal it, saw war and tried to stop it.

"Those of us who loved him and who take him to rest today, pray that what he was to us, and what he wished for others, will someday come to pass for all the world.

"As he said many times in many parts of this nation to those he touched and who sought to touch him, 'Some men see things as they are and say, why. I dream things that never were and say, why not.'"

As the music of the pontifical mass began, Mr. Kennedy wept.

I sat on the footstool close beside him and grieved for him in his loss. I had thought we were completely alone in that lonely, empty house until I looked up to see his chauffeur of many years standing in the doorway, crying.

He was there to be with a man he called his friend.

He came into the room and stood quietly at the foot of Mr. Kennedy's bed. Then the three of us said a silent rosary while the final remains of his son were honored.

Much later we watched as a train, draped in black, slowly carried the mourners from New York to Washington. Along the miles between, through cities and across farmland, people lined the way.

It took eight painful hours for the train to reach Washington, and it was dark when it arrived in a dreary bleak rain.

The cortege moved slowly past the Capitol where Bobby had served as a Senator and on past the office in the Justice Department that had been his as Attorney General.

The people, drenched and weary from long hours of waiting, lined the streets and bowed their heads as Bobby passed by.

Slowly they crossed the bridge to Arlington, and by a flowering magnolia tree, near his brother, they buried him.

In the light of a thousand flickering tapers, Bobby, Jr., and John Glenn folded the flag which had covered the coffin. The astronaut handed it furled to the son, and the son handed it to his mother.

Ethel Kennedy clutched the flag in her arms and walked slowly to the casket. She knelt in the wet, glittering grass for a final prayer. One by one each of her children knelt beside her. Then Teddy, guiding his mother, came. And Pat. Eunice. Jean.

When it was over, Mr. Kennedy gave a long, agonizing shudder and covered his face.

I turned off the television and lowered the lights. A million thoughts later he fell asleep.

When the family returned from the funeral, I was startled by their recuperative powers. His children came rushing past me, smiling, saying, "Hi, Mrs. Dallas, how's Dad?"

They talked to him about the funeral with great excitement.

"You should have been there, Dad."

"Daddy, there were people by the thousands."

"Did you watch it on television, Daddy?"

"Oh, Grandpa, it was fantastic! And the train ride. . . ."

"Daddy, Teddy was magnificent, absolutely magnificent."

Mr. Kennedy's eyes darted to each one, puzzled in a way. The talk then switched to Bobby's son, young Joe, and they told him about how he went through the train, all by himself, shaking hands with everyone, thanking them for coming.

"Dad, he's got *it*. You should have seen him."

"Nobody put him up to it, Daddy, he did it on his own."

Mr. Kennedy looked suddenly very tired, and his children, sensing this, left the room as they had come.

"See you in the morning, Daddy."

"Get a good night's sleep, Dad."

"Rest well, Grandpa."

"Good night, Joe, dear."

Later, when the house was quiet, Jacqueline Kennedy came alone. She pulled up the footstool and sat by his bed, and they were silent in their thoughts.

Much later, as she stooped to kiss him good-bye, she whispered, "We'll miss him, Grandpa."

23

Two of the Kennedys had been assassinated, and the loss was felt throughout the country and within the family. The magnificent Kennedy dynasty that Mr. Kennedy had dreamed of and that had twice electrified the nation with its extraordinary sense of power and surging youthful vision had been almost completely decimated. But there was still one son left, and everyone looked to Teddy Kennedy to see whether he would try to fill the vacancy left by his brothers.

Almost from the moment of Bobby's death, speculation had it that he was the only possible contender in the election. But anyone who had seen him with his family at that time would have known that seeking high office was simply not possible for Teddy. He realized that he was being sought only as a sentimental talisman, and despite the building pressures, he was in no state to take on such a responsibility.

It's quite possible that he could have succeeded purely on the basis of the fact that he was a Kennedy, but the whole family had been made painfully aware that the Kennedy charisma seemed to have turned into a curse. They knew that the fever they generated was the primary element in their extraordinary success, but they were equally aware that this same fever had been the root of destruction. They had received universal adulation, but they had also been the target of an all-consuming hatred. They had seen the murder of two sons, and they lived with the horrifying whispers of "If he runs, somebody will get him too." I doubt if time can ever erase the gnawing fear that haunts their every move. It was not easy to bury the shattered bodies, and it will never be easy to risk it yet another time.

There were already violently extreme feelings about Teddy. He was a Kennedy, and that's all most people could see. Very few people knew anything about who Teddy Kennedy really was. And in a way he did not know himself.

Over the years that I had been on the case I had seen many changes in Teddy Kennedy. When I first came to the family, he was always full of laughter, fun, and high style. Perhaps the major trait that had separated him from his brothers was that they were all "Kennedy," whereas Teddy is more a Fitzgerald. His brothers inherited their qualities from their father, but Teddy radiated the qualities of his grandfather, the controversial "Honey Fitz." His flamboyance, his hale and hearty political mind, his quick wit, his tendency to cut corners, his smile— all are Fitzgerald.

Perhaps this is why Mrs. Kennedy adored him above all her other children. Time and again when she would hear him in the house laughing and singing, she'd say, "Teddy was our surprise baby, and he's brought more joy into our lives than we ever thought possible."

There had never been any jealousy in the family over this youngest child. Everyone loved him—perhaps to a fault.

Mr. Kennedy was no exception. He doted on his youngest son. No matter what Teddy did, there were no stern looks or reprimands, no impatient frowns. In happier times Teddy would burst into his father's room, and at the sight of him, Mr. Kennedy's face would light up.

"Hi, Dad." He'd laugh. "Havin' any fun?"

Mr. Kennedy would chuckle and wink—and was always amused at his son's energy and impatience.

I remember an incident during which his father was being given a physical examination in his home, and the EKG machine would not operate properly. Teddy impatiently roared to the specialist attending his father, "Quit fooling with that damned thing and buy a new one."

A brief check showed that the machine was not broken; the

aide had simply not plugged it in. But Teddy's impatient reaction had been to ignore the cost involved. His solution was "buy a new one," not try to make it work.

Teddy was always open and spontaneous with his mother. She was never teased or joshed by her other children, but Teddy would often run up behind her, grab her around the waist in a hearty bear hug, and laugh. "How's my girl? Havin' any fun?" She would chuckle and pat him affectionately.

That's what life had been all about: fun. And there was nothing to indicate that it might ever be otherwise for Teddy Kennedy. He had plenty of time to grow up. Plenty of time to worry about accepting responsibilities. Plenty of time to develop an image, and more than enough time to settle down and become serious.

But time ran out on Teddy, and his father couldn't help him.

I remember a day, after the President's death, when Cardinal Cushing was spending the weekend with Mr. Kennedy. Teddy had gone with them on their daily outing on the boat. After lunch the cardinal and Teddy sat near Mr. Kennedy and settled down for "good conversation."

The subject of responsibilities came up, and the cardinal turned to Teddy and began almost lecturing him on the right and wrong sides of life.

"Always remember, Teddy, it's not what you gain in life that matters, it's not what you can gain by being a Senator that matters. It's whether what you do, as a man, is right or wrong. You must learn to ask your heart whether the act you are doing is proper, in the sight of man and God.

"Never listen to people who flatter you, for their loyalty will be as slippery as their tongues.

"Learn to face your responsibilities, and you will learn to face yourself. That's the important thing to learn, and it's the hardest thing a man can do. Face himself.

"Don't idle your time by looking at the gray areas in life. Look for whether it's right or wrong, and act from there."

Teddy listened attentively, and his father was completely absorbed in studying his reaction to the cardinal's advice. His eyes were riveted to his son's face. Teddy was receiving the same sound direction from the clergy that his father would have given, had he not been so completely handicapped by his stroke.

The expression on Mr. Kennedy's face at that time caused my thoughts to go back to a story Mrs. Kennedy loved to tell. When she was in a particularly nostalgic mood, she would relate how her husband would always devote himself to his children during the dinner hour. As they were eating, he would say, "Now I want each of you to tell me what you read in the papers today and what you think is noteworthy."

One by one they would discuss whatever they felt was of particular interest to them.

Mrs. Kennedy would end her story with a chuckle. "Teddy was so young," she'd say, "he'd usually report on his favorite sports figure."

This habit of thinking and learning how to draw conclusions was an important part of the Kennedy training. Mr. Kennedy expected his children to learn about the world in which they lived and draw intelligent conclusions from their involvements.

Mrs. Kennedy said so often, "My husband was wonderful at such times. He would mentally spar with the children, challenging their thoughts, forcing them into heated but productive debates."

Teddy had been too young to participate in these family think tank sessions.

Also, unlike his older brothers, he never received the benefit of his father's political guidance. His compulsive determination was not tempered with the discipline of his father's experience. The two older boys had operated on a pattern that was set by Mr. Kennedy. No mistakes were made in their careers. They did not rush precipitously in erratic maneuvering. They remained calm and, by doing so, generated excitement. By the time Bobby was twenty-seven he was campaign manager for his older brother, and this experience made him tough and aware.

Teddy, on the other hand, had been practically handed his political start. He has always worn the label of "coattail politician." The Kennedy image had been created before he stepped into the picture. He didn't have to work hard as his father and his brothers had worked. It was all there waiting for him.

Perhaps this is why Teddy has always generated such extreme reactions. He got his political career because he was a Kennedy, and from the very beginning he was either loved for being a Kennedy or deeply criticized for being a Kennedy. His bitterest critics often said that Massachusetts was bought for him as a political ornament on the Kennedy tree: "A nice toy for Teddy to play with." And in the beginning Teddy was very playful. He has natural tendencies as a skilled showman and politician; but he had been young, and with his brothers carrying the heavy responsibilities of their offices, he didn't have to take things that seriously. There was always time.

Then, suddenly, John Kennedy was dead.

Life became a shocking reality for Teddy when his brother was assassinated. He was shattered. The killing confused him, frightened him, matured him.

Then his own life was drastically affected in a most personal way on that fog-ridden night when Senator Birch Bayh pulled his unconscious and damaged body from the gnarled wreckage of a small chartered plane.

Personal pain became a reality, and the Teddy Kennedy who had once bounced into a room like an animated cartoon began carrying himself with a new caution and dignity.

Everything had been bigger than life to him until he clung to it by a thin thread. His haunting brush with death changed him in ways that were perhaps unnoticeable to the world at large. But those close to him could see the difference.

He became much closer to his father after the plane crash and all during his slow, painful rehabilitation. The President had been drawn close to his father because of his own suffering, and I saw the same thing take place with Teddy.

During the winter after the plane crash the estate next door to the Kennedys' in Palm Beach was rented for Teddy so he could recuperate in the Florida sun.

"He wants to be near his father," Mrs. Kennedy explained, "but not in constant contact. He's undergoing such critical therapy by learning to walk again that he felt it would not be good for his father to see him all the time."

Teddy believed it might be upsetting for his father to see him wearing a brace and using a cane; but Mr. Kennedy had other ideas, and after Teddy moved in next door, he took an intense interest in working out in the pool himself. He once more started his exercises.

One morning he was in the shallow part of the water and was doing exceptionally well in walking using the parallel bars that had been installed for him right after his stroke. He made one complete round while, unknown to him, Teddy was watching.

When he realized how difficult it was for his father, he called out, "Wait a minute, Dad. We'll do it together."

Unassisted, he walked down the ramp and into the water. He linked his arm in Mr. Kennedy's and proceeded to walk the exercise path with him. A photographer was present, and the picture of the two of them in the pool appeared in the next issue of a national magazine.

Seeing the photographer made me aware of a significant difference between Teddy and the other boys. They were known for their shrewd political involvements, and before and after the Presidential election (with the exception of the inauguration portrait and the family portrait taken the night of the election), there were no pictures of the President with Mr. Kennedy. It was the same with Bobby.

Teddy, however, literally thumbed his nose at the "controversial association" and said to the world, "This is my dad, and I don't give a damn who knows it."

Neither of his other sons would risk the political consequences, but Teddy could not have cared less. Mr. Kennedy knew this and loved him for it.

He understood why he had been closeted during his visits to the White House, and I'm sure he was the first to agree that it was best that way. Nevertheless, he loved Teddy's attention.

Mr. Kennedy was usually quite exhausted after his exercises in the pool with Teddy, and I would prepare him for his nap by massaging his legs, hoping to relax him. One time he looked down at himself and shook his head sadly. The paralyzed limb had shriveled over the years from uselessness, and hoping to encourage him, I said, "Please keep trying, Mr. Kennedy, please. There is so much left for you to teach your children. None of us can know what's in store for us or what kind of illness may strike us down. Your children are seeing you fight through every obstacle, and now, look at Teddy and how well he's doing. It's from you he's learned how to fight his new handicap—and it will be from you that he will get the inspiration to overcome it.

"Don't let him slacken. You know better than anyone the frustration he's going through, so you keep trying. As long as he sees you making the effort, he won't give up. He'll make it, and that will be the greatest inheritance you could ever give him."

He reached out his hand for mine and, in a gesture I'd come to understand, pressed it to his cheek.

Teddy had always been the spoiled one and had seemed to expect his father to humor him and give him whatever he wanted, but after his accident, he took special interest in observing every move his father made. Once he had pranced in and out, lighthearted and apparently unaware of his father's painful condition. His visits were always brief, boisterous, and frivolous. He never had the time to stop and consider the courage and fortitude it took for his father to live.

After his slow recovery, he would sit for hours with Mr. Kennedy, watching a game on television and would discuss the plays seriously rather than just root for his favorite team like a high school student.

Often there were times when Mr. Kennedy would fall asleep while watching the game. Teddy would tiptoe across the room and quietly turn off the set. Then he would settle down in his father's easy chair by the bed and wait, studying his father's features until he would awaken.

Mr. Kennedy would look around as one does coming out of a nap and see his son with his long legs stretched out in front of him. They would look at each other and smile.

Teddy came to love reading the newspapers to his father. Mr. Kennedy would prop himself up in bed during these sessions and put his hand behind his head to get comfortable.

So many evenings Teddy would come by and stay until long after his father was asleep. He would fix his covers or get up and softly lay his hand on his forehead or adjust the nightlight. Where once Mr. Kennedy had reached out to touch the son, now the son strove for contact.

The relationship that grew between these two men was powerful in its gentleness, strong in its understanding, and unique in its love.

Teddy had passed through his own crucible. The fires of pain and death had tempered his fiber and finally caused him to put on a new and cautious sobriety.

But Teddy had no sooner achieved a level of maturity that would have enabled him to play a significant role in the resurging Kennedy dynasty when Bobby was killed. With his brother's death, Teddy became a man haunted by loneliness and responsibility.

He was left in complete solitude with his brothers gone. The virility that he had shared with them was no more. His world, which had once vibrated with men, was extinct, and he was left in a lonely universe of fatherless children, grieving widows, and aging parents.

I remember seeing him sitting on the steps of the porch, watching the children at play: Bobby's, the President's, his own. From the pain in his eyes, I could tell he knew there was no way for him to replace their losses. He tried valiantly, but it was too much. He would exhaust himself on weekends taking all the children out in the sailboat even though to do it meant hours of "taking turns." He made a devoted attempt to fill the vacancy in the First Lady's life and even went to Greece with her on one of her visits. But the traumatic chore of coping with Ethel after Bobby's death was perhaps his most trying and complicated effort, for her reaction was disturbing and frightening in its intensity.

Ethel was driven by hysterical, almost uncontrollable grief when her husband was killed. She was pregnant at the time, but when she returned to the compound after the funeral, she startled everyone by taking on wild frenzied tennis matches.

She seemed never to be alone and was always hunting a tennis partner. She would get opponents on the court and banter unmercifully. Everyone knew it was best to let her win. She would throw the racket uncontrollably if she lost the set and ridicule her opponents until, for their own peace of mind, they would let her have the next game. As the days wore on, the tennis games became harder and harder. She could not seem to play enough or win enough.

She also had a jukebox installed in the garage of her home, and music would blast out day and night. The records were played so loudly that Mrs. Kennedy would come in, her fingers pressed to her temples, and say, "Please, someone, call Bobby's house and tell them the music is disturbing Mr. Kennedy again." It would stop for a while, then begin as loud as ever.

Her maids were terribly concerned over the loud, boisterous parties and the twenty-four-hour jukebox. "It's giving the children the shakes," one of them said. "They even shake picking up their rooms in the morning."

Jacqueline Kennedy seldom joined in any of these parties, but after Bobby's death she and Ethel seemed to become closer. They would talk together in the afternoon, but when Ethel's guests tried to join in, the First Lady would slip off quietly.

One evening Ethel had a houseful of people. Teddy and Joan were there, and everyone decided to take in the nine o'clock movie at the big house. I watched them as they crossed the lighted lawn. Ethel was with Andy Williams. Teddy had his arm draped around Joan. The other people were full of laughter and gaiety. It was, to all appearances, a lighthearted group of partygoers; but their laughter sounded hollow and forced, and their faces seemed to be masks. The true emotions had been pushed far down inside where they could not be felt.

This is not surprising because it seemed as if death had been hounding Ethel Kennedy like a curse in its tragic recurrence. A few months after John Kennedy's murder her own brother had been killed in a private plane crash. Eight months later his widow was having dinner with her children, and a piece of meat lodged in her windpipe. She choked to death while her children watched in helpless terror. Then Bobby. Four violent deaths in only five years.

She was running, running, running, all the time, and it was not surprising when she finally took a bad fall on the court, exhausted. Everyone—doctors and nurses, family and friends —had tried to warn her that she "had to let up," but she threw back her shoulders and snapped, "Let's have at it."

After her fall Louella Hennessey was called to nurse her. She seemed almost to be forcing another tragedy. Louella was brought in to keep her in bed for the sake of her baby, but that was almost impossible. Bobby's secretary had also come to the compound to help clear up his papers, and it became so difficult for her to work that she asked if she could come to my place every night "to get away from that house of sorrow."

Ethel could not sleep. She would toss and turn for hours, weeping. The secretary said one night, "I could not stand it any longer, seeing her like that, I mean, so I blurted out, 'If you think Bobby is in heaven, why don't you ask him to help you?'"

She said Ethel sat up in bed, tears streaming down her cheeks, and cried, "My God, I have. I do! I go to sleep thinking about him."

Ethel Kennedy loved her husband. He was her life. With him gone it was almost as if she had nothing to live for.

She had always been shy around Mr. Kennedy, and with Bobby gone, she would never come to visit him without some of her children along.

"Grandpa," she would say, "this is Christopher," or "This is Matthew." She would always ask them to perform little things for him—a prayer or a song. She would sit on the edge of her chair, watching the children, and an expression would come over her face of utter sadness.

She and Bobby had chartered a sailing yacht before he had

left for California. They planned to take the children on a cruise when he returned. Ethel would not cancel the yacht, and Teddy, hoping in some way to substitute for his brother, took them on the vacation.

As the time drew closer for her to have her child, the atmosphere around the compound was filled with anxiety. Ethel did not seem to be able to let up, and everyone felt the chilling threat of yet another tragedy. They desperately wanted her to have Bobby's last baby very much, and I remember the look on Teddy's face the day she fell on the tennis court.

"She can't lose the baby," he said. "She can't."

And when Rory Kennedy was born it seemed to reaffirm the continuity of life against the inexorable pattern of premature deaths that had been stalking the Kennedys.

In the fall Jacqueline Kennedy broke away from the shadows of her past and startled the world by marrying Aristotle Onassis. Many people turned against her because of this, but the Kennedy women, with the exception of Eunice, attended the wedding. Eunice's family blood ties were apparently too strong. She often said, "Once a Kennedy, always a Kennedy."

Mr. Kennedy was not disturbed over the marriage, and it did not alter their relationship.

I remembered back to our conversation and her long walk, and I had to feel that she made the right decision. Indeed, after her official period of mourning had been over, there was much speculation over her future. For a while the press had linked her with Lord Harlech, and he visited the compound several times as guest of the Kennedys; but anyone who saw them together could tell at a glance that she was not interested romantically. She was not aloof from him, but whenever they were together, she always looked as if she were alone.

Mrs. Kennedy, however, was very impressed with him and gave a special luncheon in his honor. She sent out word that everyone was to be prompt, and everyone was, except the First Lady. She decided to go water skiing alone. Mrs. Kennedy was very upset and waited quite a while, but rather than keep her guests waiting any longer, she finally seated them in the dining room. The First Lady came in when the luncheon was halfway through, and she never made any excuse or apologies for her tardiness. It was her way of saying, "I'm not interested in Lord Harlech."

Everyone watched very closely, and any man she was seen with was thoroughly discussed and debated. When she finally made Mr. Onassis her choice, many people were shocked into anger or disappointment.

I remember the first time I saw him at the compound. He had an incredible sense of vitality and command about him. He came walking across the lawn with his thick hair combed straight back from his swarthy face, and he seemed to be eyeing everyone somewhat sardonically.

He had on an open-necked shirt and a pair of cotton twills. Compared to the other guests, he looked a bit too careless to be smart. His jeans were not old enough to be fashionably faded. They were just, I suppose, a little shabby-looking.

He seemed to be lording it over the rest of the guests. His manner suggested that he did not have to dress up to impress the "jet set." He had originated it, and he looked at the world as though it had a price tag that he could easily afford.

And perhaps it was this air of crude confidence and power that disturbed everyone. He didn't seem to be a proper match for the gracious widow of the handsome young prince. But I often thought of Mr. Kennedy's acceptance of the marriage, and it gave me some understanding of why she chose him.

The President was thirty-six years old when they were married. She was twenty-four. There was a need and a reaching out, even then, for the security of an older man. Her constant devotion to Mr. Kennedy was still another expression of this need. Where could she have gone after the death of her husband except to a father, to a man who, in so many ways, paralleled Mr. Kennedy?

Onassis is a self-made man of questionable financial reputation. Consider Mr. Kennedy. Onassis has a strong fascination for show people. Consider Mr. Kennedy. Onassis has long enjoyed an amorous reputation, openly sporting a mistress from the entertainment world. Consider Mr. Kennedy, and his reported lengthy affair with one of Hollywood's most beautiful actresses. The political dogmas of Onassis are highly controversial. Consider Mr. Kennedy and his ill-fated ambassadorship. Onassis is often reported to operate his oil empire inches inside the law. Consider Mr. Kennedy and his notorious securities manipulations. Mr. Onassis is European. Mr. Kennedy, though first-generation Irish, continued the strong native ties and habits. Mr. Onassis operates on a worldwide basis, and Mr. Kennedy's holdings were equally widespread.

It would have been difficult for Jacqueline Kennedy to have found a man who was like her father-in-law in so many ways.

Seeing her during her widowed years gave me cause to ponder about the man she would choose. I believed her devotion to the President's memory would prevent any possibility of an American for a husband. I felt she would logically gravitate to a man many years her senior, who would never, in any way, be competition to the memory of her husband.

As a widow she did not, at any time, create controversy or concern among the family. She remained quiet and kept to herself. When she did entertain, it was with a small, gracious dinner party. She seemed more concerned over her children's welfare than over anything else and for the most part concentrated on them.

I have a vivid memory of her with Caroline shortly after the President died. The little girl was sitting by herself at the edge of the beach staring out across the water. Her legs were tucked up with her arms locked around them, and her chin resting on her knees. It was a dark, cold day, and the wind had been high. It caught her hair and blew it about her face angrily. She made a desolate picture huddled so alone in deep despair.

I watched as her mother left the house and walked down the long sweep of lawn toward her. She stood behind the child for a moment, hesitating, and I could almost read her thoughts of *What can I say? What can I do?*

Then, like a child herself, she sat down beside her daughter, and for a long while they remained side by side, not touching, only looking out toward the colorless rim of the horizon.

Finally, Caroline struggled slowly to her feet and offered a hand to lift her mother. They were silhouetted against the gray sky, and I could see the wind strike hard against their bodies. The waves that day were strong and angry, and all the trees had gone bare. As they walked slowly down the beach, the flag, at half-mast, crashed and dipped against the slapping wind.

Caroline leaned hard against her mother, and without stooping or bending low, Jacqueline Kennedy wrapped both her arms around her daughter and held her pressed close. They walked to the edge of the water, almost into it, it seemed, then began a solitary walk along the deserted beach.

Jacqueline Kennedy cupped her hand around her daughter's head and pressed it against her as if to keep away the stinging wind, and I knew she would provide the child with the strength that is necessary to suffer a great loss. She shielded her until the sharp pain had settled into a dull, eternal ache. She set an example for her to follow, and as the years passed, the little girl was able to pick up the task of living and find a solid foundation based on love and understanding.

Her father was gone, but her mother never flinched or withdrew from her obligations. She handled the loss, as a widow and mother, quietly and taught her only daughter the grace of dignity.

After her marriage, she still maintained her home on the compound and saw to it that both of her children remained Kennedys.

24

THE FALL SEASON came to a close, and the atmosphere around the compound became as desolate and mournful as the lonely windswept beaches of the Cape. Teddy spent as much time as possible with his father. Rumors were still popping up in the papers and on television about his Presidential aspirations, but he would invariably say to Mr. Kennedy that he was too busy looking after "our family" even to think about it. Mr. Kennedy would reach out his hand to touch his last son.

The Kennedy family was shrinking. Jean became more concerned over her personal life and more remote. She stayed very close to her own children and husband. She still sat with her father, but the visits were usually brief. She was a Kennedy, but she was also very conscious of the fact that she had her own family. Her visits to her mother were also brief. To find Jean, you would have to look for her children and her husband, for she would invariably be with them.

Pat, divorced from Peter Lawford, would visit often but, like her sister, would not stay for any length of time. She was restless and seemed to move without any purpose.

Although the President's widow had married and was reported to be spending the majority of her time on the Continent, she remained in close contact with Mr. and Mrs. Kennedy. And, strangely enough, she and Mrs. Kennedy seemed to be drawn closer together after her marriage.

Ethel could not shake her grief, and we seldom saw her alone. Also, her daughter Courtney had not been able to pull herself out of the shock of having seen her father killed. When she was invited to visit her cousin Caroline in England, everyone at the compound tried to build her enthusiasm for the trip, but her only response would be to shrug and say, "Oh, well, I guess I just have to go." It was only a few days after her arrival in England that she phoned her mother in tears, homesick and distraught. Ethel was deeply disturbed and sent for her immediately, but somehow when she returned, she seemed a bit more alive and willing to participate in activities around the compound. Perhaps those few days away had reawakened a strong sense of family in her.

Eunice, as Mrs. Kennedy so proudly said, found her place in life when her husband, Sargent Shriver, became ambassador to France. She had never before considered it important to spend time or money on a personal wardrobe, but she wrote her mother that as an ambassador's wife, she realized she was representing the people of the United States and should look the part. From that time on, whenever Eunice would fly home, she would bring with her the most exquisite wardrobe I have ever seen. None of the other Kennedy women could compare with her new and regal sense of culture and fashion.

She was not around the Cape a great deal in person, but she would phone her parents from Paris or wherever she was every night. Mr. Kennedy would smile as she told him about meeting De Gaulle or Queen Elizabeth or other important dignitaries and nobility. She was constantly telling him to "get well and come on over." When Pat or Jean were on the Continent visiting with her, they would all get on the phone and talk to him. These phone calls lifted his spirits.

Through all this, Teddy was left in his solitude.

He had tried hard to fill in the gaps and take his place as the masculine head of the family, but he also needed understanding and companionship. In this need he turned, instinctively, to the man whom Mr. Kennedy had selected when they were children to be his companion and playmate: Ann's brother, Joe Gargan. Joe was an extremely likable man, but he had always been a shadow in the background. He was the one who carried

Teddy's sails and cooked special breakfasts for him and his guests every Sunday. With Bobby's death Joe was unexpectedly in the position of confidant and adviser. He was not a Kennedy, but like his sister, he found himself a position of power and influence that he had never had.

Teddy also turned to his mother, and despite her age, she tried to do whatever he wanted.

Once he even asked her to go sailing with him, which she did, even though she detested being on the water.

She had often said to me, "It's so senseless going out on those small boats just to be tossed around by the waves. It's not my idea of 'fun,' and Mr. Kennedy can have it."

But she knew how the loneliness was affecting Teddy, so she put aside her feelings. She dressed very carefully for her day on the water, and when we all complimented her on her outfit, she smiled. "I must look good for my son."

Teddy called for her at the house and grinned from ear to ear when he saw her. They spent several hours together, and when she returned to the house, I asked her if she had enjoyed herself. She let out a tired sigh and said, "It was very pleasant."

Another time, just before the Cape closed down, he asked her to go ice skating with him on the rink Mr. Kennedy had donated to the people of Hyannis Port. She told me, laughingly, "I haven't been on skates for thirty or forty years, but Teddy wants me to go with him."

She got all dressed up in a black outfit, for she was still in mourning for Bobby. Although she seemed slightly embarrassed in her woolen togs she looked very natty—and off they went together.

One of the most beautiful pictures of her was taken that day with Teddy at the ice rink—beautiful in the sense of its being a graciously aging mother with her son. She loved it so much that she always kept it on her dresser.

She tried hard to make things easier for her son, and despite her own grief, no mother could have given more of herself.

But his ultimate loneliness was painful to see.

Mr. Kennedy was not doing well at all after Bobby died, and that fall there was speculation that he would not be able to make the trip to Palm Beach. At times he was very, very poor. He was not as yet in a terminal condition, but he was visibly going downhill. Teddy, seeing this and keenly aware of it, grew more and more concerned and apprehensive.

But when Thanksgiving came and all the children were home, Teddy was like a new man. He could not see enough of his sisters. We could hear him singing again, and some of the old hale-and-hearty enthusiasm was back. It did much to pick up our spirits.

Dr. Boles came to consult with the family and he advised that if at all possible, Mr. Kennedy's routine should not be upset. He recommended that the trip to Florida be made, for he felt that Mr. Kennedy would be more prone to depression if he were kept on the Cape for the winter.

Winter in that part of the country is desolate and depressing, especially for a person as ill as Mr. Kennedy was, and Mrs. Kennedy said she would feel better in a warmer climate, so it was finally decided to open the Palm Beach house as usual.

The *Caroline* had been turned over to the Smithsonian Institution after Bobby died, and for the first time, Mr. Kennedy had to travel by chartered plane. When Captain Baird and the crew came for their last good-bye to him, he held each hand for a long, personal moment and nodded his head sadly.

We arrived in Florida about a week before Christmas, and it was perhaps the saddest holiday we ever spent. Mr. Kennedy did not show any interest in the family gathering. He was tired —almost too tired to care, it seemed. He had lost considerable weight, and even though he was quite alert mentally, his body seemed to be gradually losing its vitality. Physically he was becoming a tired, aging, worn-out old man.

He stayed downstairs for the opening of the Christmas presents, but it was a sparse celebration. His daughters had all rented places of their own, and for the first time the grandchildren had their trees and gifts at home. Only Mr. Kennedy's

children came. He opened his gifts and thanked each one, but
it was obvious that he really lacked the strength for a party.

It was a testy winter for everyone concerned. Dora, Mr. Kennedy's devoted maid, had a minor stroke at the house and was
hospitalized. I became seriously ill with a setback of the Hong
Kong flu and was put on the critical list in the hospital. Dora
and I were on the same floor, and Ann came by often to check
up on us. Mrs. Kennedy phoned and urged me to "get well and
hurry back." She said the house was operating in a state of confusion with so many sick people off work. She wanted to visit
me, but I advised her not to risk it because the flu was highly
contagious. In spite of that, everyone on the staff did come.
They stood in the doorway for brief visits and assured me that
Mr. Kennedy was doing fine.

Toward the end of my stay in the hospital, the head nurse
came to my room and said, "Rita, Mr. Kennedy is here in the
hospital, and they say he wants to see you. Miss Gargan said to
tell you he has put his foot down and will not budge. She wants
to know if you'll see him."

By that time my doctor had told me I was no longer in a
contagious state, so I said, "Of course. Please tell Miss Gargan
to let him come in."

He was wheeled just to my door—close enough for him to see
me but not too close just in case of any contagion. We looked
at each other for a moment, and then I saw him attempt something he had not done for years—he put his hand on the rim of
the wheel and tried to move the chair forward himself. Ann
was standing behind him and said, "It's okay, Uncle Joe. I'll
push you in."

He came as close to the head of the bed as he could.
He looked at me piercingly, shaking his head. His eyes filled
up, and I knew I, too, was ready to cry. He bowed his head and
gave a helpless gesture with his hand, as if to say, "What can I
do?"

"Oh, Mr. Kennedy," I said, trying to sound lighthearted,
"I'll be out of here very soon and taking care of you again. I'm
coming right back to the house."

He nodded and sighed.

"I don't want you to tire yourself, Mr. Kennedy," I said, "but I'm awfully glad you came to see me."

Ann saw that we were both getting emotional, and realizing I was trying to keep a light mood, she bent over him and laughed. "Uncle Joe, I think that's Rita's way of telling us good-bye."

He chuckled and waved his hand as she wheeled him out.

The day I walked into his room at the Palm Beach house, ready to return to work, he was smiling. Mrs. Kennedy was especially cordial, and the whole staff made me feel that I had been missed and that it was good to have me back. However, I was startled at the gloom which seemed to pervade everything. The house was dreary, and so I was very happy when Mrs. Kennedy told us we would soon be leaving for the Cape.

Seasonal migration was never easy, for everything was transported back and forth between the two houses. Linens, pictures, bric-a-brac, books, even the alarm clocks were packed—everything was moved except the furniture. It had always been a problem, but now with Mr. Kennedy requiring so much attention, it became even more difficult for all concerned.

When it was finally time for us to leave, a plane was again chartered. We all sensed that it would be Mr. Kennedy's last trip, and his lingering looks into all the rooms as he left the house gave us the sad knowledge that he also knew it was the last time he would see this home that had once been filled with the voices of his children.

Mrs. Kennedy had gone ahead to ready the Cape for our arrival, so it was a gloomy and lonesome departure.

Mr. Kennedy was depressed and kept his head down during our drive to the airport. He was listless as we removed him from the car, but suddenly, he heard a familiar voice say, "How are you, Mr. Kennedy?"

His eyes darted up, and he sucked in his breath in surprise. Then his eyes filled, and he held out his hand to Captain Baird.

The captain had received permission to take time off from

his job in order to fly Mr. Kennedy on his last trip home. Very gently, as he had always done in the past, he lifted Mr. Kennedy aboard, and since there were no compartments in the plane, he carefully selected a seat for him near the middle.

Mr. Kennedy was not able to fly in a jet, as we had learned on his trip with the First Lady, but he offered no objections to the small propeller craft that had been chartered for him.

The flight was quiet and smooth, almost silent, and after Captain Baird moved him off the plane and into the car, the two men shook hands for the last time.

Many words of criticism have been written and said about Mr. Kennedy, but the man I cared for inspired greater loyalty than any person I have ever known. I saw it from his friends, from the people who worked for him, and from his family. He grew faint, but the devotion to him waxed strong.

25

The summer of '69 began on a low, sorrowing keel. Mr. Kennedy tried hard to keep to his routine, but it grew more and more difficult. In the beginning he still went to the pool if the weather was good, and he also enjoyed taking his rides, but Mr. Kennedy was far from his usual self.

One of the men from the New York office came on business and, after having a brief consultation with him, said, "Oh, Rita, why have you tried so hard to save him all these years? Why wouldn't you just let him go? He'd have been so much better off."

"He'll know when he's ready," I said, "and so long as he still eats and still tries, he deserves every break he can get. Who are we to say that his life has not been precious to him?"

Mr. Kennedy remained alert and physically functional, and it seemed that life became more valuable to him with each passing day. I believe he knew that it would soon end, but as long as he could keep his faculties, he was satisfied.

A new warmth and understanding came into bloom between Mr. and Mrs. Kennedy that summer. They would look at each other, and one could see they were drawn closer by the many bridges they had crossed together.

Their main concern was Teddy, for he seemed to be lonelier and more lost than anyone at the compound. From the first part of the season I saw him begin to surround himself with men who seemed anxious to serve as brother substitutes. He would spend long hours with his father; but he was restless, and when he would finally pull himself away, he practically ran to Joe Gargan for companionship. He needed a close confidant, and although Joe offered him a strong friendship, it was not, nor could it have ever been, the same as Teddy had known with his brothers.

Joe was always there when Teddy wanted him, and he would do anything or agree to do anything that pleased his cousin. Joe was never too tired, never too busy.

Having seen how close they were and how much time they spent together that summer, I can understand why Teddy went first to Joe after the car he was driving went off the dyke bridge. I do not have any idea what really happened that night at Chappaquiddick or why Teddy waited so long to report the accident because almost nothing was said at the compound. The family became so tight-lipped after the body of Mary Jo Kopechne was discovered that none of us knew any more than what was reported by the press.

In truth I cannot bury the haunting issues of Chappaquiddick, for like the rest of the world, I do not know the answers— but in my heart I cannot feel condemnation for Teddy Kennedy. As I knew him, he could never have deliberately brought bodily harm to another human being. Although the facts seem cold and ruthless, and he himself admits to erratic, emotional behavior, the Teddy Kennedy I knew was a warm, loving, openhearted man.

The first time I saw him after Chappaquiddick was shortly after he had appeared before the chief of police of Edgartown, Massachusetts. He came to his father's room, drawn, downcast, intimidated. He looked up at me, briefly, and nodded his head in greeting. Then he walked over to his father's bed and laid his hand on his shoulder.

"Dad," he said, "I'm in some trouble. There's been an accident, and you're going to hear all sorts of things about me from now on. Terrible things. But, Dad, I want you to know that they're not true. It was an accident. I'm telling you the truth, Dad; it was an accident."

Mr. Kennedy reached for his son's hand and held it tightly against his chest.

"Dad, a girl was drowned. I stopped by at a party Joe was having for some of our girls from the office. One of them wanted to catch the ferry and get back to the motel on South Beach. I said I'd take her, but I turned off the wrong road, and my car went off the bridge into the tidal pond. I got out, Dad, and I tried to save her, but I couldn't. I guess, after that, I went to pieces. I walked back to Joe's, and then we drove back to the bridge. He tried to get her out, too, but he couldn't. I must have gone a little crazy, Dad, because I swam across to Edgartown. I left the scene of the accident, and things aren't good because of that.

"But I want you to know that I'm telling you the truth."

Mr. Kennedy nodded weakly, patted Teddy's hand, and closed his eyes.

The next afternoon Joe Gargan was at the house talking with his sister, and I noticed he was moving his arm rather stiffly. It was especially noticeable, for he was wearing a long-sleeved shirt, something seldom seen around the Cape. When I asked him what was wrong, he raised his brows and said, "Oh, haven't you heard? I scraped it trying to save Mary Jo."

Joe became his own man after Chappaquiddick, and he was the only one who did not seem to be going around in a state of shock—who did not seem horror-stricken over what had happened. If I were to describe his manner, I would say he was suddenly self-assured.

Mrs. Kennedy was deeply disturbed and in her desperation sent out a call for her family to return to the compound. They came from around the globe, and it was not until Teddy was safely closeted with those who loved him that the atmosphere began to seem less full of tension.

Mrs. Kennedy never talked to her son in any personal way while they were in the house. Whenever he would come over, he would visit with his father, never mentioning the accident, and then seek out his mother. They would leave the house together and go to the flagpole that stood in the center of the lawn. Whatever she had to say to him or ask him was not for anyone else to hear. She was heartbroken, but she could not risk jeopardizing her son by asking him questions that could be overheard and misinterpreted.

Teddy Kennedy, in his grief and confusion, had sought for trust and wisdom, but he had surrounded himself with yes-men for so many years that on that unfortunate July night there was no one to help him handle the accident in a disciplined, logical manner.

After Chappaquiddick, I would see him stumbling around the compound confused and alone, and I knew that his heart was broken. His hopes were dashed; his trust in human nature was shattered.

The family began arriving as soon as Mrs. Kennedy sent out the word. Jean came with her husband, and Steve immediately started organizing the shambles. He moved in fast and made logical decisions.

Pat arrived, hollow-eyed and nervous. Eunice arrived from Paris and came storming into the house, her face set. Her eyes smarting.

"Where's Teddy?" she snapped. "Where's my brother?"

I told her he was at his home, and she did not pause long enough to see her father or greet her mother. She left the house as she had entered it, in angry haste.

Mrs. Onassis arrived from Greece and turned over her home to be used as headquarters for Teddy's advisers.

Robert McNamara came, along with Burt Marshall, Arthur Goldberg, Arthur Schlesinger, Jr., Richard Goodwin, Ted Sorensen, and Pete Markham. Robert Clark, Jr., and his son Robert Clark III, who were considered the foremost vehicle accident attorneys in Massachusetts, also came.

These men, the "thinkers," the "policymakers," the "speech writers," all convened at the President's house for long hours of loud, argumentative discussion over what to do about Teddy.

Through it all, the man in question was never deeply involved. He walked around in a stupor, more alone than I had ever seen him.

A doctor from Hyannis Port was called for an examination and recommended that Teddy's spine be tapped. This was done at Teddy's house at Squaw Island. The diagnosis was "wear your neck brace," but Teddy shook his head, saying, "No, I can't do it. I can't let people think I'd be trying to get their sympathy. I can't."

I'm sure any doctor would have recommended hospitalization for Teddy, for he was apparently in deep emotional shock, but the "advisers" decided not to enter him.

Mistakes were made from the beginning, and I was shocked more than ever when I learned that he was to make a "confessional speech" that was to be televised to the citizens of Massachusetts. Even more disturbing was the fact that it was also to be televised nationally.

"They can't put the man through that kind of emotional ordeal," I thought, but when Mrs. Onassis called me to her house to give her a B-12 shot, I knew it was true.

The remnants of the Kennedy clan and its advisers were in her living room, prompting Teddy on his speech. He was dull and listless, hardly able to respond or function.

Joe Gargan came into the house and did something I had never seen him do, before. He walked right into the living room, fixed himself a drink, and stretched out in an easy chair. This was the same man who once stood outside a room until he was invited in and then waited until someone said, "Sit down, Joe."

He was now an integral and necessary part of everything. His testimony in court was the only evidence to substantiate Teddy's. He no longer dwelled on the perimeter. Not only was he needed, but his participation was crucial.

Mrs. Onassis was deeply involved in seeing that the meeting went smoothly, but it still took them three long days after the accident before they drafted what they considered to be a proper statement for Teddy to make. In the eyes of the public this puzzling delay cast an even greater shadow over his already scandal-marred image.

Mr. Kennedy's mind was alert to all that was going on around his house, but he never once sought a further explanation of the event at Chappaquiddick. It was enough that his son had come to him, and he was not interested in seeing television or reading any paper that pointed suspicion at his son.

The speech was to be televised from the Kennedy living room, and Eunice arrived at the house before anyone else. She issued orders that it was to be a private, family affair, and she wanted no one else around. She took the reins and protected her younger brother.

"I don't want anyone staring at him."

She was right. It was difficult enough for Teddy to give his speech, but to have a staff who'd known him all his life looking on would have been unbearable. Eunice was back, radiating power and strength, and her younger brother drew courage from her.

I stayed up with Mr. Kennedy, and we did not turn on the television. When Teddy had finished, he came to his father and said, "Dad, I've done the best I can. I'm sorry."

After the telecast and all the speechwriters and advisers and lawyers and hangers-on had disappeared, only the family remained. One by one they too drifted away, until it seemed that only Teddy was left. Alone again.

From that point on Mr. Kennedy failed rapidly, and a pall hung over the compound, for we all knew that it was only a matter of time.

His children would call him every night from wherever they were. They would talk to Mrs. Kennedy first, and if he was asleep, they would not awake him. Whenever two or three days passed that he had missed talking to them, he would sink into a very blue mood and stare blankly into space. I finally mentioned this to Mrs. Kennedy.

"I don't think he understands that they're calling," I said, "and it's making him very despondent."

She went to him and gently kissed his cheek. "Joe, dear," she said, "I want you to know that the children call you every night, but sometimes you're dozing, so they talk to me then. They want you to get all the rest you can."

He nodded wearily. After that the calls would keep coming

in until he was awake. He would listen to their voices and smile happily.

Toward late summer Mr. Kennedy lost his appetite, and I knew he had given up. Over the years I watched him sometimes force himself to eat, but when he finally stopped, I felt my heart sink. He barely touched his food after Chappaquiddick.

I also noticed that his eyes were tearing a lot. He would rub them with his fingers, and they rapidly became inflamed and irritated. The local doctor examined him and ordered special medication, but this did not alleviate the problem. Teddy decided to call in a specialist.

"Maybe you need your glasses changed, Dad," he said, even though he knew that his father had regular eye examinations.

When the specialist came, he shook his head sadly. "Mr. Kennedy is going blind," he said.

By then he was not a good surgical risk, and there was nothing to be done. No one had to tell him what was happening to him. He knew, and he never complained. I was particularly sorry, for it meant he was about to lose the only pleasure he had left. He would watch television for hours and lose himself in it, but now even that small comfort was fading.

The rule was still in force that no staff nurses other than myself were allowed in his room, but since he was going blind and becoming even more helpless, I went to Mrs. Kennedy and asked if it could be laid aside.

"Mrs. Kennedy," I said, "I think you're aware of your husband's impending difficulties, and I believe a nurse should be in the room with him at all times. They can't care for him over the intercom any longer. He's too weak to call out. Not only that, he's blind, and he should never feel that he's alone. This is going to be a very difficult period for him."

She thought a long moment and then agreed. She went to his room with me and pointed to a straight-back chair near the door.

"I want them to sit here," she said. "Not near him."

"Whatever you say, Mrs. Kennedy, just so long as they're in the room."

I told each nurse to tell Mr. Kennedy where she was sitting and to let him hear her voice. Then to him I said, "Mr. Kennedy, you're never going to be alone. A nurse is in this room now, and one will be here at all times. I don't want you to worry. We'll not leave you."

He raised his hand weakly, telling me that he understood, and from then on he was able to rest a little more securely.

Mrs. Kennedy would come to his room in the evening and ask that some of his favorite records be put on. The music was piped throughout the house, pouring into the rooms softly. Her eyes would brim with tears as she sat by his bed, for she was terribly affected by his blindness. She would leave him and weep, "My poor Joe. How cruel, how cruel."

His vision was gone, and even more depressing was the fact that his vocal cords were deteriorating, and he was no longer able to make strong sounds. Occasionally he would make an almost inaudible noise in his throat when he recognized Teddy's footsteps, and somehow managed to turn his head to the door and smile, but it was an effort.

As his throat tightened and he could no longer swallow, we would put an ice cube in a piece of gauze and let him hold it between his lips.

He was receiving oxygen nasally at the time, but the family decided "no heroic measures." This meant that nothing would be done to prolong his life. Ann was concerned when I did not remove the oxygen, until I explained to her that it was not prolonging his life; it was only making things a little easier for him in his final moments.

Summer died, autumn passed unnoticed, and November came as gray and as cold as I can ever remember it. Now Mr. Kennedy seemed to exist for only one thing—the sound of Teddy's footsteps. And we could tell by even a slight twitch of his fingers that he was listening when Teddy spoke to him.

On November 15, Jacqueline Kennedy Onassis arrived. She came softly, as she always had. "It's Jackie, Grandpa," she said, kissing him. He recognized her voice and nodded his head faintly. She held his hand, and even though he was blind, I know he could sense the tears in her eyes. She knew she was losing a beloved friend—one she would sorely miss.

Dr. Boles was also called on the fifteenth, and his medication orders were started. Mr. Kennedy was in pain because he would cry out a little, and even though he was unable to tell us or show us, Dr. Boles knew the man was suffering.

Mrs. Kennedy was almost constantly with her husband. Once I saw her walking along the beach all alone. I had seen the President deep in thought walk slowly along the same sands. I remembered Bobby after the assassination walk the same solitary path. And I remember Teddy, during the endless lonely months, walk with his head down, his arms linked behind his back. Now the mother, stooped and weary, walked a path of dead memories.

Eunice and her husband arrived from Paris. She kissed her father, then quickly hurried to her mother's room. At that point she wanted no one to see her weep. Sargent Shriver stayed with Mr. Kennedy and bent down to kiss him.

"Grandpa," he said, "can you hear me?"

Mr. Kennedy nodded his head.

Eunice's husband sank to his knees and said softly, "Oh, Grandpa, I want to tell you how much I love you, and I want to thank you for everything you've done for me. Without you, none of us would be anything."

He began to cry.

Hoping to ease the situation, I said, "Isn't it wonderful, Mr. Kennedy, that everyone's getting here a little early for Thanksgiving? Pat and Jean, and now Eunice."

Sargent Shriver closed his eyes and tried to keep his voice level.

"Grandpa, we're going to stick around and wait for you to come downstairs."

Then, with tears flowing down his cheeks, the ambassador to France left the room.

On November 16, Mrs. Kennedy sat with her husband all day and late into the night. That day I saw a look of utmost grief come over Teddy's face. It was the first time his father had not responded or recognized his voice.

"Dad, it's me, Teddy," he would cry over and over. "It's me, Teddy. Dad, can you hear me? Please talk to me. Please answer me."

Mrs. Kennedy crossed the room wearily and took her husband's hand.

"Joe?"

He moved his head slightly.

The next day, the seventeenth, his vital signs were very poor, and he was comatose.

Louella Hennessey arrived, and it was a great personal comfort for Mrs. Kennedy and the girls. She stayed at the big house until late that night; then she went home with Eunice.

Dr. Boles arrived again from Boston, and he knew that his old friend was past help. He sat down by the bed and said, "This man gave me the strength and courage to face many things when I was a youth. No one will ever know how much he's done for me."

Ill and feverish, Ethel Kennedy arrived from McLean, Virginia. After only a few moments in the room she had to be taken to bed.

Jacqueline Onassis sat with him through that whole night, and it was apparent that the end was near—but still he lived.

Word came from Mrs. Kennedy that all the staff nurses were discharged from the case. The local doctor had agreed to remain with him until he died. I stayed until eleven o'clock that night, and although I had been on duty almost around the clock, I knew the doctor was exhausted too, for it was the end of his day.

Medically, Mr. Kennedy was expected to expire at any moment, so I went in search of Teddy to find out if he wanted me to remain on with the doctor. He was in the living room with Steve Smith, slumped in a chair, staring moodily out the window.

"Shall I stay with your father?"

He swallowed hard and his eyes filled with tears.

Steve said, "No, Mrs. Dallas, you need rest. The doctor is taking the shift."

Teddy buried his face in his hands.

"I'll see you in the morning," I whispered to Steve and left the room.

I started across to my home but stopped and turned back to Mr. Kennedy's room. The doctor was sitting in the nurses' station, his face strained and tired.

"Is Mr. Kennedy alone?" I asked.

He nodded yes.

I slipped into his room and very quietly crossed over to his bed. His breathing was no longer audible, and I knew I was telling him good-bye. The house was quieter than I had ever heard it. Even the ocean seemed to have lost its sound. I looked at the pale man, who lay now in the care of God, and I whispered, "God keep you, Mr. Kennedy, and bless you."

26

MY PHONE RANG at six the next morning. It was the doctor asking me to come and relieve him.

"How is Mr. Kennedy?"

"No change."

I relieved the doctor at the nurses' station, and he left saying that he would call in around nine. I went in to Mr. Kennedy and found Teddy sitting in a chair with a blanket wrapped around him. He got up.

"Jackie's just left," he said. "She sat with me all night. We wanted it that way, and you know, Mrs. Dallas, I think Dad would have, too."

He folded up his blanket and stood over his father. "He had a quiet night, Mrs. Dallas. All in all it was a quiet night. Jean and Pat will be over later, and Eunice has gone to mass with Mother. Jackie went home to shower and eat, and she's coming right back, so if you think it's okay, I'll go down and have breakfast."

"I'll be here with him," I said. "Take a rest, and if there's a change, I'll call you."

"No, I'll just eat and come back up."

He left, and I sat down by Mr. Kennedy. There's an old-world expression, "Death has set in," and Mr. Kennedy was dying. Teddy had not seen the change, but a nurse or a doctor knows.

At nine o'clock the doctor phoned, and all I said was, "He's not the same."

The doctor understood.

He told me he had to go to the hospital to make his rounds, but that if I needed him, I could reach him there.

A few minutes later the phone rang again, and it was Louella.

"Eunice said Mr. Kennedy is the same," she said, "so I think I'd better run up to Boston. I left in such a hurry that I didn't have time to close up my house, but I'll see you when I get back."

"Louella," I said, "will you come over and see me now?"

There was complete silence on the phone. Then she said, "Yes, Rita, I'll be right there."

I had not said any more, for I did not want to risk one of the family picking up the phone and overhearing a discussion about their father. Louella knew why I was asking her to come, and she arrived in about five minutes.

I was still alone upstairs when she came in. She looked at Mr. Kennedy and said, "Oh, Rita, this is it, isn't it?"

I nodded.

She walked over to the window and looked out. I knew she was remembering all the years, the wonderful years, now past. I walked over to her and laid my hand on her shoulder. I knew as a friend, she did not want to be there to see him die, but as a nurse, she realized that I needed her.

"Louella, the doctor is on duty at the hospital, and the other nurses have been discharged. Will you stay with me?"

She turned and looked at Mr. Kennedy. After a long moment she said, "I won't leave, Rita."

At ten o'clock none of the family had come in, and he was getting steadily weaker. I kept my hand on his pulse and took the heartbeat with the stethoscope. His radial pulse was gone.

At ten thirty I said, "Louella, I know they've been up all night, but he's getting weaker, it's time to call them."

She began to cry. "Rita, I can't, I can't tell the family."

I understood. She was a friend, and I knew it wasn't right to expect her to be the one to break the news. I couldn't leave him to go to the phone, so there was only one way to call the family together. I was standing at the head of his bed, and I reached out and touched the alarm bell. It echoed across the compound.

Those who heard it knew that it was the end. It would never ring again.

I heard footsteps running down the hall. It was Pat. Her eyes were wide and startled.

"Daddy?"

I nodded. She saw Louella at the window, and numbly she bent down and kissed her father's face, her tears covering him.

Ann rushed in, and right after her Teddy came running into the room. He saw Pat with her face buried in her hands, crying. He put his hand on her shoulder and kept it there. "Have you called Eunice?" he asked.

"I will," Louella whispered and hurried to the nurses' phone.

In a matter of moments Eunice and her husband arrived.

I glanced out of the window and saw the First Lady running across the lawn. It was a bitter cold day, but she had not even stopped to finish getting dressed when she heard the alarm. All she had on was a pair of slacks and a short-sleeved shirt. In her bare feet, she was racing across her yard, through Bobby's and across the wide lawn of the big house, to Mr. Kennedy. She came breathlessly into the room.

Mr. Kennedy had received the last rites numerous times in the last few weeks, and once again the priest was called.

In a moment Ethel came, pale and ill. Joan came and stood beside Teddy. Eunice and her husband stood silently at the foot of the bed. Jean and Steve Smith took their places beside Eunice and her husband. The chair Mrs. Kennedy had always sat in next to his bed was still vacant.

Behind the family circle, Jacqueline Onassis and Ethel Kennedy stood close together, their faces drawn into painful masks. Ann stood quietly in the background, and Louella was in back of them all, by the side window.

At that point Steve Smith, Sargent Shriver, and Joan Kennedy stepped back quietly until only his children encircled him.

Teddy looked at me and said, "Should I get Mother?"

"No, not yet."

I wanted to spare her as much agony as I could, and even though his radial pulse was gone, there was still a slight apical count. I did not know whether he would convulse at the last throes of death, and I wanted to spare her that if I could.

"Oh, God," I prayed, "let him go quietly."

"Let me know," Teddy said. "She'd want to be here."

He watched me intently until finally I knew it was time. "Senator, you should bring your mother in now."

Pat's shoulders stiffened.

Teddy left, and in a moment he returned with his arm wrapped gently around his mother. She looked at me.

"He's going?"

"I'm sorry, Mrs. Kennedy."

She knelt down by the bed, put her head against her husband's hand, and wept in deep, grievous agony. Her children were frozen seeing her and then their father. I knew I had to do something, for they were all beginning to break.

"Will someone get Mr. Kennedy's rosary from the dresser?" I asked.

Jacqueline Onassis quietly brought it to me. I gave it to Mrs. Kennedy, and she put the cross to her husband's lips, then very gently, laid the rosary in his hand.

The room was silent for a brief moment, and then Eunice's voice came very softly in prayer. She began the Our Father, and each line was passed on from one to another until it was finished.

Eunice: "Our Father, Who art in Heaven, Hallowed be Thy name."

Teddy: "Thy kingdom come, Thy will be done."

Jean: "On earth as it is in heaven."

Pat: "Give us this day our daily bread."

Ethel: "Forgive us our trespasses."

Jackie: "As we forgive those who trespass against us."

Mrs. Kennedy's voice broke. With her head bowed, she ended the prayer for her husband.

"And deliver us from evil. Amen."

As she was saying these final brief words, Mr. Kennedy died.